# MONGOLIA

## The circle in the clouds

The missionary adventures of John and Nancy Hopkins

# MONGOLIA
## The circle in the clouds

The missionary adventures of John and Nancy Hopkins

John and Nancy Hopkins

Walking the Line Publications          South Jordan, Utah

Cover Design: Jaime Clawson
Electronic Page Makeup: Jennifer Asplund
Editing: Kim Hopkins Griesemer, Pat Hopkins, Terri Hopkins Clawson, Jessica Griesemer
Printer and Binder: Printed in the USA by Morris Publishing, 3212 E. Highway 30, Kearney,
    NE 68847, (800) 650-7888

ISBN 0-9714540-6-X

Printed in the United States by Morris Publishing
3212 East Highway 30
Kearney, NE 68847
1-800-650-7888

# contents

# About the Authors

John E. and Nancy M. Hopkins reside in Bucks County, Pennsylvania (just north of Philadelphia). They received their Bachelor of Arts degrees in Elementary Education with John continuing on to The Ohio State University where he received his Masters and Ph.D. degrees.

John taught and served as principal in several elementary schools in Columbus, Ohio and later became a central office administrator. Following the completion of his graduate degrees he was employed as an Assistant Dean in the School of Education at Indiana University, Bloomington. From IU, John was hired to work for a non-profit educational research laboratory in Philadelphia, Research for Better Schools, where he served as the Executive Director for 20 years prior to his retirement in 1996.

Nancy has been a homemaker and mother to five children during the 50-plus years of their marriage, while also serving in a variety of positions within The Church of Jesus Christ of Latter-day Saints.

John and Nancy have served two missions for The Church of Jesus Christ of Latter-day Saints, the first as humanitarian missionaries in Mongolia in 1997–1998. During this period, they coordinated the English project and John served as country director for humanitarian service couples and activities in Mongolia. Nancy taught English as an International Language (EIL) in several universities and the Ministry of Justice for Mongolia. In September of 1998, John was awarded a medal by the Mongolian Center for Children for service to the poor and needy children. This is the highest award that can be given on behalf of the children in Mongolia. Their second mission in 1999–2001 was served in the Asia Area Office in Hong Kong as Area Welfare Agents. During this period they managed church welfare programs in the countries of China, Taiwan, Laos, Vietnam, Mongolia, and Hong Kong. After nineteen months in Hong Kong (January 2001), they were transferred back to Mongolia and served another nine months creating employment programs for returned missionaries and unemployed members. They returned home in late October 2001.

John now serves as Patriarch for the Philadelphia Pennsylvania Stake of the Church, and Nancy is his typist.

# A History of Mongolia

The steppes of Central Asia were inhabited by nomadic tribes before the Mongolian nation was created. Chinese Emperors built the Great Wall of China to keep out these marauding tribes. Around 200 BC the Huns established the first state in Central Asia. They eventually split into two groups, one went west towards the Roman Empire, the other group became integrated with the Chinese and eventually created the great Han dynasty in China, south of the Great Wall.

Specifically, the Mongols were a small group of nomadic people who moved from place to place with the seasons. Alliances were formed and then changed over the years depending on their needs, and based upon the strength of various clans. The rise of the Mongol people as a nation began in the time of Chinggis Khan (commonly known as Genghis Khan), who was the first ruler of Mongolia to unite all the tribes of Central Asia. He came to power by conquering and/or making alliances with the other clans. In 1206, at a great assembly of all the tribes, Chinggis Khan was formally proclaimed ruler over all the Mongol tribes.

Chinggis began to build his empire through the brutal conquest of the surrounding nations. The Mongol cavalry was highly trained, able to shoot while riding at full gallop, and equally capable of hitting targets behind as well as in front. Bombardiers with giant catapults supported the cavalry. The army of Chinggis Khan was feared because of their reputation for mercilessly exterminating those that opposed them. However, many chose to submit rather than be killed, paid taxes, and even provided men to support the army, adding to its strength. Though these wars brought great destruction and subjugated millions, they did in fact unite both the Asian and European tribes for centuries.

The brutality of the Mongol hoards as they swept across Asia and into Europe brought terror into the hearts of everyone, even those who only heard stories of their atrocities. That terror was handed down generation after generation as, centuries later, just the name of Mongolia still brought fear and curiosity into the hearts of westerners.

Chinggis Khan, driven by a sense of divine mission, is quoted as saying, "I am the flail of God. If you had not committed great sins, God would not have sent a punishment like me upon you." For fifty years, half the known world faced a destroyer of unprecedented ferocity.

Under the leadership of Chinggis's sons, the Mongol nation expanded into Russia, China, Korea, India, Persia, Iraq, Turkey, and as far west as Austria. It became the largest continuous land empire ever known. The Mongols ruled China for 89 years (the Yuan dynasty) with its capital at present day Beijing. Eventually the Mongols were forced back to Mongolia by the Ming dynasty, which rebuilt the Great Wall of China to ensure the Mongols would never come back.

After their defeat in China, the Mongols retreated to their homeland. Caught between the growing powers of Russia and China, Mongolia fought to maintain its independence. Eventually China came into control of the area. In the 18th century, the Manchus decided to divide the country into northern and southern regions. The south was known as Inner Mongolia and the north as Outer Mongolia.

In 1911, when the Manchus were overthrown, and with Russian help, Outer Mongolia declared its independence. In 1921 a Russian general, known as the Mad Baron, led an army that routed the Chinese army, uniting all of Mongolia. However, this victory became a two-edged sword, as the Russian army became an army of occupation. This was a confusing time for the Mongolians. They seemed to be fighting everyone (the Chinese, the Russians, and themselves), but eventually, due to the socialist revolution in Russia (and with the help of the new communist regime), the Mongols defeated the Russian army and in 1924 the Mongolian People's Republic was declared. This communist government, with strong ties to Russia, remained in power until 1990. During this time the country was closed to the outside world.

After the fall of communist Russia, the Mongolian people began to hold pro-democracy rallies. In 1992 a new constitution was established, and in 1996 the Mongolian Democratic Alliance won election. As was typical with many of the European countries, the fall of communism and the rise of democracy in Mongolia became another two-edged sword for the Mongolian people. Though receiving greater freedom, the pullout of Russian forces and money brought about economic collapse and starvation. With the help of western ties, Mongolia is beginning to come back from the devastation that occurred while transitioning from a communist to a democratic state. Of course, the writing of this journal became possible only because the collapse of communism and birth of democracy opened Mongolia to missionaries and the teaching of the gospel of Jesus Christ.

# Quick Facts About Mongolia as of 1998

- Mongolia, located in the center of the continent of Asia, is completely landlocked between two large countries, Russia and China. Geographically, it is the sixth largest country in Asia and the 18th largest in the world. It is about one-fourth the size of the continental United States and in 1998 had a population of 2.5 million, one of the lowest population densities in the world. It is comprised of several ethnic groups: 85% Mongol, 7% Turkie (mainly Kazakh), 4.6% Tungusic, and 3.4% others. Four million Mongols live outside of Mongolia.

- The language spoken is Mongolian with the second language of the older population being Russian. Presently, English is replacing Russian as the second language. Some Chinese and German are also spoken. The Cyrillic script is the primary script, but the schools have recently begun to teach the traditional Mongolian script.

- The literacy rate is approximately 94%. The major religion is 94% Tibetan Buddhist Lamaism including some Shamanism. A small percentage of Muslims are found mainly in the southwest. Presently The Church of Jesus Christ of Latter-day Saints is the largest and fastest growing Christian church in the country.

- The climate typically fluctuates between 90°F in the capital city of Ulaanbaatar in July to –45°F to -52°F in the coldest month of January. It is an arid country with 80 to 90 percent of its rainfall occurring between May and September. The spring winds are devastating, blowing stinging sands similar to an arctic "whiteout." Ulaanbaatar is the coldest winter capital in the world. It is a remarkably sunny country and is referred to as "The Land of Blue Skies."

- The primary industry is animal husbandry. Petroleum, gold, coal, copper, uranium and other minerals are the natural resources but are not as yet developed due to the lack of an infrastructure. The country's major exports are: copper, molybdenum, fluorspar, cashmere, wood, hides, and skins.

- Typical salaries per month: doctor, $53; teacher, $70; laborer, $30. GDP per head of population was $359 U.S. in 1995. The rural areas operate within an almost cashless barter economy.

- The government is democratic with an elected Parliament and President. The Prime Minister is appointed by the Parliament. There are two primary parties: communist and democratic-coalition.

# The History of The Church of Jesus Christ of Latter-day Saints in Mongolia

"Elder Monte J. Brough of the Asia Area presidency met with [Mongolian] top government officials and the directors of five universities in May and August 1992. Afterward six missionary couples were sent to assist the country's higher education program and to teach others about the Church. The first couples arrived September 16, 1992, and lived in Ulaanbaatar, which is home to half the population of Mongolia. Elder Kenneth H. Beesley, former president of LDS Business College, and his wife, Donna, headed the couples. The first sacrament meeting was held September 20, 1992, in Elder and Sister Beesley's apartment. The Ulaanbaatar Branch was organized in 1993. The first converts were Lamjav Purevsuren and Tsendkhuu Bat-Ulzii, baptized February 6, 1993.

"The first six missionary couples to arrive included the Beesleys, Royce P. and Mary Jane Flandro, Richard G. and Anna M. Harper, Stanley B. and Marjorie Smith, C. DuWayne and Alice C. Schmidt, and Gary and Barbara L. Carlson. The first full-time elders were Bart Jay Birch, Duane Lee Blanchard, Brett Andrew Hansen, Jared K. Meier, Curtis Lee Mortensen, and Bradley Jay Pierson.

"On April 15, 1993, Elder Neal A. Maxwell of the Quorum of Twelve and Elder Kwok Yuen Tai of the Seventy visited Mongolia [and Elder Maxwell dedicated Mongolia for the teaching of the gospel].

"A foundation representing the Church was legally registered January 17, 1994.... The Mongolia Ulaanbaatar Mission was created July 1, 1995 with Richard E. Cook serving as president.

"Seminary and Institute classes for the youth in Mongolia began in 1996. Missionaries from Mongolia served on Temple Square and helped translate the scriptures into Mongolian."

Source: *Church Almanac 1999-2000*, pages 358-359.

# Names of Persons Mentioned in the Journal*

| | |
|---|---|
| Alfonsina | Alfonsina Lenzarini Hopkins, Pat's wife. |
| Baatar | (bah'-tur) Hopkins's driver, friend, and Mongolian "son." |
| Ball, Elder | Nick Ball, red-headed young missionary who also played Santa Claus at several school parties. |
| Batbold | (bat'-bold) Mission driver and "Man Friday." |
| Bayarmaa, Dr. | (by-ar-ma') Neurosurgeon and Church member. |
| Bayarsaikhan | (by-ar-sack'-hun) Building #7 handyman. |
| Beesley, Elder & Sr. | Ken and Donna Beesley, first LDS missionaries to Mongolia. |
| Benson, Elder | Joseph Benson, young missionary. |
| Buck, Elder | David Buck, young missionary. |
| Butkhuyag | (but-hoy'-yag) Director of Social Policies in Moron. Later moved to Ulaanbaatar where he and several members of his family joined the Church. |
| Buyankhishig, Sr. | (boy-an-hish'-ig) Mongolian sister missionary. |
| Campbell, Elder & Sr. | Welfare Services Senior Missionary Coordinator, Church Office Building. |
| Cantwell, Elder | Scott Cantwell, young missionary. |
| Carlson, Elder | Gary and wife Barbara were among the six couple missionaries initially sent to Mongolia. |
| Cerveny, Elder | Ralph Cerveny, young missionary. |
| Chris | Christopher, Hopkins's son. |
| Coil, Elder | Andy Bush Coil, young missionary. |
| Cook, President & Sr. | Richard and Mary Cook, first Mongolia mission president and wife. |
| Cox, President & Sr. | Gary and Joyce Cox, second Mongolia mission president and wife. Had served in Mongolia before being called back to serve as president. |
| Dan | Dan Griesemer, Kim's husband. |
| Dolona, Elder & Sr. | (dolan) Gary and Molly Dolona, medical tech missionary couple. |

---

*It is impossible to correctly anglicize the pronunciation of the Mongolian names and their sounds as they are unique to their language, but we have included approximate representations of the sounds as we heard them.

| | |
|---|---|
| Doya | Interpreter and former member of John's TOEFL class. |
| Enkhbold | *(ink'-bold)* Served as temporary companion to an American elder before serving a full-time mission in the States. One of the translators of the Doctrine and Covenants and Pearl of Great Price. |
| Enkhmaa | *(ink-ma')* Hopkins's interpreter and guide during their early days. |
| Enkhsaikhan | *(ink-sackh'-un)* Baatar's wife. |
| Enkhtor | *(ink'-tor)* Young man at Magicnet, internet access provider. |
| Enkhtsetseg | *(ink-tset'-sig)* Nyamdorj's mother. |
| Enkhtuvshin, Pres. | *(ink-too'-shin)* First Mongolian convert, district president, not married to Sr. Enkhtuvshin. |
| Enkhtuvshin, Sr. | Secretary to mission president, interpreter, and "Girl Friday." |
| Erdenetsetseg | *(air-den-tset'-sig)* A member of John's TOEFL class who eventually served a mission on Temple Square following which she became the first Mongolian full-time employee of the Church. |
| Flake, Garry | International Director of Humanitarian Services. |
| Gallia | Good friend who wears a medal awarded by the government for having 11 children. |
| Ganbold | President of the Hovd branch. |
| Gantulga | *(gan-toll'-ik)* Keyboard student. |
| Gerelsaikhan | *(ger-el-sack'-un)* Keyboard student. Served a mission to Japan. |
| Groberg, John H. | Asia Area President, The Church of Jesus Christ of Latter-day Saints. |
| Groberg, Sr. | Jean Groberg, wife of John H. |
| Hague, Elder and Sr. | Robert and Deloris Hague, a missionary couple from Yakima, Washington. |
| Jennifer | Jennifer Asplund, Hopkins's youngest child. |
| Jeremiah Clawson | Terri Clawson's son. |
| John Asplund | Husband of Jennifer Asplund. |
| Jones, Lloyd | Missionary who taught Nancy. |

| | |
|---|---|
| Khavtgai | *(hawft'-guy)* Baatar's brother. Professor, branch president, counselor in district presidency and co-translator of the Doctrine and Covenants and the Pearl of Great Price into Mongolian. |
| Kim | Kim Griesemer, Hopkins's oldest daughter. |
| Kinnison, Elder & Sr. | Gary and Victoria Kinnison, senior missionary couple who lived in Erdenet, located in the north central part of Mongolia. |
| KJ | Kim Grant Hopkins, daughter-in-law, married to Chris. |
| Lamb, Elder | Jonathan Lamb, young missionary. |
| Lenore | Lenore Ferguson, John's sister. |
| Lowther, Elder | Jared Lowther, young missionary. |
| Lubsanjav, Dr. | *(lub-san-jav)* Noted professor in Mongolia, leader of the movement to return the teaching of Mongolian script to the schools. A Buddhist and friend of the Dalai Lama. |
| McIntire, Elder | Bernell McIntire, missionary coordinator of EIL in Mongolia. |
| McSwain, Elder | Harry McSwain, Area Welfare Agent, Hong Kong. |
| Miller, Elder & Sr. | Jo and Lew Miller, missionary couple and first director of the Service Center of the Church in Mongolia. |
| Munkhtsetseg | *(munk-tset'-sig)* Sister missionary on Temple Square and major translator of the Book of Mormon into Mongolian. |
| Munkhtuya, Ms. | *(munk-toy'-yuh)* Director of Khan Uul district orphanage. |
| Nadmid | *(nod'-med)* Dolona's interpreter. |
| Nemu, Mr. | Printer used by the Hopkins's. |
| Nyamaa | *(nee-mah')* Driver for couples. |
| Nyamdorj | *(nee-yam'-dorj)* Young boy who received wheelchair from Deseret International Charities. |
| Oogie | *(oog'-ee)* Teenage member of the Church. |
| Oyun, Dr. | Doctor at Khan Uul District Social Welfare Center and mother of Doya. |
| Oyunga | *(oi-yun'-ga)* Baatar and Enkhsaikhan's daughter. |

| | |
|---|---|
| Parkinson, Elder & Sr. | Jim and Kerry, CES couple, assigned to Darkhan for part of their mission. |
| Pat | Patrick, Hopkins's fourth child, second son. |
| Rolfson, Elder | Vann Rolfson, young missionary. |
| Sandwijav, Dr. | *(sawnd-wee-jav')* Chief surgeon of the only oncology hospital in Mongolia. |
| Shipp, Elder | Daniel Shipp, served his mission previously and returned to Mongolia while we were there. |
| Sessions, Elder & Sr. | Garold and Pauline Sessions, CES couple, assigned to Erdenet in the summer. |
| Sosor | *(so'-sir)* Early convert to the Church, cleaning lady, and dear friend. |
| Staley, Elder & Sr. | Owen and Superla Staley, Humanitarian couple assigned to Boy Scout project. |
| Sumya | *(soom'-ee-ya)* Interpreter who later served a mission in Chicago and then attended BYU-Hawaii. |
| Swenson, Elder | Devon Swenson, young missionary. |
| Terri | Terri Clawson, Hopkins's second oldest daughter. |
| Theurer, Elder & Sr. | *(tire)* David and Gayle Theurer, mission doctor and wife. |
| Torgerson, Elder | Ben Torgerson, young missionary who several years later returned to Mongolia and with a Mongolian sister translated many hymns for the official Mongolian hymn book. |
| Tserendulam | *(tseran-dew'-lum)* Enkhmaa's mother from the Gobi Desert. |
| Mrs. Tumenbayar | *(too-men-bye'-er)* Director of Police Children's Shelter. |
| Ulaankhuu | *(oo-lawn'-who)* Director of Mongolian Blood Center. |
| Unruhjargal | *(un-ruh-jar'-gal)* "Unruh." Keyboard student and university student studying voice and opera. |
| Voros, Elder | Jeremy Voros, young missionary. |
| Wilstead, Elder | Damon Wilstead, young missionary. |
| Wirthlin, Joseph B. | General Authority of The Church of Jesus Christ of Latter-day Saints. |
| Yerolt | *(yur-olt')* Branch president. |

## Names of Places Mentioned in the Journal

| | |
|---|---|
| Baganuur | *(bah-gan-nor')* |
| Darkhan | *(dar'-hahn)* |
| Erdenet | *(air-den-net')* |
| Gorodok | *(gor'-dock)* |
| Hovd | *(hövd)* |
| Khan-Uul District | *(hawn-ool')* |
| Khara Khorin | *(ha-hor'-in)* |
| Muren (Moron) | *(moor'-on)* |
| Nalaikh | *(ni'-lack)* |
| Saynshaand | *(sain-shand')* |
| Sukhbaatar | *(sook-baa'-ter)* |
| Tuul | *(toll)* |
| Ulaanbaatar | *(oo-lawn-baa'-ter)* |

# Current Map of Mongolia

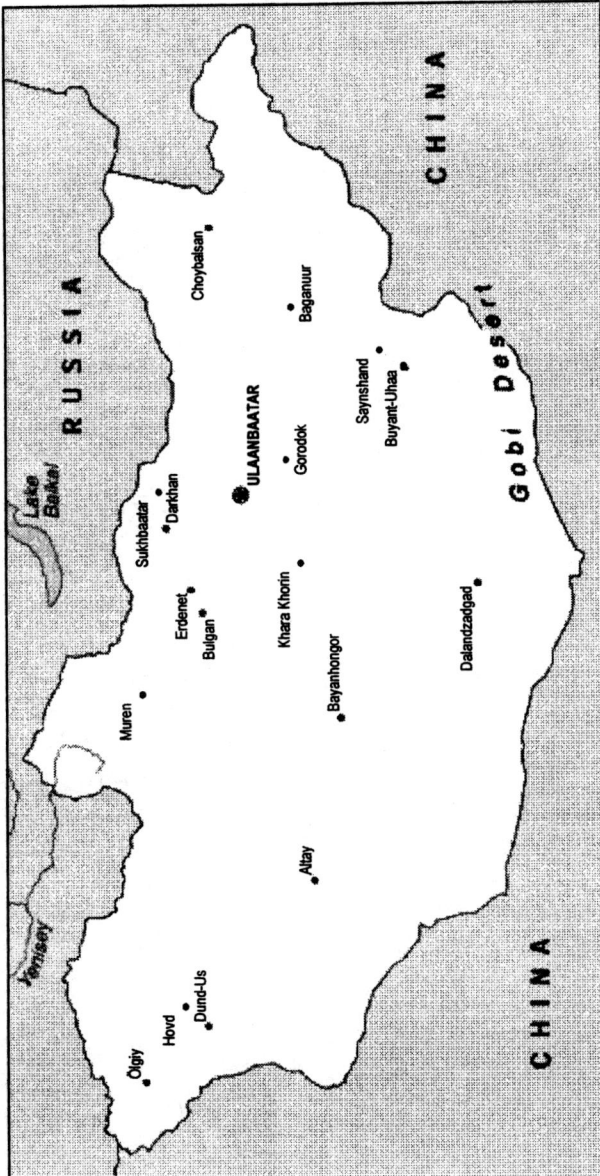

RUSSIA

CHINA

Lake Baikal

Yenisey

Choybalsan

Baganuur

Saynshand

Buyant-Uhaa

ULAANBAATAR

Gorodok

Darkhan

Sukhbaatar

Erdenet

Bulgan

Khara Khorin

Bayanhongor

Dalandzadgad

Muren

Gobi Desert

Altay

Hovd

Dund-Us

Olgy

CHINA

# MONGOLIA
## The circle in the clouds

The missionary adventures of John and Nancy Hopkins

Visit our website:

*www.walkingthelinebooks.com*

and click on "Interactive Mongolia Site."

This website contains pictures of the people
and places in Mongolia referred to in this book,
separated into chapters.

# preparations

## Introduction

*John*

After years of vaguely thinking we probably would go on a mission some day, we began to think more seriously about it when I retired at the end of June 1996. We approached the idea cautiously, as is our wont. If we were to go, we said, we would go after a full year of retirement so we could do all the traveling, remodeling, and resting that we had in mind. We planned, too. We would be willing to leave on or about August 1, 1997, because (1) that was 13 months after my retirement, and (2) our son Chris's lease would expire July 31 and he could move into our house the next day. Thus, we would have the benefit of a house-sitter we could trust and Chris could save a down payment and become a homeowner rather than an apartment renter.

We had our own criteria for the mission, of course. We would go for 12 months tops—in case we didn't like it. It would be a service mission rather than a proselyting mission because neither of us handles rejection very well. A mission in education or family history would be fine, thank you very much. And we would serve in an English-speaking country, of course. Finally, we would serve in a temperate climate because we do not function well in hot, humid weather.

Well, as will be shown, only one of our criteria was met (Chris's lease notwithstanding!). We won *big* on avoiding hot, humid weather. As Nancy said, "One more demonstration that you should be careful what you pray for!"

Even though we received little that we asked for and expected, we feel fine about all of this. It dawned on us that our "criteria" were an attempt to set bounds and impose conditions on God (and the "Brethren"). Consequently, we backed off to the point where we were comfortable thinking that we would be willing to serve in any non-proselyting way in which our talents and abilities could best be used.

We continued to carry the underlying tension felt by every missionary — *where* am I going to serve? — but the broadening and deepening of our commitment to serve a mission seemed to us to augur well for the quality of the experience. We were pleased with this.

## The Lord Takes Charge
### *February 22, 1997—John*

In early February, as Nancy was waiting for me to complete my high council responsibilities at stake conference, she read through a list of mission opportunities posted outside the stake president's door. She had browsed through the list before, but this time her eyes were drawn to the listing of a need for a curriculum developer in Vladivostok, Russia. As I had devoted the bulk of my professional life to curriculum development, it seemed to her to be a template for my experience and qualifications. The date the person was needed was already past, but she decided to check it out anyway.

What followed was "interesting," if you are a non-believer, and "the hand of the Lord," if you believe in such things. When Nancy called about the Vladivostok posting she was referred to the International Coordinator of the Humanitarian Services division of the Welfare Department (not, as one might expect, the missionary department). Thus, we found ourselves launched upon a previously-unknown-to-us back channel to serving a mission which resulted in our knowing where and when we were going to serve before our papers were formally submitted, and the stake president learning about it *after* the family, the ward, and even many in the stake!

The pace that followed was somewhat breathtaking. Planfulness, conservatism, and control were scattered to the winds in yet another demonstration that "the best laid plans of men aft gang a'gley."

The brother we were talking with, Elder Campbell, asked us to send him — better yet, *fax* him — copies of our mission papers, resumes, and the cover pages of our passports. Chris faxed them after Nancy lovingly re-typed all 10 pages of my resume. Then we left on a four-day trip to Atlanta.

On Monday, February 17, I went on from Atlanta to Miami to visit my mother. Nancy returned home where she received a call from Elder Campbell asking whether we could leave on a mission April 1st or would we have to wait until April 30th. Since Nancy knew that we were now fully committed to the mission, and in the spirit of "getting on with it," she said we could be ready the first week in April. The die was cast. We still didn't know where we were going, or what we would be doing, but we now knew with surety that we were going on a mission. Further, Elder Campbell instructed us to have the stake president send our completed missionary papers to him, rather than the missionary department. He would attach a "recommendation" that the Brethren generally honored unless they detected a health reason not to. Thus, we also knew that we were going on an *international* mission. We didn't know where yet, but were told Vladivostok and the Eastern European countries were under consideration (e.g., Hungary, Romania, Bulgaria). Kim (our eldest daughter) was certain it would be the latter, because we would then be perfectly situated to break the roadblock we were experiencing in our research on my Perzo and Wirbick family history lines.

We quickly scheduled interviews with the bishop and stake president for Sunday, February 23rd so they could complete the appropriate sections on our missionary papers.

## We Receive our Unofficial Call

*February 25, 1997 —John*

Brother Campbell called. He had on the line with him, in a conference call, Elder McIntire, a senior missionary serving as the coordinator of an English project in Ulaanbaatar (*oo-lawn-baa'-ter*), Mongolia. Elder Campbell said that the people in Mongolia had been sorely concerned because the McIntires were scheduled to leave and no one was on the horizon to assume responsibility for the program. They were worried that the program might flounder and fail in the absence of someone to lead it. And then, Elder Campbell said, we came along in the nick of time and would we be willing to assume responsibility for the program?

Nancy and I talked with the director for a while, to learn more about the project and its activities. Elder Campbell then suggested we hang up, think about whether we were willing to go to Mongolia, and then let him know whether we would accept the still-informal call.

Nancy and I hung up, looked at each other, and thought about it for a few minutes. We would be gone 18 months (not 12, as we had stated in our mental criteria), but we would have agreed to go for 24 months had that been required. Another of our criteria was that we would serve in an English speaking country, but the message obviously got garbled as we would be teaching English rather than basking in it. It would be a humanitarian mission all right, but we would be studying the missionary lessons in the Senior Missionary Training Center (SMTC) in Provo, Utah and would be teaching missionary and new member lessons at nights and on the weekends. Both of us felt it didn't matter that the call would be to serve somewhere near the end of the earth.

We prayed about it, felt good about the call, and phoned back a few mintues later to say we would be happy to serve in Mongolia. We definitely *are* going on a mission!

Elder Campbell discussed reporting dates with us. We will report to the SMTC on April 30, my 65th birthday! After six weeks of training, we will travel to Mongolia and arrive just one or two days before those whom we are replacing leave. All of this was another testament to us that the Lord's hand is in this.

## Report to the High Council
### *February 27, 1997 — John*

The stake president had me report to the high council the circumstances surrounding our decision and call (though we *still* haven't received an official call yet). I told them the circumstances were really quite remarkable. I recounted how the listing had captured Nancy's eye at stake conference (even though we had both perused the exact same listing in prior versions and had been unmoved by it) and how that had led to the current toboggan ride.

I told the high council that we knew the weather conditions were bitter, but that we were really unconcerned about that. We felt quite serene about going because it felt right. Further, I told them that they should be aware (as we are learning) that after devoting a life of leadership and service to the Church, as they all were doing, that it was the natural thing to go on a mission. It's part of the natural progression which the Lord (through the Church) makes available to us, and we should not hesitate to step up and take advantage of it. I urged them to file the thought away in their minds and begin immediately to see themselves going on a mission in their later years lest they fail to grow and progress to the full extent the Lord makes possible for us.

## The Lord's Other Hand
*February 28, 1997 —John*

While the Lord's one hand was ensuring that our going on a mission was proceeding according to His plan and His schedule, the other hand was quite busily engaged in producing one of those acts of loving kindness that makes us love Him so. Starting months before we focused on the idea of going on a mission, He set into motion a series of events that led to our seeing every one of our children and my mother and sister just prior to our having to leave them for at least 18 months.

Way back in August, no doubt prompted by the Lord since she is so close to Him, KJ (Chris's wife) launched a secret drive to provide a surprise birthday party for Nancy's 65th birthday. The result was that on January 23, 1997, Nancy walked into her kitchen to find Kim, Terri, and Jennifer (our three daughters) and 40–50 other people smiling at her and wishing her a happy birthday. The point of this particular story is that we were able to see three of our children when we weren't expecting to and hadn't made any specific plans to do so.

Shortly thereafter, we heard from Pat (our son who lives in Bologna, Italy) that he and his boss might be flying to Atlanta to attend a massive sports equipment convention. Their plans were soon finalized and we made arrangements to fly to Atlanta to spend four days with them. We had a good time together, which was fortunate, since the earliest we would have seen him otherwise was in May when we planned a trip to Italy to visit. And, as it further turned out, we would not have been able to make that trip since we were reporting to the SMTC April 30th, and would have had to go for at least 18 months without seeing Pat if it weren't for the Atlanta sojourn.

Finally, before any of the mission events began to occur, we decided that I would continue on from Atlanta to see my mother and sister for a few days while Nancy returned to Philadelphia to take care of our joint duties in the Family History Center. Later, after the mission events did occur, we realized that we must have been prompted to make those plans, otherwise I would not have seen Mom or Lenore (my sister) prior to our being gone for 18 months.

All in all, it is clear to us that the Lord used His other hand to set in motion a set of decisions and subsequent events which placed us in the extremely beneficial position of being able to see almost all our loved ones prior to our being separated from them for the duration of our mission. For this, we are humbly grateful and very appreciative. We would not have been able to pull that off had we tried, but with the Lord all things are possible.

## Natural Progression

*March 2, 1997—John*

The reaction of others to our going on a mission to Mongolia has been remarkable in and of itself. Members of the Church are thrilled and laudatory, as might be expected, but several of the stalwart members have felt the need to say that we are their exemplars—that they look up to us and follow (or hope to follow) our lead. We hope this is true as far as going on a mission is concerned. The stake president remarked, while interviewing us, that it had been a long while since a couple from the stake had gone on a mission, and this surprised us since there are many, many who could have done so. People are willing to become temple workers, it seems, but haven't felt the need or the capacity or the opportunity to serve a mission.

People who are not members of our church have been equally praiseworthy. The many patrons of the Family History Center who have commented have admired the dedication and/or the commitment that has led us to take this step. Our general care physician was frankly jealous that he couldn't do something just like this—he is hankering to volunteer his medical skills to some backward peoples who would be greatly benefited thereby. The staff at our dentist's office were so intrigued that they felt the need to participate somehow, so they put together a "care package" of dental floss, toothbrushes, and similar materials sufficient to last us the 18 months of our mission.

## Information Abounds

*March 4, 1997—John*

When was the last time you read something about Mongolia? Probably not any time recently. Nonetheless, when we found out we were headed for Mongolia it suddenly seemed like it was the hot topic of the month.

On first hearing, Terri (our second daughter) leaped into the Internet like a gazelle, of course, and rounded up a dozen really good sources of information. Did you know, for example, that *The Washington Post* publishes the three-day weather forecast for Mongolia on a daily basis? She also discovered that MagicNet is the now-privatized company that used to be the national communications agency, as well as the rates that it charges for Internet access in Mongolia. All of this while I was lumbering through Yahoo and could only come up with the meanderings of a Norwegian philosopher about the "real" reasons behind Genghis Khan's success.

When word got out in the ward, we were instantly given two articles of *National Geographic* on Mongolia and a large, illustrated map of the country. Another ward member visited a local book store and picked up the *Lonely Planet* edition on Mongolia — one of a series of booklets on out-of-the-way and *really* out-of-the-way places.

Then the calls started to come in (starting from Salt Lake City) that the *Church News* for the week had a two-page spread on the Church in Mongolia and had we seen it? We did see it when our copy arrived in the mail ten days later, and we searched every picture for clues about this place — "How short he is!" "She certainly looks well dressed," and "Look at those mountains behind Ulaanbaatar!"

The week was capped with a phone call from a member of the ward who had served his mission in Singapore. He assured us that we would find ourselves working with truly lovely people even though they were ostracized by their families when they joined the Church. He recounted a couple of stories about such people and said they tried to invite them to dinner often to offset the impact of their ostracism.

He, too, remarked on the *Church News* article and said that within the past ten days he had been in Salt Lake City with two German associates of his company. He had taken them to see the film, *Legacy,* and one of them, in particular, was very impressed with the message. So, the ward member took them across the street to Temple Square where they were met by a guide who showed them around. Our caller was struck at the time by the guide, and wondered, for example, where in the world people had just one name. He found out when he read the *Church News* article; she was one of the two Mongolian missionaries pictured in the article!

It's interesting to note that we are surrounded by a wealth of information, of which we only become aware when there is reason for us to reach out and tap into it.

We hope to add to the information flow through our journal entries. Though we are aiming them primarily at our family, Chris has just completed the structure for a web page that will enable anyone and everyone to tap into it and share the adventure with us should they so choose. 'Tis a wonderful age, indeed.

## Busy but Quiet
*March 22, 1997—John*

We are in a period reminiscent of the latter stages of World War I, where the opposing sides in The Great War hovered in the trenches most of the time but occasionally sallied forth to engage in tremendous bursts of energy. We are in a waiting period. We go forth each day to purchase another few things that have occurred to us, but, for the most part, we are waiting for the official notice that we have been approved to work in Mongolia and should report to the SMTC on April 30.

We have moved from "unofficial" to "semi-official" status in that regard. We received a telephone call two days ago from the welfare department stating that the Brethren had approved our call, and that we would be getting a single-page letter to that effect from the Brethren "sometime." (This doesn't entirely set our minds at ease since we have heard stories in the past couple days of young men who didn't get their letters until they had been in the MTC for several weeks, and of others who were told one thing but found something entirely different in the official letter.)

Our preparations now focus on the house so it will be in good order while we are gone and so Chris doesn't have to mess with it much while he is house-sitting for us. During the week we employed others to cut the hedges in the back yard down to the ground, which gives us a view from the kitchen window that we haven't seen for 20 years (and which Nancy hates). We also had the two apple trees pruned, trimmed the two fir trees that stand at the corners in the front of the house, mulched the gardens, had a leaking window repaired in the sun room, and installed new lattice work around the bottom of the sun room.

Nancy began to pack yesterday. She filled one huge suitcase with nothing but medicines, over-the-counter drug store items, and packets of dried foodstuffs. It would be fine if that left us three suitcases to pack our bulky winter shoes, coats, gloves, thermal underclothing, and so forth, but we still have much miscellaneous stuff to pack, so at this stage we are not at all certain that we can get from here to there! We look at it and we contemplate, but we don't do a lot since we're not at all sure what we can or will be able to do! So, the days go by and we are busy, but we are not "ready," not by a long shot.

## It's Official

*March 23, 1997—John*

Our "official" letters/packets arrived! We have to send back our acceptances and get a series of *shots*. Boy, do we ever need to get *shots!* There are at least six of them (typhoid, polio, hepatitis A and B, etc.), and, in addition, we will probably get an immunization in the SMTC for meningococcal meningitis. It's interesting to see that some of the shots on the list are ones that are required for Mongolia and no other stake or mission in the entire Church! We're not troubled, though; like lambs, we go willingly to the (whatever).

## Easter 1997

*March 31, 1997—John*

Few places in the world are as beautiful as Bucks County, Pennsylvania, in the spring. The dogwood, redbud, azaleas, forsythia, and magnolias combine to create a wonderland of beauty. Throw in the tulips and daffodils for an additional good measure. The beauty here isn't concentrated in a particular place, like the Hanging Gardens of Babylon, so it isn't a matter of comparing Bucks County with the Seven Wonders of the World. Rather, it is a matter of being able to drive for miles and miles and seeing beautifully maintained homes, yards, and subdivisions, all prepared by their owners to reflect and reinforce the beauty that the Lord (and his operating committees) have made available to us. It is sensational and soothing at the same time.

We continue our preparations for departure. There is still much to get and to do, but this has been going on long enough that both of us are feeling that we wish we could leave tomorrow. Enough, already! is the feeling. Let's get on with it!

12

One "preparation for a mission" began to take shape Easter day with an extended, expanded Family Home Evening. Terri and Chris arranged for us to be linked to the rest of the family through the Microsoft Game Zone. There we can play games with other members of the family and send concurrent messages back and forth. John played a game of checkers Easter evening with the folks at Terri's house, lost badly, and found that he was playing against 10 people who were sharing dinner at Terri's. Then two of our grandsons decided to stay with us overnight, and we continued to enjoy their company into the evening and on Monday morning.

It was fun to interact with members of the family and we look forward to more of it when we all get together today at 3:00, including Pat and Alfonsina this time. Let the games begin!

We rededicated our house yesterday, so it is ready for us to leave and Chris to move in. The house has been helping us by advancing the breakdowns due to occur before we leave—so the plumber is due tomorrow to fix some leaks and replace some faucets, and the repairman is due as well to fix a dishwasher that suddenly sounds as though it is grinding metal. We're actually pleased that these things are occurring so we can get them repaired before we leave.

## Fidgety

*April 4, 1997—John*

We're fidgety. Now that we're into April we'd like to get on with it, but there is practically a whole month to go. And the longer we mark time the more things we think we need and the more buying sorties we make. The pile of things we have to take already far exceeds our ability to get it to Mongolia, but we continue to add to the pile daily, nonetheless. It doesn't make sense, of course, but the psychology may be that when we buy things we give ourselves a sense of progress that the calendar doesn't permit. How's that for a rationalization!?

Another thing we do to simulate progress is to pack. We know how to pack. Having raised a family of five kids we're actually pretty good at packing. But this packing has some pretty difficult requirements. We have to lay out things for the month of April. Then we have to lay out things for the 5½ weeks in the SMTC. And then we have to lay out things for 16 months in Mongolia. Some of these things are overlapping, but many of them are not. Then everything that's left has to be packed and stored in the basement so Chris and KJ can move in when we leave.

We tackled the master bedroom yesterday, but were worn out by the item-by-item decisions that have to be made about which time period is right for the item. At this rate, we'll get to the end of the month with things just half-packed and worn to frazzled lumps by the decisions that have had to be made.

In the mail today was a package that may permit us to make some *real* progress even though we are still at home. We received a manual and some cassette tapes that offer a "basic course" in Mongolian. We listened to the first side of the first tape over lunch, and the sounds struck us as being beyond the capacity of the human throat. We're hoping it was only because our mouths were filled with ham sandwich at the time because our first efforts to speak Mongolian were not promising at all. The manual also informed us that it would show us the basics of written Mongolian, but that it probably wouldn't help much because most written communication is in the Russian Cyrillic alphabet. Not very promising news for a couple who is going to Mongolia to "communicate."

We were surprised during the past few days by weather news about Ulaanbaatar. Terri had shown us that *The Washington*

*Post* provides three-day forecasts for Mongolia. We've been watching them during the past month. Then the *Post* changed its display a couple of days ago and the weather information changed at the same time! The forecast had been showing typical high temperatures of 29° to 32°F. The new forecast indicates that the high for today and tomorrow is 70°F, and that's exactly the same spring temperature we're enjoying in Bucks County today. Sunday the high temperature goes back to 24°F, and the low temperature 4°, but the cold weather picture is not nearly as bleak given the new weather displays. The historical low temperature for Ulaanbaatar is given as –30°F, which is considerably better than the -40° to –50°F we've heard about. Further, another couple in the stake got their mission call to Winnipeg, Manitoba, Canada, and when I checked it out on the Internet I saw that their winter temperatures get down to –30°F as well, so all of a sudden Mongolia isn't looking so fearsome. The practical difference may not mean much when the temperature gets that low, but it *seems* a lot better.

Now, back to tape 1, side 1, and the basics of "greeting" in Mongolian.

## Slippin'

### *April 10, 1997—John*

By now the days are just slippin' by. When there was a month or more to go, the days seemed to drag by and we felt like it was never going to end. Suddenly, we are saying to each other that there's just *two weeks* to go and *how are we ever going to get everything done that needs to be done before we leave?!?!?!*

We bought another "jumbo" suitcase yesterday. We've begun to pull things off the pile atop the bed in Jennifer's room and to stash them into suitcases. Well, we ran out of suitcases before we ran out of pile, and we still haven't begun to pack the *clothes* we have to take with us. We're prepared for lots and lots of illnesses, food shortages, gadget deprivations, and so forth, and we have lots of outerwear to handle the cold and wind, but we don't have any inner clothes to put under our outerwear!

We're also busily putting away lots and lots of fine things and little glittery things that would attract the eyes (and "pingers") of an inquisitive grandchild. With Chris and family moving in when we move out, all agree that it would be wise to put away these attractive nuisances. So, John worked in the kitchen today, putting away the good dishes, and Nancy worked in the living room/library putting away fine things from the wall unit.

The pace is quickening. We haven't begun to run yet, but we certainly are moving a lot faster than we were two weeks ago. Now that we have the Mongolian language tapes we're so busy wrapping things up that we find it difficult to get time with the tapes, and after a busy day of packing we go to sleep when we *do* use the tapes! Such is life, I guess.

## We're OFF!

*April 25, 1997—John*

Well, at least we've started our engines. The suitcases are packed (eight of them, counting our carry-ons but not counting a shopping bag full of teaching materials which we hope the airlines won't notice). The stored items are all in boxes and toted to the cellar. The house is clean, thanks to two days of effort by Nancy—one day for the upstairs and another full day for the downstairs. The radios and CDs have been put away; the TV goes into a box and down to the cellar tonight. KJ is having us for dinner tonight, so the pots, pans, everyday silverware, and miscellaneous other kitchen gear have all been put away. Chris has been bringing in boxes from his attic (fearsome thought) and storing them in whatever niches remain in the cellar. He will put our suitcases in the van the last thing tonight, to save time in the morning when we leave early for the airport.

More wonderful things happened during the past two weeks. Word of our mission is spreading like the proverbial ripples upon the water, and we've been hearing from dear friends from the near and distant past. Probably the most distant message we received (in terms of time) was from Nancy's roommate while she was in Bethany College (Bethany, West Virginia). We also heard from the elder who taught and confirmed Nancy in Columbus, Ohio, many years ago (Lloyd Jones). He was pleased and proud that we were going on a mission (as well he should be, since it was just one more fruit of his labors). We were touched by his offer to provide some financial help if we needed it.

Our kids have been actively involved in preparing us to go. Thanks to their good efforts, our laptop has been set up so that we can converse with all of them just as though we were talking to them on the telephone. We had a wonderful time during the past ten days having "phone" conversations with Pat and Alfonsina (his wife) in Italy, and all for the cost of a *local* phone call! The quality of the sound is excellent; it is easy to tell who is talking just by the sound of their voice.

The kids also set us up to play games over the computer, so we've been playing checkers and other games with one another. While the games are underway, typed messages can be sent concurrently. Sometimes the games have reminded me of a ladies Tuesday afternoon bridge club, as the card game gives way to the more interesting conversation that is being typed out below. The game really slows down during those times.

Nancy and I were set apart by the stake president last Sunday. First he released us as Family History Center director and high councilor, respectively, and said some kind things about our work in these callings. Then he proceeded to set us apart with his counselors assisting. He gave us blessings that spoke directly to the things we hoped for and were concerned about. We left feeling, in spirit as well as in deed, that we were Elder Hopkins and Sister Hopkins, prepared and ready to do the Lord's work.

Early tomorrow morning we leave for Salt Lake City where we will spend five days with our three daughters and their families and then into the Senior Missionary Training Center Wednesday morning. We are ready.

# senior missionary training center (SMTC)

## Packing Our Cares and Woes

*May 1, 1997—John*

From April 25th to April 30th we spent five wonderful days in Utah with Kim, Jennifer, and Terri and their families. The flight out was uneventful but fraught with lessons for us. We paid $250 in excess weight and baggage fees in Philadelphia but still carried with us four bags, two down overcoats, Nancy's raincoat and wide-brimmed hat, and Nancy's purse. It was too much.

We staggered and stumbled and fought our way up the narrow airplane aisles and back again. Our bags caught on every seat as we went by, causing us to lurch, pull, bend, and strain all the way. When we reached our assigned seats, some of the bags were heavy, and it was awkward and difficult to stow them overhead. The passengers behind us in line resented the delay, so in Denver (and later in Salt Lake City) we waited until everyone else was gone before we deplaned, and in Denver we took advantage of early boarding "for those who needed a few extra minutes" and had our bags stowed before the others had to get by. In Salt Lake City, I put on both down overcoats over my suit-before loading up our carry-ons. It must have been a funny sight as we puffed our way through the terminal and out the door to where Terri was waiting with the van.

We knew we were lucky we hadn't had heart attacks and that we'd never make it to Mongolia lugging so much stuff. The next day, we went out and bought yet another jumbo-sized suitcase — our fifth. Then we spent all day Tuesday rearranging our mountain of stuff to redistribute the weight and reduce the amount we had to carry. We also pulled out a large amount of heavy instructional materials because the Church welfare department agreed to box and ship them for us. But would you believe, at the end of the day we had filled our new jumbo suitcase and hadn't eliminated a single bag from the ones we carried from Philadelphia! The bags were lighter, because we had gotten each bag under 70 pounds, but in so doing we had filled the new bag with the excess weight and left empty space in the other bags. We were bummed out Tuesday night by all the effort and the realization that we hadn't accomplished much despite the effort.

Early Wednesday we loaded everything into Terri's van once again and left for the SMTC. I was lounging in the back with the bags. At the first stop sign I thought my life was over as the bags lurched forward against the driver's seat and, on the other side, against me and the passenger's seat. Fortunately, they stopped before they overwhelmed me and we continued on our way.

Our mission got off to a great start. The first people to greet us were the parents of a former bishop in Doylestown, our home ward. They have invited us to have dinner with them some evening. The first day in the SMTC involved us in meetings from 8:30 A.M. to 9:30 P.M. (we didn't even have time to unpack). Ours

20

is a large contingent because there is a group of 26 senior missionaries (11 couples and four single sisters) being prepared to go to Thailand. The Bangkok mayor is a non-member graduate of Brigham Young University and he has undertaken, through BYU, to have this group teach the elementary school teachers of Bangkok how to teach English to their pupils. Two others are going to Hong Kong, six to Vietnam, and we are going to Mongolia.

The senior missionaries are wonderful people. One of them is 85 and leaving on his fourth mission (he left on his first mission the year before we were born). The instructors are excellent, the Spirit is very strong, and even the food is good. We feel we are well launched on our great adventure, exhausted though we may be.

## If You're Lucky, You'll Be Sent to Outer Mongolia
*May 2, 1997—John*

The main message of the SMTC is already clear; we are to do all that we can do, and give all that we have in order to provide an opportunity for the Spirit to witness to the truthfulness of the message during that interaction. So yes, we are to improve our knowledge of the gospel. And yes, we are to improve our presentation and teaching skills. But in the end our job is to cultivate and sustain discussions which enable the Spirit to do its work. Our personal love and concern for each of God's children is an important element of the work, of course, because any insincerity on our part will belie the message of the Spirit. But if we truly care, and if we are willing to reach out and speak up to others, we will be doing our part. And if we do our part, we will be blessed for our obedience.

Touched and stirred as we were by this message, we nonetheless cut class on the second afternoon! Instead, we went to a

21

session of Women's Conference on the BYU campus where the topic was: Search for Truth in Outer Mongolia. The panel included the first couple into Mongolia in 1992 (Brother and Sister Beesley), the first mission president (President and Sister Cook), and a Mongolian sister (Munkhtsetseg) who is on a mission in Salt Lake City and who is devoting half her time to translating the Book of Mormon into Mongolian.

We were astonished to see the number of people who came to the session. The large amphitheater (with possibly 1000 seats in all) was filled nearly to capacity. Who would imagine there were that number of sisters interested in Mongolia? And they cared! An intense spirit came into the room that brought tears to the eyes as the hardships and joys of service in Mongolia were unfolded. Near the end of the session, following an appeal for more missionary couples, Sister Cook announced that there was a sister in the audience who was going to Mongolia (accompanied by her husband—after all, it was the *Women's* Conference!) and asked us to stand. The entire assembly happily and heartily applauded us at some length.

When Nancy first heard we were going to Mongolia, her first thought was of her mother's oft-repeated admonition that if she was bad she would be sent to Outer Mongolia. Two members of the panel repeated the very same story, so the parents of people our age must have used that forbidding message a lot. Today, though, it seems the opposite is true. The general perception seems to be that if you are lucky, you'll be sent to Outer Mongolia!

The way people treat you here can do a lot for one's self-esteem. Last evening, as we were walking to the store next door, a car stopped in front of us and the young woman who was driving asked if she could take us someplace. She asked where we were serving and expressed sincere admiration for our willingness to go to Mongolia. A bit later, a young man approached us at the checkout counter and repeated the conversation, except that he was patting me on the shoulder and rubbing my back the whole time! And then he came back and rubbed my arm some more! I keep thinking that this is all well and good *but we haven't done anything yet!*

I know that we will serve (and all this praise would make it hard to back out), but conditions in Mongolia have improved markedly every year since the first couple went there in 1992. Brother and Sister Beesley were the real pioneers, and it is they who have earned, and deserve, all the praise and acclaim. The thought crossed my mind that Mongolia has in some strange way become the mission-of-the-month and anyone associated with it reaps unusual attention. The couples going to Vietnam, Thailand, and Hong Kong are doing no less, yet there is not the same degree of glamor attached for some unknown reason.

## We Are to Care for Every Single Individual
*May 5, 1997—John*

I'm impressed with the caliber and message of our church leaders. We've all had the experience at one time or another of receiving an instruction or hearing about a new program that left us thinking: "I don't know that I totally agree." Well, we heard directly from the mouths of some church leaders today and I believe their unfiltered message is one with which we all would agree.

We were scheduled off the BYU reservation today. Our meetings were held in the Church Office Building in Salt Lake City. There we listened to a number of church officials, including the head of Latter-day Saint Charities, a general authority from the Fifth Quorum of the Seventy, the General President of the Relief Society, and (her husband) the Director of Hosting Services for the Church. They told us in sharp, clear terms that in those countries where the government did not want us to proselyte we were not to sneak around and try to do so anyway. They want us to represent ourselves and the Church with real integrity. We are to work hard at our assignments and look for service activities we can perform in our off hours that will have a direct, positive impact on one or more people. In so doing, we will be letting our lights shine to such an extent that people will *know* we are different. As they puzzle about the cause of that difference, the Spirit will tell them what they need to know—without our having to open our mouths.

Nancy attended a number of conferences in Salt Lake City in the '70s where the leadership of the welfare program gave her a view of the Church welfare program that was more lofty, generous, and expansive than the view usually held by people in the mission field. Nancy's understanding of the program was a vision that had the power to stir the heart and inspire one to action; other members often had a more pecuniary view. Our lessons today indicated that Nancy's view is still held by the Church welfare leaders, and that they truly desire and intend for us to care for every individual in the countries where we serve, and that we exert our energies toward helping every one of them—more if that is possible. It is a vision that has the power to motivate, inspire, and challenge those of us who care.

We had an interesting personal experience today. We learned that we will have to move to various locations in and around the campus each day for the next four weeks. We also learned that the BYU shuttle system that is supposed to transport us to these various locations is an unreliable beast. So, we arranged to have Terri transport one of Kim's cars to our meeting place so we can use it while at BYU. We were to meet Terri in the lobby of the Joseph Smith Building at 4:00. At 3:50, we entered the lobby and Nancy instantly recognized that the lady standing in the far kitty-corner was a dear friend from Bloomington (Indiana) whom we hadn't seen for 20 or more years. After a few moments of joyous reunion, on impulse I placed my head close to hers and told her what an important influence she had been on us during one of the best periods of our Church lives. Both of us cried, of course, but I could see that she appreciated my words. We parted soon after.

On the way back to Provo, I thought about the "coincidence" of our meeting. Our friend still lives in Bloomington, so it wasn't that she often stands in that lobby. She'd only dropped by to take care of a couple of matters pertaining to her daughter's wedding. And we, of course, hadn't known she was going to be there when we arranged to meet Terri in the lobby. During our evening meeting, it struck me that the Lord had likely arranged the whole thing so I could be the means through which He could answer one of her prayers. (She is so close to Him that I know He would move Heaven and Earth to respond to one of *her* prayers!) So I think He surveyed the Salt Lake Valley, identified someone whose presence would be meaningful to her, and then set into motion the conditions and circumstances that led to my making the meeting appointment, to her being in the lobby to take care of a few things, and to Nancy's instant recognition of her across 20-plus years and a large hotel lobby.

## Life in Mongolia (by Videotape)

### *May 23, 1997—John*

Another busy week comes to a close and, as usual, something new appears on the horizon to continue the process of stretching us—forcing us to grow. As part of our training to teach English to people who speak other languages, each evening we present lessons for two hours to members of the Provo community who are not native English speakers. The week was much better in terms of our preparing lessons. After spending dozens of hours learning what was between the covers of the various manuals, workbooks, and other resource materials provided us, we have finally developed some ability to find with dispatch the information we need to fulfill the needs of our students. Thus, instead of spending 10 to 12 hours in lesson preparation every day, we were getting it down to 6 to 8 hours per day. We were reaching a level of comfort. Then, of course, it became time to stretch.

We attended Mongolian Culture Night on Friday evening. Three returned missionaries gathered together the six young missionaries studying in the MTC to go to Mongolia and we two senior missionaries for a presentation of various things Mongolian. They showed us the garb they had brought home with them, slides of the Mongolian people they had baptized who are now leadership figures in the country, and a videotape taken by one of the original senior couples. We were fascinated by the tape since it displayed pictures of the apartments where we will be living, the schools where we will be teaching, and the streets and buildings of Ulaanbaatar itself. Though four years have passed since the video was shot and changes have undoubtedly occurred, it nonetheless gave us our first glimpse of the environs where we will be living and working.

The apartments are of poured cement construction, as anticipated. The interiors are coated with a chalky material that is painted an institutional color up to the five-foot level and thus stabilized. The surface above the five-foot level is not painted, and according to the returned missionaries thus remains a chalky material that rubs off when touched. There are three bedrooms of a size that one can just walk around the edges when a double bed is installed. A small kitchen and smaller bathroom and "storage room" (closet) round out the facilities.

The bathroom was amusing from a distance; it will probably be much less so when we have to actually live with and use it. The video showed the lady of the house turning off the running faucet in the bathtub. She turned, and turned, and turned, to no avail. The fully running water cannot be turned off—some leaky faucet! The shower head is attached to a hose that you hold above you as you shower.

Then the video showed the laundry device. It is a metal rectangle about the size of two clothes hampers, side by side. One lifts the device into the tub and then fills one side with water from the shower hose. Roughly five shirts are placed into the water and washed. From there, they are moved to the other side where they are spun vigorously. While that is happening, the first side is emptied of soapy water, refilled with clean water, and the spun clothing is placed back in the first side to be rinsed in the clean water. The rinsed clothing is then either put back into the spin side or immediately hung to dry on hangers throughout the apartment—dangling from doorways, from light fixtures, wherever. The arms of every chair we saw were draped with socks that were drying. After washing has been completed and the washer has had time to drain, it is lifted out of the tub and placed in the hallway until the next wash day.

The returned missionaries gave us a helpful hint about using the chalkboards in the country. The surface of the boards is so rough, and the chalk has so much "rock" in it, that one cannot readily write on the boards. They taught us to hold the chalk in one hand and a wet cloth in the other. To write, you scrub the surface of the board with the wet cloth and then write on the wet surface before it has a chance to dry. This is the only way one can write on the chalkboards.

We saw an amusing sequence about using the public buses. Apparently there are always more people using the buses than

there is space available. And the Mongolians do not have the tradition of getting into line. So, as the bus arrives, the driver slows
to a crawl, and the people who are getting off jump from the
front and middle doors while the people who are boarding
gather at the back door and jump while the bus is still moving
forward! At some point, the bus driver decides he has been there
long enough and guns the bus forward to the next stop.

We've been told that pickpockets are common among the
masses of people jammed on the bus. They use razors to slice
through wallet pockets and through the bottom of backpacks, after which they simply empty the contents and hand them off to
another person, who hands them off to a third person, following
which they all jump off at the next stop. I think we'll try to use
taxis whenever we can.

We had two inspiring meetings during the week with officials of the humanitarian services department of the Church. This
is the department that attends to the survival needs of distressed
peoples and nations, and devotes Church resources to building
the capacity of nations and peoples to improve themselves. We
are part of those "Church resources" because we will be helping
the nation and people of Mongolia to improve their lot in life by
helping them to relate to the affluent Western democracies. There
are a hundred couples like us serving throughout the world. By
the end of the year there will be 65 such couples in Asia alone. It
is good.

## In Search of ... The Gift of Tongues
### May 28, 1997—John

We've completed a week of tutoring in the Mongolian language and, surprising to me, it's possible that we actually
learned something. It's a jumbled mass in our heads right now,

but we can already see that we have better command of the Cyrillic alphabet. We've been eyeing the alphabet for weeks — even have it written on the white board in our room so we can study it in the niches of time available to us — but the second half remained beyond our ken. Now that we've begun using it in words, however, we are better able to remember that the "P" is the "err" sound, and that the "H" is really the "N" sound, and so on. There are four letters that look like "Y" and distinguishing among them continues to elude us, but we definitely made good progress during the week. Today we copied a hymnal with 20 LDS hymns that have the Mongolian language and the Cyrillic alphabet. We think that seeing the words in relation to the familiar LDS melodies will further help us decode the language and build vocabulary at the same time.

Further, we were able to gain a sense of the tenses that are used in the Mongolian language and the suffixes that are associated with them, even though we are as yet unable to apply them. Their sentence construction remains a complete mystery, however. We've learned that the verb always comes last, but that's all.

The time devoted to language instruction created an additional pressure on our evening English language teaching, of course, so the week has been very demanding. TGIF reached the level of a fervent prayer today. We really *need* the weekend break. We'll use it to bring some order to our notes and scratchings about the Mongolian language. Perhaps greater orderliness will also bring with it greater understanding? One can hope.

Most of the people with whom we've been receiving EIL (English as an International Language) instruction are leaving Monday for Thailand. A large contingent is headed to Bangkok to teach the elementary school teachers there how better to teach English. Four couples remain, heading to Hong Kong, Indonesia, Vietnam, and us to Mongolia. We have been touched, and moved, and impressed, and inspired by our compatriots. They are such good people and their quiet examples of courage, dedication, commitment, and caring have been a constant inspiration to us. It has been a constant pleasure to be in their company and we will miss them. Oh yes, they are very quick-witted, too.

Elder Joseph B. Wirthlin was the speaker at the Tuesday evening devotional at the MTC, and he continued the recent trend of mentioning Mongolia. He reported that he and his wife will be leaving in early June to visit China, Nepal, Hong Kong, and Mongolia. If he visits the other countries first, as seems likely, there is a good chance we will be in-country when he arrives in Mongolia and will undoubtedly have a chance to meet him.

On Thursday the young missionaries "kidnapped" us, took us to their classroom, and there made us join them in a stirring rendition (in Mongolian!) of *If You're Happy and You Know It Clap Your Hands*. We did well in the clapping hands, patting knees, and stomping feet parts, but the Mongolian words were pretty much a bust. They plan to sing this song around half of the world. I think we'll pretend we don't know them!

## The Final Countdown

### June 1, 1997—John

It's ten days before we leave for Mongolia and time is really speeding up. We completed our EIL classes and conducted our final evening class. We had been told that we would get quite close to the students we taught in the evening classes and that proved to be true. It was a sad parting on both sides as we said goodbye and they wished us well on our missions. Some of our students were members of the Church and some not, but they all wished us well in our endeavor. The sad part is we'll not see them again as they are in most cases returning to their own countries or our paths simply won't cross again.

Gary Carlson, the husband of one of the original couples that went into Mongolia in 1993, came over Monday night and installed the Cyrillic alphabet in our computer. Now our work looks very professional and at least gives the appearance that we know what we're doing. When talking to Gary, we can tell that he wishes he were going back with us. He made friends with some of the Buddhist monks while there, including the leader of one of the prominent monasteries, so we are taking to him one of the presentation books about the Church entitled *The Mission* as a gesture of respect.

Last Saturday, Jennifer and her family moved from Logan to Draper where John has a new job. On Sunday we went to South Jordan for Jeremiah Clawson's ordination as an Elder in preparation for his leaving on a mission to Chicago North. His older brother is already on a mission in south Brazil.

Yesterday we purchased a vegetable brush (a must in Mongolia). We are told we will have to first scrub all vegetables with the brush and then soak them (even after they are peeled) in Clorox water before eating them!

This week our daily schedule changes — we begin attending classes again from 8:00 A.M. to 8:30 P.M. We are to receive additional instruction about Church welfare, charities, and humanities. We're so fortunate to be here. It exceeds our every expectation.


## SMTC Retrospective

*June 11, 1997—John*

Our visas to stay overnight in Beijing have not been received, so we will not be leaving for Mongolia Monday as planned, but the delay provides a good opportunity to look back and consider our stay at the SMTC since we completed our training yesterday.

Our final session was an opportunity to give feedback on the training program to one of the Church's area managers. The members of our group offered some suggestions for modification and improvement, all right, but the overriding sentiment was that we felt good about our preparation and were ready to go. Certainly Nancy and I feel that we have been well served by the staff of the SMTC. We feel prepared to teach English, and that is something we would not have said when we first came here.

Of equal or greater importance, we feel spiritually bolstered and strongly supported by the Lord and the Spirit. We know that we have been chosen by the Lord to do this work, and we know that the Spirit will help us do whatever needs to be done to succor his children in Mongolia. We recognize that we are His instruments and are both proud and thankful to be such.

The clear, steady progression of events, circumstances, and "coincidences" that brought us to this point are a major element of this knowledge. There is no question in our minds that the Lord made it possible for us to be in this place at this time to do the task that lies before us. Of such things are firm personal testimonies built.

Our association with the other couples in the SMTC and our training staff has been another major element. We are in awe of the spiritual maturity of our associates and the dedication which has enabled them to override all obstacles in order to be here. What came so easily and naturally to us required Herculean effort for some of them. Physicians in active practice have closed their practices in just two weeks and reported to the SMTC. Successful small businesspersons have turned their businesses over to their children or others in order to answer the call. Couples 70, 75, and even 85 years old are embarking on their second, third, and fourth missions to serve the Lord. People from humble backgrounds are plunging into the unknown to do that which they are called to do, even though they have no knowledge, experience, or background for the work. As for the staff, they have consistently displayed a knowledge and love of the scriptures that is impressive. Who wouldn't be humbled in the face of such dedication and understanding?

Nancy has written extensively in her reports to the ward about a third element, and that is the knowledge one gains about the worldwide work of the Church that had been largely unknown to us. The Church is supporting, through humanitarian services, literally thousands of projects aimed at helping the poor and the needy around the world. They range from $100,000-plus donations of medical equipment to $70 micro-grants to help individual entrepreneurs start a business. And, of course, with these donations of equipment and cash there goes the untold value of the missionary couples who freely donate their knowledge, experience, and personal abilities to make the equipment work and the entrepreneur succeed. It is a vision and a work that is worthy of a worldwide Church headed by the Lord himself because we couples strive to leave the recipients with the capacity to continue without us, thereby ensuring continual growth and progress into the future. As one teacher taught us, we are doing more than teaching them to fish. We are teaching them everything they need to know about the entire fishing enterprise, so they will not falter or fail over some aspect which is new to them. Only then do we leave them to continue on their own.

So yes, I'd say we are as ready as we're likely to be. Ready to contribute our time, talents, money, energy, and training toward helping the people of Mongolia help themselves in whatever ways they think best. It is a mission we are at once proud and humbled to serve.

*Note: Our visas arrived shortly after this was written. We left for Mongolia later that day.*

# June 1997

## The Trip

*John*

Our trip to Mongolia was uneventful and, contrary to my expectations, not at all demanding. Which is not to say that it wasn't hectic at times. We'd been told that everyone that passed through Beijing had an airport story, but we didn't have much difficulty there.

We were met by the mission president and some missionaries, escorted to our apartment building, and were relieved and thrilled that they (rather than we) carried our luggage up the three flights of stairs needed to reach our apartment. We had arrived in Ulaanbaatar and were excited and pleased to be there.

## First Days

*June 17, 1997—John*

While traveling in from the airport in Ulaanbaatar, the mission president and his wife mentioned that they and the members had fixed up our apartment for us and expressed the hope that we would like it. After walking up three flights of stairs at this high altitude, we were so out of breath when we walked into the apartment that most of our concentration was on just staying upright. But we couldn't help noticing the Cheshire grins on people as they helped us into the apartment or came to visit shortly thereafter. They were there to see us, but they were equally interested in getting a look at the apartment.

And no wonder! Members of the branch and the senior couples had spent *nine days* just prior to our arrival stripping off the old wallpaper, removing worn contact paper, clearing away left-over items, and moving every item of furniture so they could paint all of the floors in this three bedroom apartment! The wallpaper is a light blue with delicate figures in it. The floor is painted a complementary blue — painted personally by our mission president! And the walls that are not papered are painted slightly more than halfway up in the same blue as the floor. It is an institutional style, but essential with this construction because the unpainted portions of the wall leave chalk dust on your hands and clothes any time you touch them.

We had visitors the rest of the day — to see us and to see the apartment. We enjoyed watching them look over the portions of the work they had done, to see how it looked now that the place was finished. And it looks great. No outback outpost here. We are comfortable, well looked after, and very appreciative of the members and couples who worked so hard and long to prepare a pleasingly attractive and comfortable apartment for us.

One of our more memorable visits was from a group of eight or nine Young Women. They proceeded to sing a couple of hymns for us *a capella* and to recite the Young Women's motto, all in Mongolian. It was charming. Our problem was that initially we couldn't tell by looking which were the young women and which were their leaders. It was only after the leaders took charge that we knew who they were. This is a continuing problem

for us—Nancy was surprised when the "deacon" who was preparing the sacrament on Sunday stood up afterward and conducted the service! We are told the problem is common among
non-Mongolians.

Friday evening (the first evening in Mongolia), we had a
delicious dinner with the couple we are replacing. The meal ban-
ished all thought about the scarcity of provisions here. Not only
was it hospitable, but it was necessary for two reasons: first, we
were (and are) such neophytes in terms of food preparation and
managing drinking/washing water that we had to be protected
from ourselves; and second, after all the work that the members
put into preparing our apartment, neither the stove nor the
refrigerator worked and we couldn't have prepared a meal for
ourselves had we wanted to—which we didn't. (These appli-
ances weren't fixed until three weeks after we'd arrived.)

Two senior men subsequently got into the electric box in the
hall, jiggled the breakers for a while, and combined the wires
from our apartment with the breakers powering the sisters'
apartment next door. That restored the electricity, and it works
well as long as we both aren't operating strong electrical appli-
ances at the same time. If we do, the electricity fails in *both* apartments and we have to go into the hall and jiggle the breakers
once more. Eventually Elder Sessions, one of the other senior elders assigned to another city for the summer, came into Ulaanbaatar for groceries and was able to remedy the problem.

Our time is consumed with little things like that and with
preparing water for consumption. Boiling water to drink is a bit
of a chore, but one must also have boiled water to wash and rinse
the dishes, brush one's teeth, and for any other tasks that involve
things that go into the mouth. Too, we haven't developed a routine yet, so we are endlessly walking from one room to another
to find or pick up something we need to work somewhere else.

We're hoping this phase passes quickly because all tasks take longer than they should, and you get the feeling that you are slogging through molasses. Yech!

There is another form of water management that occupies our attention. We've been told that the entire city will be without hot water from June 17 (later today) until June 24. Now this does not create as much distress as one might think because when the hot water *is* on it is available only occasionally—like 6:00 to 7:00 A.M. Thus, we have already learned that when you brush the hot water pipe and it is warm, you quickly jump into the tub and take a bath because there is no telling when the next opportunity will arise. My predecessor told me he was up at 3:00 A.M. going to the bathroom, brushed the pipe and noticed it was warm, hopped in, took a bath, and then went back to sleep for the rest of the night.

Since we had no stove or refrigerator, for Saturday breakfast we had peanut butter and some crackers that were in the apartment's pantry. For lunch we varied the menu by having peanut butter and jelly sandwiches. But we had delicious dinners with other couples Saturday and Sunday evenings, and it was a real pleasure getting better acquainted with more of our colleagues.

The fact that most of us live in the same stairwell might suggest the kind of "fortress" mentality that often develops among small cadres of Americans in foreign countries, but that is not the case here. First of all, everyone that we've met is genuinely taken with the love and spirit of the Mongolian people. Second, they want to be out among the native Mongolians because there is so much to do and so little time to do it. So while they may not always enjoy everything the Mongolians eat, for example, there is no hesitation and no reluctance to get out amongst them to get things done.

I, on the other hand, am still developing that attitude, which led to an amusing episode. Elder McIntire and I had a 10:00 A.M.

appointment on Saturday with the executive director of the foundation that supports our teaching work in Mongolia. He decided we would take a bus to the meeting rather than a cab. Well, I had heard that pickpocketing was rampant on the buses, and one of the elders who traveled to Mongolia with us had already had the experience of finding someone else's hand in *his* pocket while they were taking a bus in from the airport on Friday! Further, on the way to the bus stop, Elder McIntire regaled me with stories of times that he had caught pickpockets in the act and wrestled them to the ground(!), so my feelings weren't the most serene when we got on the bus. Nothing happened during the trip but I must have been a funny sight as I tucked myself into a corner, used my arms to protect every valuable and part of my body, and kept turning back and forth to keep an eye on every person within five steps. It was a nerve-wracking experience (I got a sense of how women must feel when they have to protect themselves everywhere all the time). I didn't want to get paranoid about the people I'm here to help, so I resolved right then not to carry money or valuables that I didn't want to lose. Now I leave home my credit cards, temple recommend, driver's license, and so forth, and only carry the amount of money I can afford to lose in a day. It is doing wonders for my peace of mind.

On Sunday we walked to church with another of the senior couples. We were welcomed by many new people—there must have been 80 Mongolians in attendance. By the time we left, I had been named "keeper of the keys." I now have the keys to the closets where the sacrament preparation materials and the portable organ are kept. It is my job to be there early each Sunday to open these closets and also to carry in my pocket (in case of emergency) two slices of bread for the sacrament. Nancy was abducted by the Young Women and carried off to their meeting. While sitting in the Aaronic Priesthood meeting, I heard the Young Women singing, and it was truly beautiful. The men sang too. It could not be described as beautiful.

## Some Stories

*John*

We were coming out of the mission home yesterday morning and noticed there were three cows on the corner that weren't there when we entered. As we were passing them on the way back to our apartment building, a man sitting on the curb near them gave a loud, long cry. Nancy recognized it as the same cry we had heard before in Ulaanbaatar but hadn't recognized as a street peddler's call. Nancy then realized that this is the way they solved the problem of keeping milk cold and clean as it is transported. They just bring the cows right to the doorstep so there is no problem of transportation, cooling, or purity.

When one is on a ship, one accepts the need for door sills that will keep sea water from sloshing into every room. Since Mongolia is a landlocked country far from any significant body of water, we can't figure out why they have raised door sills at every internal and external door. We have learned to keep our eyes down as we walk (lest one literally fall into an open manhole), but we still trip ourselves several times a day as we stumble over a door sill.

The temperature here has been in the 95°F range for the past several days, and the high altitude and clear skies combine to make the sun blistering hot. In the evening, the west sun streams in the windows in our long wall, so the apartment gets very hot. Yesterday, we bought a portable fan to get some relief. The price was $39.95 and it was on sale at ten percent off. When the man showed me on the calculator how much the price was in Mongolian dollars ("tugrugs"), it didn't square with my mental calculations of 800 tugrugs to the dollar times $40 equals approximately 32,000 tugrugs, less ten percent, or 28,000 plus tugrugs. So he went through the calculation another time, and I said that wasn't right and went through the calculation yet another time to show that I was right. Eventually, the Mongolian lady with us pointed out that a ten-percent sale in Mongolia doesn't mean they reduce the price by ten percent; it means that you pay the full price and they give you gifts in the approximate value of ten percent of the purchase price! So we paid the full price and they gave us as gifts a new audio cassette tape and two wires to run between a TV and a VCR. We could have had batteries as gifts but they didn't have the AA size we were looking for.

Drivers travel at full speed in their rickety old cars. (Several times we have seen drivers using hand cranks to start their cars—honest!) Their driving reminds one of the bull ring where the skillful matadors show their bravery (and risk their lives) by moving ever closer to the horns as the bull thunders by. Mongolian drivers don't actually aim to hit pedestrians, but they certainly don't mind coming very, very close as they whiz past. In that sense, the drivers in Mongolia are the bulls and the pedestrians are the matadors. In our case, however, we just don't like to put all our faith and confidence in the driver's judgment that he will, indeed, miss as he goes past, so we pedestrians and most drivers act as though we are fair game every time we cross the street. Some of the senior couples think the drivers actually speed up as you cross so they can give you a really close brush-by.

Most streets are lined with metal shipping containers that people use as storage places or garages for their cars. (Everything is locked up here lest it be carried away by a burglar, a street person, or a child gang.) The streets around our apartment buildings are no exception and the children around the city *love* to climb atop them and run pell-mell from one end to another, leaping and jumping as they go. Since they are metal, the sounds of their journeys thunder and clang through the neighborhood. In the evening, when the doors and windows are open to let in some air to offset the heat of the day, it gets so loud that two people sitting in the same room can hardly talk to each other. Fortunately, the sun goes down at 10:15 P.M., and by the time the dark actually settles in at 10:30 P.M. the kids are home because it is too dangerous to jump from one metal container to another in the dark.

Tuesday and Thursday evenings for the remainder of June and all of July we will be teaching "community evening classes" in which we and three sets of missionaries provide free English instruction to whomever wishes to come. The first night we were prepared to teach about 100 students in five classes — two beginners classes, an intermediate class (which Nancy teaches), an advanced class, and a TOEFL[1] preparation class (which I teach). About 100 people showed up all right — 50 of the ones we were expecting and 50 more who were brand new! I hadn't made any provision for interviewing new students, so chaos reigned while we tried to sift and sort the walk-ins to get them into the right classes. Eventually people got into classrooms and teachers taught.

Afterward, as we were riding home, we noticed a long, long line of our students walking back to the city (the place where we teach is about 1½ to 2 miles outside the city) in the hot, hot evening sun. It sobered us immediately to realize that our students value English so much that they are willing to walk long distances to get free instruction. Of course they do a lot of walking in the normal course of events so it may not be as big a deal for them. But as tired as we were after teaching the class we couldn't help but feel humbled by their drive and thirst for English.

Earlier I mentioned the open manholes. The covers are off the manholes because street people live in the tunnels that undergird

---

[1] TOEFL stands for Test of English as a Foreign Language. The TOEFL, for which my students were preparing, is a test used by US and Canadian universities to determine whether non-native English speakers have sufficient English fluency to be admitted as students.

the city. It is where the steam pipes are, and in the winter they are able to stay alive by living in the steam tunnels. Nancy noticed one group of street children where the older ones were teaching a very young child how to eat the raw meat clinging to a bone they had found behind the meat market. The street people (including children) are often seen rummaging through the trash and rubbish that the people in the apartments discard in metal containers to be burned once a day. One of the first things the senior couples taught us was to discard our trash every day, before the food remnants spoil, and to package our food discards separately so they wouldn't be soiled and filthy for the food rummagers. This, and the thirst for English described above, demonstrate how much we are needed and it reinforces our gratitude that we are here.

## The Countryside

*John*

The impact of "the countryside" is all-pervasive in Mongolia. We had been told in the SMTC by former missionaries to Mongolia that the people wore boots with turned-up toes because they honored the earth so much they didn't want to risk digging into it with their toes. We also learned that many of the population lives a nomadic life on the steppes, moving their homes as their flocks and herds deplete the grass in one area to take advantage of the bounty provided by Mother Earth (my term) in another area.

And whereas some missionaries-in-training were told that the people in their nations considered the head sacred and not to be touched (even affectionately) by others, in Mongolia it is the foot that is sacred because it is the part of the body that comes into contact with the provider of all good things, Mother Earth. The people pack themselves onto the public buses, eyeball to eyeball and cheek to jowl; nonetheless, to step on another's foot is a major offense requiring an immediate and abject apology, including a handshake and a spoken (in my spelling) "ooch-la-rye" (slight trill on the "rrr," please).

We've seen more evidence of this feeling about the country-side recently. (I guess everything is recent since we've only been here a week!) Nancy was asking the members of her class where they were born and most simply answered, "The countryside." A few were born in Ulaanbaatar, but most were born "out there." When one stops to think about it one realizes that many (if not most) of the babies are born on the steppes without the benefit of hospitals, medicines, or anything other than the experience and the wisdom of the family members who are with them. It works, obviously, but I wonder about the fatality rate.

I talked with a young man who is unemployed except in the summer when he acts as a guide for tourists. He would like to go to university but cannot save the money. Still, he is going to take three weeks in the heart of the summer, immediately following the national holiday—Naadam, July 11–13—and "go to the coun-tryside" because his parents fear for his life otherwise. They are afraid he will die unless he recharges with the "pure" air, and the "pure" water, and the "pure" milk that he will get at home in the countryside. We know these things might be germ-ridden and polluted, but it is part of the national soul and spirit that the countryside is so clean and pure that it offers rejuvenation to all who live and visit there.

One of our interpreters told us, in all seriousness, that her dad was beginning to suffer the diminution in eyesight that comes with age and so he went to the countryside to get cured. Sure enough, the long, long sight lines in the countryside reversed the effects of age and he could see as well as he ever could when he returned from the countryside.

The grip of parents appears to be very strong here. A young woman practicing her English on me yesterday said she had just graduated from high school (which goes through the 10th grade) and wanted to go on to post-secondary schooling. Her parents were amenable but insisted she must first spend a year with them in the countryside in order to prepare herself physically and emotionally for the challenges of post-secondary education. Another told me that his parents (in the country) were insisting that his post-secondary studies be in the hospitality industry because they wanted him to be in a position to show others in the world how beautiful it is in the Mongolian countryside. The parents of yet another student are requiring him to go outside Mongolia to study forest conservation so he can help save "the countryside."

Veterans here tell us that Ulaanbaatar in general will become a ghost town following Naadam, and our English classes will have few to no students in them because almost everyone will "go to the countryside" until September. Not too long ago it was a Godsend that the ties to the countryside are woven so tightly. When the Russians pulled out of Mongolia in 1991, they stripped the country of everything portable. The people in Ulaanbaatar were in danger of starving during the harsh winter that followed. In response, the people from the countryside came to the city, gathered their family members, and took them back to the country to recover and survive.

Yesterday was another very hot and dry day. Nancy and I went to the Institute choir practice at 6:00 P.M. (Nancy is the choir director). At 7:00 P.M., just as we were having the closing prayer, a half dozen young men and women bounced into the room, eyes flashing and huge grins on their faces. They had spent the day in the countryside. They'd walked two hours out into the country, spent the day near a body of water that "came up to their chins" (the Tuul River, I think), walked two hours back in the blazing heat, and were so thoroughly rejuvenated that they literally couldn't stand still. They were "sorry" that they missed choir practice, but it was understandable (wasn't it?) because they had "gone to the countryside." They then proceeded to take the long walk back into Ulaanbaatar, chattering and bouncing as they went. Nancy and I sagged in exhaustion just watching them.

Today at church a gentleman was talking to me about the interstate highway system in the United States. I told him that it was true that one could drive from the East Coast to the West Coast without having to stop for a red light or a stop sign. (He asked me, "What if you wanted to eat?" and I told him you could pull off the interstate in that case.) He is just leaving on a business trip to eastern Mongolia; it takes 33 hours to get there by bus. As he said, the roads are not very good in Mongolia. He marveled that there were asphalt roads throughout the United States (he'd seen them on television) and speculated what an interstate highway system could do for Mongolia. But then he stopped and realized there never could be such a highway in Mongolia because it would despoil "the countryside." He contemplated the desecration for a moment and then put it out of his mind because it would never happen.

Nancy and I have looked at the rolling hills just outside the city and they are lush, green, and beautiful. There is an undeniable attraction to them, even for us. One of these days we are certain we, too, will go to the countryside (with our own food and water rations, of course) and then perhaps I will be able to add a personal note to the mystique of "the countryside."

## The Black Market

*John*

For some time we've been traversing the city back and forth, entering one anonymous (signless) establishment after another buried within warrens of nooks and crannies of equally anonymous buildings. Each shop seems to specialize in one type of product (e.g., office supplies, used auto parts, TVs, VCRs). We have been using a young Mongolian lady (Enkhmaa) to locate for us the shops that possibly might have the items we need and a Mongolian driver (Baatar) to take us there. Usually we have come away empty-handed, despite this knowledgeable local assistance, because that which is available for sale yesterday often is unavailable for sale today. The senior couples speak often of sources they have discovered only to find on a return trip that the proprietor has evidently sold out the one and only shipment he or she had and gone out of business.

Nonetheless, we had managed to whittle down our list of needs to a relatively few things that, everyone assured us, could only be obtained (and could be obtained more cheaply) at ..."the black market." Thus, we resolved to visit this place that is evidently tolerated by the government because it is either a symbol of democratic entrepreneurship or, more likely, a place where people can get the things they need when the systems of government fail to provide them. The black market helps to ease the pressure on the government to function better.

So at 1:00 P.M. on a clear day, with the summer sun blazing down upon us, we had our driver take us to the outskirts of town. To get to the market we had to pass through one of the ger[2] (gair) districts wherein live the members of the working class who cannot afford housing in town. It was sobering to observe a long line of people queued up with their pans and jugs to get water at a solitary faucet. We knew how difficult it was for us to maintain a pure water supply for ourselves with plenty of water available right in our apartment; how much more difficult it would be for those who must go to the public faucet for every drop of water they need to drink, cook with, and maintain some semblance of hygiene.

---

[2] A "ger" is a felt and canvas covered portable structure in which reside more than half of city residents and all residents of "the countryside." Each family has its own ger or home.

We were further sobered when we asked about the masses of people moving along both sides of the road and were told they were all going to and from the black market.

As we approached, we were entangled in a glutted, endless mass of honking, sputtering vehicles of all types, proceeding intermittently without order of any kind. Eventually, we agreed we would meet our driver "over there" and debarked (with some difficulty since there were so many people outside we couldn't get the car doors open) to wend the rest of the way on foot.

We tried to get in a nearby entrance but there were so many people we couldn't get near it. Our trusty guide took us to another entrance where you had to pay to get in, so it was approachable. We paid our tiny entrance fee and entered.

Mongolians have a particular method they use to get through crowds. When the bus arrives at a bus stop, for example, and they want to be sure they get on before it leaves, they place their forearm against the back of the person in front of them and exert a steady pressure to propel the person forward. It feels very much like you're the blocking back for the runner who is following behind. You're the cannon fodder to be expended for the greater good of the person who is ready to walk over your back to get to the goal. Simple and straightforward as it is, the method works well enough when everyone is moving in the same direction, as toward an open bus door. As we shall see, the method works less well when approaching a four-way intersection with traffic moving in all directions simultaneously.

*Everybody* was using this technique at the black market. After we entered the gate, amid a mass of fellow travelers, we started up a dusty path with booths on both sides. People, peddlers, carts, animals—all of us were trying to use the same space at the same time. Enkhmaa (our interpreter and guide) led the three of us with Nancy in the middle and me following behind. Naturally I was being pushed in the back all the time. If/When there's a glut of humanity ahead, the Mongolian answer is to simply keep pushing the person forward until you wind through the tangled mass. I got used to that, treating it as a touch of local color. Since I'd given all our money to Enkhmaa, Nancy and I didn't even worry about pickpockets, who we were assured would be ever present.

I was not prepared, however, to be jammed in the back by the handle of a pushcart being used like the handcarts of the Mormon pioneers. I turned around to see what was happening, only to be yelled at by a young lad who was evidently claiming some sort of right of way. Well, I put my hand on his cart handle and held him back so he couldn't/wouldn't just drive right over me and Nancy in front of me (I assumed Enkhmaa could handle herself very well, thank you). He gave me a very perplexed look. I gathered that it just wasn't done to actually *resist* the forward propulsion of this carrier of commerce. Besides which, the cart was so heavily loaded that either he could not restrain it or it wasn't safe for either of us to try to restrain it. I therefore deemed it wise, and safe, to fight our way to the side so the cart could trundle on by.

Onward we proceeded, caught in the midst of a seething, jam-packed, cheek-to-jowl crowd reminiscent of the bus service during rush hour. The heat, the noise, the confusion, the pushing, the dust, the whole bizarre business of it all combined into an experience quite foreign to our delicate western selves. If there weren't some things that we just *had* to get we would have turned around quickly and gotten our abused and offended persons out of there.

But onward we pressed (literally!). We found the linoleum we needed to finish some shelves and surfaces. We lugged four meters of it to the fabric place where we were unsuccessful in finding any drapery material heavy enough to keep out the heat generated by the western sun. One more purchase we *had* to make—some tools to use in maintaining the fragile elements of our water system.

At this point the pickpockets entered the scene. Evidently one had spotted Enkhmaa as the carrier of our 10,000T bills when she pulled the bills out of the bib of her overalls to pay for the linoleum. (Nancy was the keeper of the 5,000T bills which she had promptly stuffed into her bra.) Nancy noticed this character maneuvering to get a look into Enkhmaa's bib. Finally, he moved down the path in front of us, turned, and started walking toward Enkhmaa to bump into her head on. Nancy called a warning to Enkhmaa, who promptly crossed her arms over her chest, and the character moved on.

After his efforts to get into position to steal the money were thwarted, we pressed forward toward the tool aisle. We then came to a four-way intersection where the gridlock was complete. Enkhmaa wiggled through, somehow. Nancy surged (was pushed) forward. I followed—and discovered that I had no idea which way they had gone. No way to stand in the middle of the intersection to call or look one way and the other. I was merely propelled forward as one more piece of rudderless flotsam. I grabbed hold of a piece of stand and pulled myself out of the racing tide. Then I began to bellow and wail, but to no avail. Finally I hurled myself back into the stream, headed back to the intersection and discovered Nancy to my right. Enkhmaa had been sent to find me so Nancy and I both howled and wailed for a while, until we saw her bobbing through the surf, headed back to rescue us from our eddy in the flood.

As we were moving down the tool aisle, looking at all kinds of reconditioned junk, I noticed another man hovering over my back with obvious designs on our money. I gave him my best stare; he barely noticed. Then I gave him a hard glare; he stared back. I warned the others and we watched him while trying to look for tools and tacks. We couldn't do both; I don't know how the Mongolians see anything on either side what with having to watch out for the surging people and for your person as well.

Finally we found a claw hammer and some used screwdrivers. Nancy found some tacks that were smaller than what she needed but we took them anyway just to get out of there. We started back to the gate. On the way a young man's pack caught on Nancy's bag as he was pushing around her so he gave her a push. She pushed back and the young man got an amazed look on his face—evidently it is okay to push and shove, but you can't do it meaningfully or intentionally. That appears to be against the rules!

We went looking "over there" for the car, hot, thirsty, dirty, ruffled, and bushed. We found it and as we were trying to get up a slight grade to the roadway (where the traffic was at a dead standstill, of course, but with everyone sounding his or her horn nonetheless) our car stalled and died. After several efforts to restart, Baatar coasted backward, lifted the hood, and proceeded to dismantle the carburetor! We sat, baking in the hot sun. A driver who had pulled into the exit we had intended to use, thereby sealing us into a cul-de-sac, came smilingly over to help. He helped use rags to wipe the carburetor parts clean, then manned the crank to start the engine (the battery, by this time, was stone, cold dead). No use. Take more engine parts apart and clean them. Reassemble. We continued to sit. Finally, wonderfully, the car started. The driver moved his car to unplug the exit, we roared onto the roadway (without stopping to see whether there was any traffic coming) and sputtered our way down the hill and into the town.

It will be a cold day in Mongolia before we visit the black market again. But people say we will get over it in 3–4 months and will, indeed, go back. I doubt it.

As postscript to this entry: Baatar said someone had poured salt into his gas tank and that's why the car had stalled. We were told before we arrived that this is a favorite vandalism, so he's probably right. Further, a couple of the elders who traveled to Mongolia with us visited the black market yesterday. Veteran elders carried their backpacks in their arms; one greenie didn't and had his pack slashed. Another bought himself a "deel" (*dell*), the colorful outer garment worn by Mongolians. It, too, was slashed when his backpack was slashed with a razor to see what contents could be stolen from the pack.

Thus ended our adventure for the day, and the week, and the month.

## Some Random Thoughts

*Nancy*

Most of the Mongolian people are extremely honest. We had been told before coming that it would be a choice experience working with these people because they are basically innocent and sweet. We were not prepared for their genuine honesty.

As I struggle with recognizing the correct denomination of tugrugs, I have learned I can depend on their complete honesty as I fumble and falter while looking through the wad of bills we have to carry since a can of soup costs 800–1000 tugrugs (about one U.S. dollar). The other day at the market, I handed a woman a 10,000 tugrug bill when it should have been 1,000. She sweetly smiled at me (in a motherly way although I'm probably much older than she), shook her head, and handed it back to me, pointing to the 10,000 bill and showing me 1,000 on the calculator. I indicated to her that I was "loony" and she laughed. She could have taken my money and I would not have known any better. The calculator is an invaluable tool in UB (Ulaanbaatar). All vendors and store clerks communicate with we non-native speakers through the calculator. They punch in the numbers and that's how we know how much to pay. It is a marvelously efficient means of communication.

We referred to the "taxi cab" system earlier in one of our entries and it provides another example of the trustworthiness of the Mongolian people. I would never hitch a ride at home but it is most common here. When you get tired walking (and there are great distances) you hold out your hand, palm down, and wiggle your fingers. Eventually someone stops and picks you up. If you have a Mongolian walking with you, he or she will tell the driver where you're going. If you're not that lucky, you try to convey the best way you can where you want to be dropped off. Fortunately for us, most people in Ulaanbaatar know where the Mercury Market is so we just mention that and we're close to home. The driver pushes his/her odometer button and away you go. We have used this method several times. I resisted at first but have now relaxed and have even enjoyed several air-conditioned rides. One of them gave us an opportunity to teach our Mongolian escort, Enkhmaa, about air-conditioning. This is a real marvel to her. Everyone charges 200 tugrugs a kilometer (25 cents). The driver shows you the odometer at the end of the ride and that's what you pay.

Enkhmaa is in the advanced English class. She loves learning obscure English words and the missionaries love feeding them to her. She goes around mumbling, *mock, regurgitate, illuminate, disgraceful,* and then asks how to use them in a sentence. Then she turns them around on the missionaries and tells them, "You should not mock me," or "Your smile illuminates the room."

Since she does this all the time, I was caught unawares as we were setting up my classroom one evening and she was asking me about various words and how to use them in a sentence. After five or six of them, I noticed she was writing all the sentences down in her well-worn notebook. A light bulb went off in my head and I asked if I was doing her homework. She really giggled about having put one over on me. She serves here as a branch missionary but has sent in her papers for a full-time mission. She would like to go to Africa because she was raised in the Gobi desert and thinks it would remind her of home.

John and I (at 65) are considered quite old here. Life expectancy is not that of the United States. In my English and other classes I let them ask me any question they want. The second question (after "How many children do you have?") is always "How old are you?" When I reply "65" they always respond as a group, "Oh-h-h-h-h."

Many years ago my father explained to me how the motor control mechanism in the human brain automatically adjusts the height we step up or down when negotiating stairs. Normally the first step you take is noted in your brain and then each step afterward is the same distance and you don't need to check the height of each rise for each step—it is an automatic response. It doesn't work here in Mongolia. Over here, one step has nothing to do with the step before or after it and if you're on automatic it can be a jolting experience. I've had to catch myself several times so as not to tumble down a flight of stairs.

Ice cream doesn't melt in Mongolia. Kids can stand out in the blazing sun with their ice cream in a cone and it never drips. They can set it down and it remains the same. I saw them unloading some cones at the market yesterday and they're already made up, stacked sideways in a large metal container to be transported. Then when they arrive at the market they are placed into a cooler. We've never tried one to see how they taste as we had been warned by the medical personnel in the SMTC that the milk is not pasteurized and we should avoid local milk products. We'll never know if it's really cold. They have excellent cheese here. It's all imported from Holland and Germany.

John has taken on an added responsibility while we're here. The Mongolian internet provider is called MagicNet, through which we now have our personal access. It is owned by Data-Com, which has an information page about Mongolia and the area around Ulaanbaatar. Upon reading it in the States, John thought it could use some editing and polishing (of course). When we were in their offices arranging for our service, we became acquainted with a lovely young man who installed the necessary systems into our computer. He spoke excellent English but when he became aware we were English teachers and would be teaching that evening he asked if he could come. He wants to be able to take the TOEFL test and that's the class John is teaching. John told him we'd be delighted to have him and he did show up. The next week he brought his brother and sister. He has attended regularly ever since. His name is Enkhtor. Anyway, John showed him some ways that their information could be improved and suggested that this might be a service he, John, could perform for them. Enkhtor talked with the boss (they call him "the master") and he was delighted to get this free service. So John is now editing for MagicNet.

The Church has purchased a building in the center of Ulaanbaatar which is presently being remodeled and is referred to as the Central Building. Remodeling is a tremendous undertaking as it is quite cavernous and old. The work is mainly being done by one of the senior elders with several local helpers. They found that the insulation in the attic was simply black, filthy ash and all had to be removed. This took days, taking out a sack at a time. When the senior elder would arrive home after a day's work he looked exactly like the West Virginia coalminers I remembered from my youth. The only things that were white were his teeth and his eyes. He's not a young man and I truly feared for his health. At the end of that terrible task they had removed twelve tons of ash! Can you imagine the disaster it would have been had there had been an earthquake while a church service was underway?

The original missionaries here did wonders with packing crates. All their support materials had been crated in Salt Lake and then shipped here: books, food, and teaching materials of all sorts. The wooden crates have been turned into book cases, desks, storage shelves, pantry shelves, and so on. Someone was pretty handy with a saw, hammer, and nails. It provides us with plenty of storage space and each apartment is well equipped as a result.

As an English teacher here I feel a tremendous responsibility. Those who are in our classes hunger to learn to the point that they write down every word you say or every word or sentence you write on the board. They all carry well-worn notebooks for this purpose. They remind me of the blue books we used for final exams while in college. They use every bit of available space on each page and reinforce the covers with wide strips of clear tape. Our first night of class, John and I gave each of our students a new book to use during class and you would think we had given them pure gold. Every day I learn from them how much I take for granted. They teach me more than I teach them.

Speaking of being taught by my students: Genghis Khan is pronounced "*Chinggis Han.*"

# July 1997

## Fourth of July in Mongolia

*John*

Yesterday we celebrated the birth of our nation at the U.S. embassy in Ulaanbaatar. The embassy staff had been casting about for several weeks to locate some group that would volunteer to help them stage the celebration, to no avail. So, they turned once again to the group that regularly pitches in to do the work; Mission President Cox, Nancy, and another senior sister met with the staff three weeks in a row to plan. The staff seemed a bit nervous about conducting this *big* event, so at each of the three meetings the planning covered every facet of the afternoon in excruciating detail.

The party lasted from 3:00 to 6:00 P.M. (we got there at 1:00 P.M. to set up). It included a welcome from the charge d'affaires, a reading of President Clinton's July 4 proclamation, and the playing of the Star-Spangled Banner and Mongolian national anthem. Then there was an hour of eating, a raffle, and a showing of *The Wizard of Oz*. Last year the big raffle prize was a round-trip flight for two to the United States! We missed out on that goodie—this year's grand prizes were one $10, one $20, and (drum roll) one $40 telephone calling card that can't be used until you return to the United States!

The mission president volunteered to prepare the ice to put into plastic tubs with water to cool the beer and sodas (both donated by Beijing bottlers). Since you can't buy ice in Ulaan-baatar—anywhere, any kind—he fulfilled his assignment by clearing out the small chest freezer they have at the mission home, filled three pails of water, and then put the pails into the freezer for an extended period before the Fourth. It worked per-fectly! At the end of the warm summer afternoon there were still small chunks of ice remaining but all of the drinks were gone.

Nancy took responsibility for preparing and conducting games for the children. We put chalk marks on the ground for hopscotch and four-square. Nancy had little plastic fruit figures and teaspoons ready for relays and was prepared to play duck-duck-goose (whatever that is), but the little ones were more inter-ested in eating with their families than playing organized games. She would round up a few kids but they would soon wander away; thus there were no organized games.

The other senior sister volunteered her husband to prepare a board with diamonds, hearts, and circles cut out of it to throw bean bags through the holes or darts at balloons fastened to the surface of the board. This turned out to be the hit of the celebra-tion, with kids in line most of the afternoon to take a turn.

I, in the meantime, kept the condiment table clean and well stocked. People grilled their own meat and then came by my table so I was well positioned to observe and talk with this par-ticular group of American expatriates. We have them all, right here in River City. We have the organized groups, like the Peace Corps and Believers in Christ, and we have the lone, backpack-ing citizens of the world, cruising their way through life. We have the clean-cut families and the beer-drinking, scruffy-looking, foul-mouthed, fun-and-sun seekers. But just like the mustard, ketchup, relish, and diced onions on my table, it was all pure American. At first the people tended to stand off alone or with their groups. Then as the day wore on, they began to mingle, the Frisbees came out, and by the end of the day a large number of them were hooting and hollering together in a no-holds-barred volleyball game just outside the gates of the embassy.

We took down the decorations we had taped around the embassy grounds, rolled and packaged them carefully for next year's celebration (and the year after that, and the year after that...). I was thinking about one type of unspoken exchange that occurred during the day. The mission president had given the young missionaries the option of wearing or not wearing their name tags at the celebration; the only stipulation was that everyone had to do what the group decided would be done. Our missionaries decided they would wear their name tags even though, in the past, some expatriates had shown decided coolness toward them when they met on the street.

## Some Domestic Observations

### John

Life in Ulaanbaatar (at least during the summer) is nowhere near as stringent as we had feared. Given enough time and enough searching one can find at least a primitive version of almost anything. It is the time and effort that it takes to do even the simplest things, though, that contributes a great deal to our present schedule which has us arising each day at 6:00 A.M., going like gangbusters until 10:00 P.M., and then collapsing into bed only to arise the next morning to do it all over again.

What follows is intended to provide you some glimpses of

the little domestic things that consume so much of our time, attention, and effort. This cavalcade of "minor" details will enable you to get a sense of the grappling we've had to do to regain a feeling of control and order in our lives. The loss of that feeling of control has contributed as much as anything else to the niggling frustration and fatigue that we have felt since our arrival. I've heard some veteran members of the Church comment on the danger of becoming overloaded with *things,* and the consequent need which follows to be constantly managing your *things.* After three weeks in Mongolia I would like to add to that the danger of being controlled by our *routines.* Thinking positively, I'm hopeful that our little struggle to establish new routines here demonstrates that we aren't fossilized yet and that we will somehow benefit from this opportunity to revive our flexibility.

I fear that this will be interpreted as a griping or complaining piece about the hardships of serving a mission on the "frontier." It isn't. We are not the slightest bit irked about being here. Rather, it is an effort on my part to explain to you (and understand for myself) the factors that go into the adjustment we are having to make.

**BOILING WATER.** When our son Chris returned from his mission to Taiwan, weeks passed before he could bring himself to drink water from the faucet. After just three weeks we're getting a sense of the discipline that you get into with respect to water. When we arise in the morning we put on a kettle to boil some water. After it cools, which takes a while, we then boil more water to do the dishes (see **WASH DISHES** below). Then we boil more water to have on hand to replenish the water we use in cooking. Then we boil more water —just because we know we're going to need it.

Each cycle takes half an hour for the water to come to a boil and then boil briskly for 20 minutes. Frequently we lose track of the time the boil started and when it is safe to turn off the heat.

We really should have brought our little kitchen timer with a bell that could tell us when the 20 minutes were up. Sometimes the kettle clicks itself off before we return to check on the water and we don't know whether it clicked off early during the 20 minutes or in the 19th minute, so you are left each time with the conundrum of just how long to boil it again (or some more). Then it takes a couple of hours to cool, so sometimes we pour the boiling water into a pan to cool while we boil yet more water. There are times when we seem to have bottles, cooling pans, and boiling water everywhere we look in the kitchen.

BATHING. Some mornings we do not have hot water, so we have to wait until some water boils and then pour it in the tub. The kettle holds enough to fill two one-liter or liter-and-one-half bottles. That seems like a lot when you are filling bottles with a funnel, but when you pour a kettle-full into the bathtub it looks like a teacup-full. You add a little cold water, step into an essentially dry tub, and take what amounts to a sponge or washcloth bath. It is a most unsatisfying procedure.

On the other hand, when we do have hot water it is a *very* satisfying procedure. There is no water conservation here. Every fixture drips, splashes, or gushes water all the time. The toilets in some apartments (not ours, thank goodness) run full bore—there is no stopper so the water just gushes like a mountain stream. Thus, we have no reluctance whatsoever to fill our tub to the brim with hot steamy water when we have it. I've learned in Ulaanbaatar that it's hard to beat the experience of slipping into a steamy bath up to your neck and soaking for 10 or 20 minutes. I don't think either of us has missed our shower back home.

COOKING. The building maintenance people worked on the electrical box in the hall yesterday and we see that the wires for our apartment are now disconnected from the sisters' apartment next door and reconnected to our very own set of breakers. Now we both can use our stoves at the same time. But the heating elements on the stove are so sl-o-o-o-o-w that cooking can be an excruciating experience. For example, Nancy mixed up a batch of brownie batter using a goodly amount of such precious ingredients as chocolate and walnuts, only to have the oven literally burn the surface of the mix. She and I scraped off the burnt crust and baked the remainder. When she put on a smooth coat of icing, one could hardly see that a near-disaster had occurred.

But there's more that makes cooking a very complex activity here. Ingredients can be had but it's sometimes a struggle to find them. Then there is milk. We have to use powdered milk and it becomes another procedure, like boiling water, that you have to think about and plan ahead to use. It gets to the point where you hate to use milk because that will mean you have to make more, which means opening packets and using some precious boiled water, which means finding more packets at the market and boiling more water in the kettle, and the cycle goes on and on....

EATING. Yesterday Nancy discovered she had some space between her waistband and person. And I spent some time gouging a new hole to tighten my belt. There is food here, but getting the food, cooking it, and cleaning up afterwards becomes such a hassle that one subconsciously reduces the amount of food one prepares and eats. The result is that one loses weight even though there is plenty of food around. That plus the extra walking we do here that we wouldn't do back home apparently is having a salubrious effect on our waistlines.

WASHING DISHES. Washing dishes is entwined with boiling water and eating. We have to use hot boiled water to wash our dishes and the same to scald/rinse them after they are washed. Due to the pressures of boiling water, we've learned to rinse the dishes, pots and pans, and silverware in tap water first and *then* wash them in as little boiled water as the conscience will allow (to conserve the water). Since the heated water is too hot, we must add boiled water from the refrigerator to cool it down to the point where we can skip our hands through it while washing the dishes. Then we empty the precious boiled water down the drain, rinse the basin, and use another precious supply of boiled water to rinse the dishes. We hate to use the boiled water but you must, so it becomes another of the little daily struggles that wears us out.

This applies to eating, too. You don't want to eat peanut butter sandwiches all the time so you prepare something more substantial. But that requires the use of more cooking utensils, and so forth, which becomes an inner struggle because that will require more water for washing and rinsing and on and on and on.

FAN MANAGEMENT. I've written previously about luggage management and water management but we have other forms of activity that require managing as well. We have a floor fan, a table fan, and a little fan that can be mounted in the rather narrow windows we have here. As the day progresses and the sun moves from the south wall to the west wall of our apartment, and as cooking occurs in the kitchen, we spend a good deal of time moving these fans around for maximum cooling effect. As evening comes upon us we try to anticipate the heat in our bedroom and shift the fans in there to cool it off before we retire for the night.

PHONE MANAGEMENT. The mission president has arranged phone service for our apartments but the service runs off a local switchboard inside the building. This requires two of us users to serve as switchboard managers. Since there are only two couples in the building at the present time, we and the other couple take turns handling all incoming calls. The other couple receives all incoming calls from midnight to noon, and we receive all incoming calls from noon to midnight. We answer the ring, find out who is wanted (which can be a circus if the caller only speaks Mongolian), and then punch in the desired extension. If the called party isn't home the call switches back to us after a certain number of rings and we try to explain that the caller will need to try again later. Each call only takes a moment to process but the phone seems to ring and ring just as we are settling down to get a little rest. We have adopted the policy that we will not answer the phone after 10:00 P.M. and it seems to be a wise procedure. The other couple reported they have gotten calls at 2:30 and 3:00 A.M.; they are more conscientious than we and have gotten up and answered them!

ROOM MANAGEMENT. The young missionaries use the couples' apartments as places to hold discussions. Since there are just two couples in residence at the moment it is not unusual for us to have four to six discussions in our apartments each day. This afternoon, for example, we had three discussions going on in our apartment while Nancy was getting dinner in the kitchen. The only other room not in use was our bedroom so we both perched on stools in the kitchen and watched the water boil.

COCKROACH/FLY MANAGEMENT. We don't have cockroaches or houseflies at home so this struggle is just one more new and different routine we are having to work into our daily lives. One cannot hope to win the war against these critters. The mission president arranges to have our apartments "bombed" regularly, to kill the cockroaches, but they just emigrate from the non-LDS apartments and the problem is soon back to its former proportions. Pat advised us, from his experience in New York City while attending Columbia University, that the only solution was to keep all foodstuffs in cans or plastic bags and put out "roach hotels." So we do that, but it means that *everything* we want has to be dug out of a package and then securely repackaged. This is another thing that discourages us from preparing food and eating.

As for flies, we have homemade screens on several windows but they congregate in the stairwell and enter the apartment every time someone enters or leaves. Since that happens constantly, due to the missionary discussions, I try to "manage" the situation by hurrying people in and out. Unfortunately, they don't seem to understand and I think they feel I am discourteous because I am not lingering and chatting with them through the open door. Consequently, I spend a considerable amount of time chasing down flies with my fly swatter in hand. We took the offensive recently by hanging a sticky fly strip in the landing just outside our door. We got a lot of pleasure from seeing the carcasses accumulate on the fly strip in a short period of time but we're probably going to have to move it. It hangs down right in the middle of the landing and we think the other tenants are probably not very happy about having to dodge the sticky thing on the way up and down the stairs—particularly at night when they can't see where it is hanging!

DUST—EVERYWHERE! Finally, a word about dust. The streets around the apartment building are not paved. Thus, when the wind is blowing, which is often, there are great billows of dust all around. When the wind isn't blowing the cars that go by generate their own clouds of dust. We have to keep the windows open because there is no air conditioning. So, we have dust everywhere in the apartment all the time. We hung a wall sampler in the living room that our daughter, Jen, made for us. It is completely and thoroughly covered with dust. We bought a new vacuum sweeper in an effort to fight back and then nearly asphyxiated it the very first time we used it. There was so much dust and so much imbedded dust not previously picked up by the old, leaky sweeper we replaced that we almost blew out the filter. We had to stop cleaning to empty the filter, wash it, and wait a day while it dried.

But the presence of dust is another ongoing fact of life. We cover the computer and printer with a dish towel when we are not using them in the hopes this will slow the invasion of dust

into their inner workings. We noticed that the new fans we purchased already have dust-rimmed blades and will have to take
them apart to be cleaned. Again, it is just one more thing that
contributes to our having to learn many new sets of management
procedures to maintain a style and standard of life that we feel is
appropriate, even in a "frontier" situation.


## Nancy's Notes

*Nancy*

Before we came to Mongolia we had many questions about
what food would be available. The first missionaries here lost 30
pounds and we were expecting some tough times in procuring
food. Much to our surprise, during this past year increasing
amounts of food have been coming in from the European countries, Russia, and Japan. There are also several "booths" at the
market next to us that cater to Americans and we can get
Planter's peanuts, Oreos, Nabisco Wheat Thins, Jif peanut butter,
M&M's, Snickers bars, Nestle's Quik, pretzels, Tang, mandarin
oranges, cocoa, and those imported Danish cookies you get in the
States. Last weekend we found a distributor of Sprite and Fanta
and bought a case of each.

Uncle Ben's spaghetti sauce and meat sauce are available.
Perdue chicken was here once but the majority of the time it's
Tyson—legs only. They must save the white meat for the U.S.
consumers. You should have seen me asking the two girls behind
the counter if they had any chicken breasts. Since I don't speak
Mongolian I do a lot of gesturing and picture drawing, so I was
beating my chest and pointing to the chicken. Finally the two of
them caught on to what I was trying to convey and started really
giggling. We all had a good laugh but I still had to go home with
legs and thighs.

This past weekend we went to a Japanese store called Sapporo and found Campbell's tomato and cream of chicken soups. John was also delighted to find Frosted Flakes in which was a prize of Tony the Tiger. Enkhmaa promptly claimed it for herself — 21-year-old that she is. The market next door only has a European brand of corn flakes. I found Hellmann's mayo there today.

There is a brand of canned fruit and vegetables called Hosen which is exceptionally good and is what I choose. They also pack whole mushrooms which are delicious. There is a German brand of jam and jelly which is out of this world and the German cheeses are plentiful and exquisite.

They bring bread (Italian style) in here by the truckload. You can also find round loaves and the standard rectangular loaf — none of which is the soft variety we are used to in the States. I've seen elders walking around with a loaf of bread under one arm, eating it as they go.

We have bought beef although some couples will not. It is not refrigerated and lays out on the open counters where they will cut it to your size and specification (wish I had learned to recognize my cuts before coming here). One of our last purchases before leaving Utah was a pressure cooker. We made the purchase at the suggestion of one of our group at the SMTC who is a microbiologist on his way to Indonesia. He told us that cooking our food under pressure would kill the bacteria. We've had a couple of good pot roasts and boiled potatoes. In some places they still use human excrement for fertilizer so we stay away from the fresh vegetables. He also told us that the skins of grapes are a natural anti-bacterial agent. I looked at some the other day but they were too dirty for me, anti-bacterial or not.

When I make vegetable soup I empty a couple cans of the Hosen mixed vegetables into the pressure cooker and it tastes exactly as though I had cut them up myself. If you do use fresh vegetables you scrub them well with a brush and then soak them in a solution of Clorox and water.

I brought a supply of Carnation powdered milk with me but it is about gone. They don't pasteurize their milk here so we don't use it. Enkhmaa helped me find some Russian powdered milk at the market. I mix it with powdered coffee creamer and it makes a pretty good milk. The powdered milk, sugar, flour, and rice at the market are all out in open bags. When I told one of the other sisters that I didn't know which was which she said you just wet your finger and stick it in and taste it. I haven't been able to do that so took Enkhmaa instead. Oh yes, I needed some powdered sugar for my Texas sheet cake the other day and a kind Mongolian merchant took me to one of the other vendors where I could get it. The yolks of the eggs are a very light yellow — reflecting the type of feed they use, I guess. They only have brown eggs.

I really miss saltine crackers. They have the English-type "cream crackers" so I have resorted, from time to time, to sprinkling salt on them. I was missing Campbell's soups until we found them this week. They have brands that sound similar, like Kimball's. Can't fool us!

The first week we were here we lived on canned corned beef (very good) and peanut butter sandwiches since we had no refrigerator or stove. I think it was a good way for our bodies to adjust gradually because we did not experience any of the initial intestinal upset that most couples suffered.

They have a jar here filled with what looks like the peanut butter and jelly combination that you can find in the States except it's white and dark chocolate. I have not and will not buy it as I don't want to get hooked on that delight. I have seen some of the young elders and sisters using it and smacking their lips but I know my weaknesses.

I have gotten used to seeing young boys unloading and carrying whole dressed sheep into the market. They leave the tail on—the elders say to increase their virility. We've stuck to beef and chicken and I made chicken tetrazzini last night.

We went to the market today with a sizeable list and found everything on it. We even found cheddar cheese this time. They have predominantly gouda and edam. Our string bags were filled and weighed us down as we hopped the stile to our apartment building.

John had to make a new hole in his belt Saturday, making it smaller. I have also noticed a looseness around my waist. It's not from the lack of food but from walking everywhere. Maybe we won't lose 30 pounds but we'll take any we can get. Don't feel sorry for us! The only thing we lack is hot water and a good plumber!

## Some More Stories

### John

I compared the driver/pedestrian situation here to bull fighting with the drivers being the bulls and the pedestrians being the unwilling toreadors. Well, it turns out the pedestrians have the same mentality. I was coming back from a district council meeting following a big rain. Since there are no storm sewers the rain just accumulates in the streets (gutter to gutter) and in huge puddles which have to be circumvented as one travels from point A to point B. I was crossing between two huge puddles on a six-inch-wide wall, umbrella overhead, when I saw that a Mongolian couple had begun coming toward me on the same wall! It never crossed their minds that they should wait until I had reached the other end. So between these two huge mud puddles we did a delicate dance getting around one another while trying not to fall off the wall. With me holding the umbrella it reminded me very much of the clown at the circus doing tricks on the low wire and I was the clown. We all made it safely across so I guess they knew all along what they were doing.

I can't adequately describe how prettily the Mongolians dress their little girls. When they're out playing they dress just like the boys. But when they are dressed up, and it can be any occasion, not just a Sunday or holiday, they have the most elaborate, frilly, lacy, ribbony nylon dresses you can imagine. To round out their outfits they have matching hats, with bows and ribbons of course, and often wear gloves — sometimes to their elbows. They *really* dote on their little girls and it is marvelous to see. But they don't sequester them. When there were horse races during Naadam the little girls were competing on an absolutely equal basis with the boys, and there seems to be little discrimination in the workplace. The women here seem to work, play, and compete on an equal footing with the men.

We attended the first half of a circus. The acts seemed amateurish to us (ruined by television) so we didn't stay. But our attitude toward the circus was not helped when they took 30 minutes at the beginning to sing the praises of some kids who were taking the night away from the English Olympics to be there. They had speeches from several dignitaries in the English Olympics movement but my favorite moment occurred while the representative from the American embassy was speaking through a interpreter. She was half-way through her redundant remarks, lauding the kids for learning English, when a fellow in the audience yelled, "Well if you really care, why don't *you* learn Mongolian!" A good point, I thought. Any seasoned politician in the States would have ignored the comment and gone on with his or her prepared remarks but she chose to make some lame remarks about not having teachers as good as the Olympic teachers, and, besides, she was spoiled by having such great translators at the embassy, etc., etc. It helped me get through the interminable remarks to see that one of the speakers who was inflicting such pain on us was squirming a bit herself.

Missionaries stay in the mission home the night before they go home. I assumed it was to ensure they got a timely departure for the airport so nothing would go awry during the last hours. When I mentioned this to Nancy she said that was probably part of the reason. But not all. She had heard that the Mongolians that are taught by the missionaries sometimes become distraught, to the point that the returning missionary doesn't get any sleep the night before he/she leaves due to all the knocks on the door. That was confirmed for us last week. Two sister missionaries were in the mission home the night before they left. A woman who had been converted by one of them had found out she was leaving and became distraught. She sat in the stairwell outside her door and wept for four hours! In the morning we found that either she or some other devoted convert had painted on the wall outside her door, "_____, I love you!" We've seen similar things happen when senior couples who are in other cities return to Ulaanbaatar for a day or two. The phone rings incessantly as Mongolian members and friends seek to track them down so they can get in a quick visit while the senior couple is in town. The senior couples seem to be so snowed under by all this attention they are happy to get away again!

We've been here long enough that we've attended some evening meetings that went on past sunset (10:15 P.M. at this time of year). Finding one's way home after dark is no picnic in Mongolia. There are no street lights on the roads we take home and the open manholes that are a hazard for automobiles during the day become a definite threat to the pedestrian wending his or her way home after dark. You just can't see very well. One learns from experience that a flashlight is a genuine need after dark to avoid falling into an open hole. The same applies to the stairwells in the apartment buildings. There are no lights. You work your way up the stairs in pitch darkness. Some prior tenant rigged up a fluorescent light in the hallway outside our door (we're on the third floor of a five-story building) and it is our job to plug in the light every night before dark. We may have been careless the first little while we were here, not used to the routine and all, but after we experienced that pitch black stairwell a time or two we became very careful to plug in the stairwell light at night. If it becomes necessary, we'll leave it on day and night just so people don't have to grope their way up the stairs because we have forgotten to plug in the light.

Since it was the national festival time last week we also were able to attend a night of folk dancing and music. Unlike the circus, it was wonderful. The music, the dancing, the costumes, and the singing were all excellent. There were a couple of male singers who did something we were told is called *throat singing*. They sounded like they were playing mouth harps but with their vocal cords, not instruments. There was a female singer who used her vocal cords to do the equivalent of "triple-tonguing" by a trumpet player. And it sounded good, too. There was also a woman who played an instrument like a cello which sounded like a rich violin even though it was only two strings attached to a pole! I couldn't figure out how it resonated so richly since there was no wooden box around it.

My favorite was the orchestra. It was composed primarily of Asian-type string instruments of types we've never seen before played like banjos and guitars but which they were able to make sound like a symphony orchestra. When they played Shostakovich they sounded Russian. When the audience gave them sustained applause at the end their encore was a waltz by Strauss and they sounded like an Austrian orchestra.

Hearing that reminded me of the time we traveled in Wales, Ireland, Scotland, and finally ended up in London. We hadn't acquired a taste for the foods in the British Isles yet so were hungry for some back-home food. I still vividly remember being in Piccadilly Circus in London when we saw some people carrying a bag with a McDonald's logo on the outside. We actually chased them down to find out where the McDonald's was and proceeded to stuff ourselves sick when we got there. The Strauss waltz was a bit like that. We sat there and soaked in the western music. I even directed it a bit. We weren't the only ones, though. There were quite a few westerners there and they all appreciated this gesture by the orchestra. 'Twas a great night.

I've been volunteering my editing skills to one of the communication companies over here. I figure that much of the world's image of Mongolia stems from what they see on the Internet and if the English is poor they are more likely to think the country is not yet modern. So they've been feeding me their copy and I have been putting it into better English. The manager called me in the other day and asked why I was doing this. I gave him my reason (to help Mongolia's international image) but he still can't fathom it. At any rate, I had my reward the other night while I was editing through seven pages of a new announcement outlining their services to potential customers. I got all the way to the end and then broke up. The last line was this: We hope our service will enjoy you!

So, if you've been reading through these essays I can only say: We hope our service will enjoy you. Bye.


## Non-Violence
### John

First the caveats. I've only been in Mongolia for five or six weeks, and I don't even see (let alone understand) the local "evening news" so it is quite possible that there is murder and mayhem happening all around us and I just don't know it. *But*, based on my own observations it appears to me that there is not a lot of violence in Mongolia. This single fact seems to have widespread ramifications for how the people here act among themselves and toward one another.

I do remember that I've written about pickpockets and drivers that seem deliberately to aim for pedestrians but the drivers normally miss the pedestrians (thank goodness!) and the pickpocketing isn't really violence against a person. Indeed, when people catch the pickpockets practicing their "trade" (I'm told) all they do is twist their arm until they give back the booty and then they send the pickpocket on his way with a hostile stare or two.

Let me give you some evidences of non-violence. And we'll start with the drivers since they seem to be a favorite subject.

All Mongolian drivers seem to covet the same space. They drive to get to a given spot—any spot—before the other guy gets there. They will cut through intersections, drive up and over sidewalks, honk their way through a covey of pedestrians, do anything to beat the other guy to a given spot. Yet when they lose to the other guy there are no recriminations. There is no yelling or finger pointing. No driver shouts at another driver. No cursing occurs. The attitude seems to be, well, I'll try to get to the *next* spot first and away each driver goes.

Here's another example. We live beside the best-stocked market in Ulaanbaatar. The day or two before Naadam (the national holiday) was bedlam around the market because everyone was stocking up for the long weekend. One of the roads leading into the market is a "T" with the foot of the "T" leading onto a main avenue. We were in an automobile on the main avenue approaching the foot of the "T" and as we began to turn left into the foot of the "T," lo and behold there was an impatient driver coming out who decided to swing into his left lane (the lane we were entering) to get out onto the main avenue quicker. There we were, eyeball to eyeball with this naughty driver. We hadn't completed our left turn so we were blocking virtually the entire intersection on the main avenue with nowhere to go. Our driver did what Mongolian drivers always seem to do in situations like these (I've seen it happen several times). First our driver just turned off his engine and then the other driver turned off *his* engine and we both sat there. Drivers all around such stand-offs always sound their horns endlessly, and there is much craning of necks to see what's going on, but everyone just sits and does nothing more than honk their horns. Finally, in this instance, enough drivers in the lane to the left of us (the proper exit lane) were able to turn right onto the main avenue and clear enough space for the naughty driver to swing to his right and go on with his life. At that point we were free to proceed, and did. But the really remarkable thing to me was that no one shouted at anyone else. No one made threatening or obscene gestures. The whole matter was treated in an entirely impersonal way. In the States, I assume several people would have pulled out their pistols and threatened to blow away the heads of several other people to get their way, but that doesn't happen here.

Latent race car drivers roar around the streets all the time, honking away at everything that moves or might conceivably move into their paths, but no one gets mad about it. When drivers honk at me I become irked and have threatened several times to Nancy to just stand there and make them stop. (Fortunately, I haven't tried that experiment yet because the driver could be so astonished at this abnormal act that he might be too stunned to stop!) But the people here just don't seem to get mad at one another on a personal level even when they are being abused by some horn-honking bully.

I believe that's the reason the "taxi" system here can and does work. If people were subject to violence they would not casually get into strange cars and be driven away by unknown drivers.

But they do. We do, too. I suppose it happens that people get robbed by taxi drivers but they are *not* afraid for their personal safety. Very occasionally we get swindled by drivers who charge us too much but we never fear for our safety.

I've seen it in the children, too. No one yells at their children, nor have I yet seen anyone smack a child. The young men (and even some boys) may carry heavy bundles or buckets around but they aren't being bullied as they do so. The worst thing we've heard so far is that some parents lock their children into their apartments while the adults are at work. This is meant to protect them from hurting themselves in the street. Apparently they do not worry about fire since all the apartments are constructed of poured cement.

Actually, no one seems to pay any attention at all to the children. The children always play in bunches and they rule themselves. They surge from place to place without the slightest amount of adult control or attention. The big kids help the little kids through tight places or onto tall garages, and if there is a problem two to four kids will band together to work the little one through the rough spot. I have never seen two children fighting with one another. The children seem to enjoy a cordial, communal, collegial society. That being the case, the adults seem to say to themselves, "Let well enough alone" and they go one way and the children go another.

As far as we can see they are in charge of themselves from morning until the sun goes down, and then they melt into the darkness (presumably to go home). The next day they are back and skipping rope, climbing garages, jumping up and down on tin roofs, and conversing amongst themselves with the endless fascination of youth for anything and everything around them.

Others may think Mongolians rude as they push each other, fudge their way to the front of the pack, never stand aside to let someone else come through a door first, and generally show no respect for the sanctity of other persons, but they don't get mad at one another over these bumps, slights, and wounds to one's dignity. Thus, when we were at the black market and we eventually shoved back at a young man whom we considered especially thoughtless, he was truly shocked and amazed that we had responded in a personal way. Why would we *do* such a thing when *he* didn't intend it to be personal?!?!

I think we are seeing an essentially non-violent society which enables the people to do many things we can no longer do in the United States. It is nice, frankly, to be able to move around without having to be endlessly on the alert lest your personal safety be at risk. Mongolia may be behind the times in many ways but it is way ahead of us with respect to non-violence.

## Our First Dinner Out

*John*

We had our first dinner out last night but getting to that point was more difficult and complicated than one might suppose. One of the students we teach at the Ministry of Justice invited us, I thought, to two events last weekend: a visit to a police station (or a ride in a police car, I wasn't sure which) on Saturday and to dinner at his home on Sunday. He said he would call.

On Saturday, we hung loose during the afternoon but there was no call. Late Saturday, our Mongolian friend was telling us that her brother, a policeman, was getting ready to attend the annual police promotion and awards ceremony on Sunday so I leaped to the conclusion that we were going to be invited to attend the ceremony Sunday afternoon and then go on to our student's home for dinner afterwards. Sure enough, Sunday after

Church we received a call from our student's daughter who asked us to meet her at 2:00 P.M. at the Gandon Temple, the headquarters of all Buddhist monasteries and temples in Mongolia. Oh, we thought, we are not going to the police ceremony but are going to visit the temple which was captured in a series of postcards our students had given us after our first week of instruction. Fine. The daughter started to give directions but I turned the phone over to our Mongolian friend to ensure we got them right. She started to tell us which buses to take and I interrupted to say, "That's okay, we'll take a taxi. Tell us where we are to meet at 2:00 P.M." She told me the east gate of the temple and drew a little map to be sure I would get it right.

We dressed and got to the temple at 1:50 P.M. It is a sprawling place, with several entrances but we calculated the direction where the sun rises and started waiting at the East Gate — or more accurately at the *two* east gates since there was an enclosure within the larger enclosure. We watched the people worship while we waited. Some were circling a pole with blue ribbons on it, touching the pole with their fingers as they circled. Others were circling a cupola with dangling bells which was burning incense. They would gently move their hands through the incense smoke and wipe it on their heads, faces, and bodies. They were also softly touching the bells to keep them moving as they circled. We saw one woman waving her wallet through the incense and guessed she was hoping for a windfall. Others were circling a white cement structure with golden spires, touching the wooden fence that surrounded it as they went. Some touched their head to certain parts of the fence. Babies were also carried around and their heads placed against the fence by their parents.

Near these structures were some six-foot long ramps. We watched as people who looked to be ancient knelt on these ramps and lowered themselves to a prostrate position, putting their foreheads to the ground. Then, ever so painfully, they arose only to prostrate themselves all over again. An incongruous aspect was that as these people were engaging in an action that obviously had deep meaning for them (else they would not have repeatedly gone through such a painful experience) little children were using the unused ramps among them as sliding boards and having a romping good time!

Time passed. We thought we must be in the wrong place and began to quarter the temple grounds. I went into one tall building and discovered inside a 50-foot figure of a woman, gold-plated. We circled the entire grounds, trying to help the daughter see us since we didn't know what she looked like. To no avail. After searching fruitlessly and waiting for a long time, we finally just went home.

The next day we discovered the key. The daughter was waiting for us at the *bus stop,* a plan which I had unwittingly upset when I decided to take a taxi since that was more convenient for us. She waited there until 4:00 P.M. while her father was at home cooking dinner for us. We were mortified and chagrined, of course, but he gamely invited us again, on Wednesday. To be certain nothing went wrong this time, after class he walked with us to the Great Square of Ulaanbaatar (Sukhbaatar Square), showed us the monument in the center of the square, and said *that* is where we would meet at 6:00 P.M. on Wednesday. Nods of agreement and understanding all around.

Wednesday arrived. At 5:00 P.M. ( we certainly weren't going to be late for *this* appointment!) we started out for the Great Square. We walked a good distance east to get to it — it took us at least 25–30 minutes to get there — and our friend was waiting. He indicated we would walk to his place and promptly started *west,* back along the very direction we had just traveled. We covered all that distance and continued onward. We reached the Gandon Temple and walked right through the grounds, continuing westward through the ger district. (At this point we thought we were going to have the opportunity to dine in a real ger.) But alas, on the far side, in the distance, he pointed out his apartment building and we continued onward. We passed the bus stop where the daughter had been waiting and continued. Finally we reached the entrance—on the *far* side of the building, of course. As is typical in Mongolia there were no lights in the stairwell so we joined hands and he led us through the pitch darkness to the stairs. Onward, up four flights of stairs, ever onward. At last, we were there.

Inside, the apartment was lovely. The walls were lined with shelves and the shelves were stacked with books. This man speaks five languages and reads in all of them, his daughter speaks four, and his young son will soon be starting his third language, English. Our host disappeared into the kitchen to prepare dinner (with his son) so the daughter sat with us while we tried the salad and nibbled items on the table. (As it turned out, she spent almost the entire meal with us, conversing but not eating, while her father and brother cooked successive courses in the kitchen. They joined us only at the very end of the meal for a period of conversation.) There were a few items we found too tart but generally speaking everything was excellent. We marveled that the vegetable and slaw salads all contained materials that had been hand-chopped into very tiny pieces without becoming pulped, and were even more impressed when we learned that all had been chopped by the young son (age eight?).

At this point I'll let Nancy take over to describe the meal itself. Suffice it for me to say, as my parting line, that we just had our first bona fide Mongolian meal—and it was Chinese!

### Nancy

We approached this meal with some trepidation. We had heard from the missionaries tales of strange foods and drinks. John had already indicated to our host after class one day that we don't drink tea, coffee, vodka, and so on. He acknowledged that he didn't either so we were relieved of that worry. (If you are served vodka in Mongolia, so as not to offend the host when you don't drink it, you dip the tip of the ring finger on your right hand into the vodka, flick it to the four corners of the compass, dip once again and touch it to your forehead. Since I was sure that I would have ended up flicking my vodka in someone's eye, I relaxed.)

The meal was beautifully presented. It was obvious the children had spent the day in this preliminary preparation. (His wife is bedridden.) The table was tastefully set with salads and appetizers of a variety of colors. Before he disappeared into the kitchen our host changed into jeans and t-shirt so as to get serious about his cooking I guess, and explained each item of food to us and assured us they would not be offended if we chose not to eat something. Then he exited with his son and we ate and visited with his daughter. We inquired as to how some of the foods were made and marveled at how three of the dishes were perfectly julienned without a machine into the tiniest of strips. Another dish consisted of cooked potatoes, onion, ham, and celery *(mislel salat)*, cut into the smallest, exactly even squares. It was what we'd call potato salad. There was a dough bread the size of rolls *(mantuu)* that was twisted and not baked as we think of — it was steamed. The daughter made these. There was a dairy product (not butter, not sour cream, not yogurt) on the table which I put on these "rolls" and I thought it was quite good. There were cheeses and goodies of all kinds and watermelon.

The main course was a bowl of perfectly cooked rice with green and red peppers cut into it, shirred eggs, and tiny onion bits. We oohed and aahed. Then stir-fried beef and green peppers arrived — cut into the tiniest strips. Then, stir-fried broccoli (they let it flower) in a sauce and a platter of dumpling-like items filled with meat *(buuz)*. Then a plate of hot, paper-thin sliced cucumbers with tomato chunks appeared followed by some other items. At this point I was overwhelmed and inquired as to how many dishes had been prepared in our honor. John counted 14. Our host finally joined us, chopsticks in hand, and ate one dumpling. I told him I was completely intimidated by their cooking prowess. None of them could think what that meant and at this point neither John nor I could explain it so they quickly looked it up in the English-Russian dictionary and found what I meant. Any thought I had of our reciprocating with a dinner invitation went right out the window. As we were heading home. John said, "I guess a pan of chicken tetrazzini wouldn't be comparable." But as I think about it now, John *has* been teaching him English for six weeks for nothing so I guess that counts for something.

The desserts were candies and cookies. I should add that the dinner plates they used were the size of bread and butter plates, so we pretty much had to eat one dish at a time. They'd be overwhelmed to sit down to a table with one of our plates. This, and all the miles they walk, promotes slim waistlines! The gift we took to their home was six Snickers bars.


## Pioneer Day in Mongolia

*John*

Every year Latter-day Saints around the world commemorate and celebrate the entry of the Mormon pioneers into the Salt Lake Valley on July 24, Pioneer Day. Three branches of the Church in Ulaanbaatar celebrated Pioneer Day today and a good time was had by all.

Planning for the event went on for a month, culminating in today's activity. Associated with it was all the angst that is part of "shadow leadership," where you want the local members to take charge, so you restrain yourself from stepping in and doing it yourself, although you want them and the event to be a big success and yet you're not at all sure that they/it will. In our case it worked. The local members came through big time. They were there at 1:00 P.M. to help with the setup, and they were still there at the end helping with the cleanup. There must have been 200–300 members who spent part of the day with us and there is no question that everyone had a really good time.

The theme was an old-time carnival and there were 15 events to thrill and amuse the participants. Included were such traditional favorites as the coin toss, the beanbag throw, face painting, arm wrestling, apple dunking, and pin-the-tail-on-the-sheep (a little local adaptation there). It was great fun for those of us from America to watch the straightforward enjoyment of the Mongolians as they played these games. We were enthralled when sophisticated businesswomen dressed in their good business suits and carrying pocketbooks lined up to get blindfolded, turned three times, and aimed at the board to pin the tail on the sheep. When they took the blindfolds off they were as excited as any little kid to see where and how well they had done. Drinks, ice cream cones (remember the ice cream that never melts?), and *khuushuur* (a favorite Mongolian meat pie, pronounced "hosher") were available for 300 tugrugs. Adults and children alike were walking around slurping on their cones as content as any child.

One of the games was a mystery to the planners. It was simply labeled "Yerolt's Game" and was to be conducted by Yerolt, president of one of the branches. Everyone was intrigued to see just what the game was. Well, it turned out to be the game we called Steal the Bacon or Steal the Flag.* I asked Yerolt whether

---

*In this game, perhaps 15–20 players assemble in a large circle and count off by fours, with the ones being one team, the twos a second team, and so forth. A set of four players (one from each team) gather in the center of the ring around an object (a sock, hat, whatever). The objective is for one of the four players, by feinting and dodging, to grab the object and successfully pass through the outer circle of players without being tagged by any of the other three players in the inner circle. If tagged, the unsuccessful thief drops out until the next round.

he had somehow learned the game in America but he said he'd learned it in Mongolia. I was in rapt contemplation of just how the same game had originated in two or more places when he elaborated. He said he had learned it as a boy in Mongolia from some Cubans who were staying at a Russian rest camp near Ulaanbaatar. So the Cubans carried it here from America. But the Mongolians played it with the same zest, cunning, and strategy as we did when we played it back in the States.

The arm wrestling was interesting because one of the Mongolian sister missionaries was the champion. (She had previously served an 18-month mission in the States and is now serving a six-month mission in her home country. This is not unusual in Mongolia.) She took on all contenders, male and female alike, and reigned supreme as long as she chose to play. Then she moved to the middle and presided over the rest of the matches; no one chose to contest her decisions since she was clearly the champ.

After a couple of hours in which everyone played games, a couple of old standbys surfaced: softball and dodge ball. As with the carnival games, the Mongolians played these games with real zest. I would not have wanted to be in the middle of the dodge ball game, as vigorously as the teams on the outside were whizzing the ball at the people between them.

At 6:00 P.M., just about everyone went into the cultural hall (gymnasium) of the building where one of the congregations meets and joined together to sing and record *Faith in Every Footstep* to send to President Hinckley. We wanted him to know that the Mongolian saints were celebrating Pioneer Day along with the rest of the world. Then a typically Mongolian thing happened. We had practiced a few times (with Nancy conducting and one of the sister missionaries playing the electric keyboard) and were *just* ready to record when the electricity went off. No keyboard; no recorder. It seemed that our good thought was doomed to fail when the mission president's wife saved the day. She had a recorder with batteries in it. So we all sang *a capella*. The recording sounds beautiful and President Hinckley will get the gift from Mongolia that he doesn't know is coming.

Since the electricity was off, the square dance instruction and square dancing that was scheduled to follow the recording session had to be cancelled. If the truth be known, we shadow leaders were not too disappointed. By then we had had a long day and still faced the challenge of getting home, one way or another (walking or by taxi). So we packed up at 6:45 P.M. and headed home, weary but happy shadow leaders, content with the performance of our Mongolian brothers and sisters as we collectively pulled off a really fine celebration of Pioneer Day in Ulaanbaatar, Mongolia.

### *Pioneer Day: Nancy's Perspective*

The celebration was held in a stadium built in the '40s or '50s by our estimation. It was the era when Russia glorified work and athletics and this was part of a large manufacturing complex in which they worked and played. The large building which the Church rents for the Tuul branch contains a huge gymnasium, on the walls of which are painted large murals of workers involved in all forms of athletics. The outside of the building is adorned with a mosaic of a woman holding a hoop. All of this is faded now and the interior murals are stained with water leaks. Glass blocks are broken out high above the gymnasium floor and during church meetings it is not unusual for a crow or two to be flying around cawing. It was during just such an occasion that the senior elder there, who is a Boy Scout representative (and in his 70s), found the cause of the ruckus, rescued a baby crow from one of the corners of the huge room, and took it outside. Soon the adult crows left and the meeting continued without missing a beat.

The stadium has also seen better days, to which John can attest as he fell through one of the boards as he was walking along the bleachers to help erect a backboard for the basketball toss. One can see the outline of a race track around the infield where local athletes no doubt competed to the roar of the crowd who would have been seated in the large stands. A backdrop to the stadium is a mountain range and upon one of them is written, in stones, the name Ulaanbaatar in the ancient Mongolian script. Today the whole stadium is overgrown with weeds and an errant willow.

However, none of this dampened the spirits of those who were in attendance (neither did the 30 minute downpour just as people were beginning to arrive). Similar to what John mentioned, the thing that touched me most was the innocence of these people as they participated in the activities. I watched as a beautiful mother, dressed in the traditional satin deel, made a covered wagon out of a round Fritos can but I was particularly touched by an older woman who let herself be blindfolded and spun around to "pin" the tail on a sheep. (We are so sophisticated in the States that we would never let ourselves become so vulnerable.) I was the photographer for the day and as I followed her and saw her happily drawing pictures at the craft booth — pictures of pioneers in covered wagons entering the Salt Lake Valley I realized that she, too, is a pioneer standing in the shadow of different mountains — in the country of Mongolia. Perhaps someday they will be writing stories and singing songs about her. I was struck by the symmetry of it all.

As I conclude my thoughts of today, I am sitting here writing this journal entry by the light of a candle, on a battery-powered computer, a perfect ending to a celebration of Pioneer Day in Ulaanbaatar, Mongolia.

# August 1997

## Some Observations

*John and Nancy*

The mission was visited this past week by a young American couple currently based in Taiwan who are responsible for arranging the translation of Church documents other than scriptures into native languages. They are overseeing the translation of some handbooks and manuals into Mongolian at the moment but travel all over Asia and are familiar with most of the Asian cultures. I heard the sister remark that Mongolia was the only country in Asia where the men usually carry the babies; in all other Asian cultures it is the women. The custom here is to wrap the babies in swaddling clothes, as in days of yore. Nancy is going to write more about this so I'll end this observation here.

Another translation supervisor was here this week; this one is concerned only with translation of the scriptures. He, too, is a widely and oft-traveled person and he offered a couple observations of interest. First, he observed that the work of translating the Book of Mormon is going well and a draft could possibly be finished in 12–18 months.* He said he had been prompted several times during his visit by Mongolian members who urged him to "get the job done" so they could (finally!) get to read the Book of Mormon. The missionaries had told them what was in it but they were eager to be able to read it for themselves. He said this kind of pressure was of the good kind; in some places the translators finish their job but to little avail because most of the population cannot read! In Mongolia, 94 percent of the population is literate and will be able to read the Book of Mormon as soon as it is finished.

The supervisor also attended fast and testimony meeting in two branches. Afterwards he marveled at the pace of progress in Mongolia. He said that the people here had progressed more in five years than the Church had progressed in some parts of the world in more than 100 years. It's true that we had a very good turnout at our branch, which was one of the two he attended. There were more than 100 people in attendance. The membership in the mission keeps increasing at a rate of 35 or more new members a month. It is August 6 and we have already had 16 baptisms this month! We should have 1000 or more Mongolian members within the next month or two. The missionaries do not engage in tracting or engage people in the street. All this is happening because the Mongolian members are referring their friends, and because strangers walk up to the missionaries (or into the stairwell of our building) and say they want to be taught about Christ. 'Tis a wonder to behold.

The missionaries have so many discussions that they often use the senior missionaries' apartments. So often, in fact, that even they are becoming concerned about the pressure and lack of privacy this imposes on us. Some missionaries were talking about limiting each companionship to one visit per apartment

---

*Note: Printed copies of the *Book of Mormon* translated into Mongolian were first distributed to the members in October 2001.

per week. Evidently this was too extreme (currently there are only three senior couples here instead of the usual five to seven) because the new rule is that there should be only one discussion in an apartment at a time—instead of two, three, or four concurrent discussions.

We had a gullywasher of a storm a few days ago complete with a barrage of good-sized hail. Evidently this is customary and traditional in the summer but it is the first one we've been through. The rain poured down in sheets. We had water come in around, under, and through windows that are so tightly sealed we can't get them open—but the water found its way anyway. I've mentioned that there aren't any storm sewers so the water just accumulates in rushing, raging rivers all around our building. We stood in the kitchen and watched two sister missionaries (without raincoats or umbrellas) virtually swim their way down the street. Several young people stopped by our apartment and we were serving towels to dry off about as rapidly as we were serving glasses of cold drinking water just a couple of weeks ago. As a result we had quite a laundry to do the following few days.

The rain evidently saturated the ground because the puddles (small lakes?) that usually drain away in a short while are staying this time. It is long enough for the mosquitoes to breed a huge population of ravenous young'uns and they are feasting on us. Perhaps they have a different formula for preparing the blood; anyway, their bites swell, and itch, and get bright red, and even hurt a little. We're hoping to get some immunity but in the meantime we are closing the windows at night and even using some bug repellent before going to bed. The smell is pretty repellent to us; we're hoping the mosquitoes will feel the same way.

We had dinner at a restaurant for the first time since our arrival. There were eleven of us in the party—the three senior couples, President and Sister Cox, and the three translation people I mentioned previously. We were too many for the restaurant to handle. Three of us went back to move tables into place and find enough chairs. For a while I wasn't sure they had enough glassware and silverware (and, truthfully, was concerned about the lengths they might go to to get some!) but after 30–45 minutes we were set to eat. Several of us ordered beef stroganoff; others got beef and mushrooms. By the time the food arrived it didn't matter to us that the two dishes looked pretty much the same—we were all pretty hungry by then. The food was actually pretty good and it was nice to have a night out for a change—the first night in a very long time. We'll have to do it more often now that the ice has been broken.

As I was typing this I heard a soft "Yippee" come from the living room. Soft because we have a missionary discussion underway in one of our rooms, as usual. Yippee because an edited version of Monday Night Football had just come on to our Mongolia/America joint television channel. We think it's not too bad that we get MNF when it is just Tuesday morning back home. We're pretty pleased, especially since one of the Eagle/Dallas games is on a Monday night. As Nancy said: Yippee!!! Nancy will be taking notes. She promised her community English class she would teach them the fine points of NFL football because all they understand is soccer. Yech!

## Nancy's Thoughts on the Children of Ulaanbaatar

The children of Ulaanbaatar have a new excitement these days. The central part of Ulaanbaatar is composed of apartment buildings, built fairly close together. There are no large, open, grassy spaces in which to play—similar to our large cities in the U.S. So, as children will, they create their own games out of what resources they do have. One of the most popular sports is playing tag on top of the metal "garages" that line the back streets of the apartment buildings.

There are several times during the day when the children gather on top of these crates. At first we didn't understand what the fascination was of running back and forth along the roofs, making a terrific racket as they did so. As we watched more intently we could see that it was an organized game of tag with all the intricacies and techniques used in the States.

Since these containers are of varying heights and widths, they create spaces to be hurtled over and places to hide in which to reach up and tag someone as they jump over. Shouts of merriment mix with the rumble and roar of their feet against the metal as they jump from container to container. The most popular ones, and the loudest I might add, are the ones directly under our apartment windows, but it also affords us a perfect view as we watch the merriment. It reminds me so much of my cousins and I when, growing up in Ohio, we'd gather each evening for tag, red light-green light, and hide-and-go-seek.

We watched with interest one afternoon as one young boy had his two- or three-year-old sister in tow. She looked so tiny but wanted to be included in the game. Obviously she was too small to leap the spaces between the containers but her brother never left her side or let go of her hand as they stood watching the others in their fun. I was impressed that he wasn't enticed by the others to just leave her. The wonderful relationship between siblings is a national characteristic here. It is not an imposition for them to be asked to care for a younger brother or sister. They're extremely loving and kind and show much affection to one another. After some time passed the brother and another boy finally figured out a way to get "little sister" across the wide chasm to the next container by using their bodies as a bridge. She skipped across in obvious glee as she ran to join the others. It was a short time later that we saw the two of them heading for home, still hand in hand, having lifted her down, somehow, to street level.

In the same vein the older inhabitants of the city are rarely out alone. They are almost always accompanied by a young grandchild who holds their hand and walks slowly with them. Upon occasion you see a young child leading a blind grandparent along the streets and around open manholes. There are marvelous family relationships here and I smile every time I see them as it reminds me of my feelings for my grandparents. Saturday, while walking uptown, John and I followed just such a pair. A bent over grandmother dressed in her native deel was being escorted by a little girl dressed in her frilliest dress, long black hair down her back. Grandma had to walk very slowly and we were impressed with the patience of the frisky granddaughter as she held back her exuberance to stay with her grandmother. Finally, as they almost reached the corner and some shade, the little girl broke their grasp and ran to the steps of a store where she was going to get a treat. Grandma found a place to sit in the shade and rest after her walk up the gentle grade to the center of the city.

The other day John and I were walking along the back streets on our way to the mission home when three little boys jumped out at us. They had made themselves Indian headdresses by tying a thin strip of red and white striped plastic around their heads. Into this they had each placed a pigeon feather. Each was carrying a wooden stick. They gave us several war whoops to which we replied in like manner. They were so tickled to have ambushed two Americans. We all had a good laugh.

Americans in the midst of Mongolians is unique enough that the children are still noticing differences in our appearance. Recently, at a zone conference one of the mission employees had a young child who wandered in and out of our meetings, sitting on various participants' laps. She eventually made her way to John's lap, and, while there kept looking up at him. Finally she just couldn't contain herself any longer and reached up to his bald head and gave it several good rubs. That really broke us up; there are very few bald Mongolians. Her curiosity satisfied, she bounced on to the next knee.

Now to the new excitement: a company has come to town to install a new telecommunications network and they are digging trenches all over town—cutting across streets, sidewalks, around buildings, and so on. This is not being done with the machinery we are accustomed to seeing at home but by manual labor—pick and shovel. Young men with bare backs dig all day and are creating intriguing piles of dirt all over town. Each new pile brings a group of children who, with great ingenuity, make them into temporary forts, grand prix racetracks, and playgrounds. Walking to the state department store the other day I saw a young girl playing house, having created a "home" for herself and a few friends using implements left laying about by the workmen.

The boys make tracks for imaginary cars to travel over. I even saw a slide made from a first floor apartment window to the top of a nearby pile. In several places the workmen have brought in a large piece of equipment to dig a large hole—usually right next to an apartment building. The kids can't wait for the workmen to finish for the night. The minute they do, they're down in these holes playing all kinds of imaginary games. Oh what fun it is for the children of Ulaanbaatar as they follow the workmen from street to street. I can only imagine all the mothers trying to get the dirt and sand cleaned up at the end of the day when the children return home.

John mentioned the swaddling of babies in a previous entry. They are tightly wrapped in the Russian/Eastern European tradition. Almost invariably they are carried by the fathers. I have never seen a baby in a back or front pack. Instead, they are cradled in their father's arms. As the child gets a bit older I have seen some in strollers.

We almost never hear crying in church. The other Sunday it happened for the first time. It was not long before I saw a counselor peer down into the congregation and a young sister scooped up the baby and removed it. I'll have to ask someone about that.

During Naadam a small boy was "abandoned" and left at a hospital. Enkhmaa's brother is a policeman and he took it upon himself to find the parents. In the meantime he took the young boy home where our young friend cared for him for about three weeks. When it looked like no one was going to claim the baby, arrangements were made for one of their cousins from the countryside to take the boy and raise him with their family. A few short days before that happened a distraught mother came to the police station looking for her missing young son. It seems she had gone to the countryside and had left her son in the care of his grandmother who had become confused and lost him. Since there are few telephones in Ulaanbaatar or the countryside they were not able to communicate this until the mother came back home. At long last "lost boy" was reunited with his family and everyone was happy. (At the time he was lost it was determined the little boy was between the age of two and three because he still had long hair. At the age of three they shave a boy's head, declaring that he is out of babyhood. They then save the long queue to give him when he is grown.)

On one of our other walks from the mission home we saw a group of young boys gathered around a smaller boy who was crying. A Mongolian man walking in front of us stopped to inquire as to the problem. The little boy's hands were all muddy and he was inconsolable. It turns out he had fallen down an open manhole and had to be retrieved by the others.

They jump rope here and even do Double Dutch. I also saw a hopscotch diagram, drawn in chalk, on the cement playground of the school next door to us. Something which I have just seen in the last several days are boys with a metal rod from a trash can that they've bent at one end. They use the rod to roll old tricycle tires down the street. I'm amazed at the ability and speed with which they race behind the tires, coaxing them around potholes, open manholes, and ditches.

There are some playgrounds around the apartment buildings with a few pieces of equipment but we seldom see any children on them. Next door to us is Russian School #3, one of the schools in which we teach English. It has one of the few cement surfaces that is flat and free of obstacles. It has become a popular place to "inline" skate. Some of the children are really good and move quite fast. A few are decked out in fluorescent-colored knee and arm pads. I watched out the window the other day as a little girl was trying to figure out how to skate backwards. Children can play here unattended without any worries, and since it doesn't get dark until 10:30 P.M. they're out late into the night. There are very few bicycles here but when you do see one there's usually a young brother on the back being given a ride. I've never seen a girl on a bicycle.

Children are well educated here and many are beginning to speak English. You soon become aware of a "language line" between those who were taught Russian in school and those who are now being taught English. The little ones love to shout "hello" to us and "how are you." They love it even more when we call back to them—and their parents are so proud of their accomplishment. Their parents appreciate our attempts to teach their children English. I was walking from the market the other day when an older woman (probably my age) dressed in her deel was walking to the market. I nodded to her and said "Sain bainuu," to which she nodded and came to me with her hand extended for a handshake. She had to go slightly out of her way to do so and I knew she was thanking me for being here in Mongolia helping the children prepare for leading the new Mongolia of the future. We're happy to be here.

# The Rainbow Ends—in Mongolia!

*John*

We traveled with the Coxes to Darkhan recently for a zone conference with the missionaries and teachers in the two cities of Darkhan and Erdenet. We started early in the morning so as to reach Darkhan for the scheduled start time of 11 a.m. A short way out of Ulaanbaatar, as we were getting into "the country-side," we saw several small, sharp rainbows. And, in a once-in-a-lifetime experience for all of us in the car, we saw not just one end of a couple of rainbows, we all saw *both* ends! The ends of a rainbow usually come down in some far distant place, beyond some building, hill, or mountain, but these rainbows came down on the *near* side of the hills and we were able to see them touch the ground. The people here would probably say, "Of course, we've been telling you about the pristine glories of the country-side," and would undoubtedly agree that the countryside is the equivalent of any two pots of gold you might expect to find at the ends of the rainbow. But for us it was a rare—even unique—experience and we all took a childlike pleasure in having seen both ends of the rainbow. One more gift from the country of Mongolia to treasure and savor over time.

The trip itself was difficult. It was four hours of dipping, bumping, sliding, bouncing, jarring, and wanting to ask when the trip would end. I'd been told that the *only* paved roads in Mongolia were in Ulaanbaatar itself. That is not entirely true, we learned. There are roads that connect Ulaanbaatar with other major cities but they are filled with potholes, ruts, and washouts that make the use of them very difficult. There had been some heavy rains recently that made our road to Darkhan even worse than usual. In some places the rain had been recent so we skidded and slipped in muddy areas along the way. Fortunately we were traveling in an off-road vehicle that has several handles you can use to hold yourself in place, so that helped to control some of the effects of our jouncing ride.

After speaking with the Darkhan and Erdenet missionaries during the first hour of the zone conference and after a quick bite of lunch, Nancy and I proceeded to visit the schools where our people will be teaching this year. We had a little difficulty zeroing in on the first school because there is a Technical University on one side of the street and a Technical College on the other. We will be teaching in the latter and eventually ended up in the right place. We talked with the director through a member who was serving as an interpreter for the very first time. She was very nervous about it—shook like a leaf the whole time. Indeed, she was so nervous she brought along a friend to serve as co-interpreter. Between the two of them they did fine except for one judgment call that I wish they hadn't made.

The exchange was going fine. I was relating the conditions we desired for our teachers to teach and the director was agreeing to all of them. Then he made a long, long statement. About half way through our interpreter exclaimed, "Wow!", but at the end all she said was "Okay." We were curious about the exchange, of course, but with nothing more to go on than "Wow" and "Okay" we wrapped up the meeting soon after and left. As we got outside, Nancy asked what the long statement was all about and the interpreter related that the director was telling her about last year's experiences. (Evidently he worked in the Technical University last year, or he works in both places, because we had teachers in the *university* last year but are starting new in the *college* this year. Thus, neither Nancy nor I expected any discussion of last year during the meeting.)

The director claimed that last year's teachers often did not show up to teach and that on several occasions they had taught religion in class. Since both teachers had gone back to America there was no way we could talk to them about it. Other teachers had told us, though, that our teachers had indeed appeared, ready to teach, but had been told by other members of the faculty that they were too busy to have English and they should just go home—so they did. We would have defended our teachers to the director had we known that he was making these charges/claims but didn't know about it until after the meeting was over. We did pass on the information to this year's teachers, and agreed that if they are told there is no time to teach English today they are to go immediately to the director and inform him they are there ready to teach but were told to go home. Then we'll see if they are really too busy for English that day. And we just don't believe the teachers were teaching religion in the classroom. The mission president has assured the powers-that-be that any of our teachers who teach religion in the classroom will be sent home immediately, and he repeatedly admonishes the teachers *not* to say anything about religion in any way, shape, or form while they are in or around their school. That is the Eleventh Commandment here in Mongolia.

We proceeded to the second school where we were scheduled to teach. Three Mongolian teachers of English have been teaching privately at night during the past three years and were slated to quit their day jobs and start their own private day school starting in September. Unfortunately our contact person had moved and so neither the phone number nor the address we had was useful. Thus we were unable to conclude any arrangements with them. (After our departure, the missionaries continued the search and we later heard the three teachers were not ready to make the jump into daytime teaching and were going to continue teaching privately at night. Under that circumstance we would not furnish teachers and will not be working with them this year.)

During our search, as we went to the contact's apartment, we learned that she lived in a 16-story building that is the *tallest* building in Mongolia. This is Darkhan's chief claim to fame. We noticed a 1997 calendar in an office where we were waiting later in the day and the 16-story building was prominently featured in the calendar. The picture was beautiful, with happy children playing in the foreground and the tall, tall building dominating the background. The reality was far different. The elevator, or elevators, in the building don't work! People on the upper floors pay premium prices to live atop the tallest building in Mongolia and have to climb as many as 16 stories any time they leave the building!

We saw the future of Mongolia at our next stop, though, and these are people we want to teach. We had had a phone call in Ulaanbaatar from the sister of a gentleman that owns and operates the television station in Darkhan. He is starting a private school in the second-floor offices in his building and wanted some English teachers. Since we couldn't make contact with the ladies who were planning to start their own school, we went on to meet with the owner of the TV station. He wasn't there (we didn't have an appointment) but his office got in touch with him in Ulaanbaatar and told us we would have an appointment with him early the next morning. He is a young, energetic man who is used to getting things done. He showed us the offices on the second floor, now occupied by the back-office staff of a bank, and said they were to move out on August 14th. He has contractors lined up to begin converting the offices to classrooms on August 15th and assured us the work would be done within two weeks thereafter. The offices were already clean, spacious, and well-lit by Mongolian standards. As he told us of the further improvements he had planned, the missionaries who were with us decided this was where *they* wanted to teach. We observed several students in a computer class he already has underway and they were young, serious, and intent. These are the people who will carry Mongolia into the 21st century and project Mongolia into the fabric of western democracies. From what we've observed, they will do just fine.

## Mine Eyes Have Seen the Countryside!

*John*

We traveled to Darkhan on Thursday and returned to Ulaanbaatar on Friday. Saturday we rested, but early Sunday morning we were on the road again for a whirlwind, out-and-back, two-day trip — six hours each way — to the ancient capital of Mongolia, Khara Khorin *(ha-horin)*. Our complement was Nancy and I, Sr. Enkhtuvshin, our interpeter, and (perched on her lap in the front seat) her young son, and Batbold (the mission driver). Our task was to inspect the teaching facilities at Khara Khorin University, a private facility with 400 students that wanted English teachers. They already have a Peace Corps teacher and a Mongolian English teacher but needed more teachers with that many students. We were also to see whether there were living facilities there adequate for our teachers; the entire town is without indoor plumbing or hot water.

Well, the countryside *is* beautiful, just as the Mongolians claim. Virtually all the four-hour trip to Darkhan and the six-hour trip to Khara Khorin passes through one after another of these huge, even vast, high plateau mountain bowls. As you enter each bowl the road is laid out for miles and miles in front of you across the floor of the bowl. The countryside probably resembles the "big sky" country of Montana, though I've never been there. All around you as you traverse the floor of the bowl, rise the rounded ridges of the surrounding hills and mountains in the far distance. It is easy to see the effects of the glaciers here, grinding, smoothing, and compressing as they made their inexorable way farther south. In almost all the places we traveled the hills and mountain peaks are rounded; there are no jagged edges on anything. Most striking of all, in the far distance, about one-third of the way up the slopes, you notice these little white dots. These are the gers, the homes of the people who live out there in the middle of nowhere. Situated as they are, the people can step out the front doors of their gers and see before and behind them all their flocks and herds and can tell at a glance where they are and how they are doing. It is a marvelous solution to the task of keeping watch over widely dispersed flocks and herds.

Everything is green at this time of year. It isn't grass, though, as our eye wants us to believe. Rather, the green comes from individual ground-hugging weeds that, when you get up close, you can see are separated from one another, leaving patches of ground exposed. Seeing this, one can understand why it is necessary for the people to keep moving with their animals—it isn't thick, rich grass they are munching, and the individual plants can quickly be cropped close to the ground by hundreds of grazers. So even though each ger has access to vast stretches of land the vegetation can sustain that many grazers only so long and then it is time to strike camp and move on to another vast stretch of land.

A stream or streams meander through the floor of every bowl, of course. It is here that the animals drink and lie or stand during the heat of the day. It is also here that the residents scoop their water and carry it back to their gers, we regretted to observe. We are told that the water is always scooped upstream from the animals but saw instances where people downstream were scooping water from streams that had animals standing in them farther upstream, so we are inclined to take with a grain of salt the rhapsodic talk about the "purity" of the countryside water.

Nonetheless, it *is* beautiful, and now it is easier for us to understand the yearning to return that seems to fill the heart of every Mongolian city-dweller. Imagine a day spent astride your faithful horse (or horses), moving sedately around the fringes of a flock or herd, each member of which you know intimately. From time to time another person lopes up to exchange a few words, a drink or two, and probably some ribald gibes. You check the sky occasionally and see in the far distance some lightning and the rain falling from a mountain squall, but it is moving away so there is no need to get the flock or herd moving. Time passes, in the eternal way of nature, and the animals begin on their own to head for the stream or head for the gers, needing only gentle guidance from the horse-riding herdsmen. The wind, the sky, the sun, the grass, the stream, the gers—all become a lullaby of peace and tranquility that have to sink deep into the soul. One can envy them their existence during the summer. However, during the winter the wind must be ferocious, ripping its way across the floor of these mountain bowls. It must be a hard life during the long, cold, hard winters of Mongolia.

But back to our trip to Khara Khorin. The paved road stops about 75 kilometers short of the "city." They are working on it and hope to have a road completed by the end of the year, but, for now, at a certain point the road stops and pathways in the dirt begin radiating out in many directions. What you do is take one; almost any one will do. Some will get you there faster and smoother than others but evidently all of them will get you where you want to go eventually. Our car had a compass but the driver didn't seem to use it. He just selected a dirt path and took it. Part of the time you find yourselves amidst a herd of grazing animals. One time we even passed a herd of camels. On the way the hazards of the road took their toll and we had to stop to change a flat tire. We tried to get it fixed overnight but without success, so made the return trip without a spare—a fact that Nancy and I bore uneasily.

102

The university facilities proved to be all they claimed. We found the executive president of the university in one of the dorms, setting up bunk beds for the students for the fall semester with the help of the chief accountant. The entire faculty had been working all summer to clean up, paint, and prepare for the fall semester. The administration had given them time in August for vacation—in the countryside, of course. We were impressed with their diligence. Many townspeople believe the university cannot and will not last—there have been schools in the building before—but if hard work can make things happen this group *will* succeed. Just as we were leaving the facility the staff presented to us four students who are enrolled in their English program. All were dressed to the nines and gamely did their best to represent their school and their classmates well. One of them had graduated from the school in June but was coming back to be in the English program. She was the designated speaker. Shaking all over, she introduced herself and told us how glad they were that we were sending them an American English speaker. It was really a nice touch. At times like these we feel that we are in the movie *The King and I,* where the children are meeting their English-speaking teacher. Often the students remind us of the children in that movie, too, as they "ooh" and "aah" at your every move and word, as with Miss Anna.

We found three condominium-type buildings near the university that offer the only hot water and indoor plumbing in town. They are thus considered to be the "finest" that the city has to offer. With some work one of them will be suitable for our teachers and it is anticipated we will send teachers there in mid-October if everything works out right. Nancy and I expect to make only occasional supervisory visits.

We stayed overnight at a countryside building that used to be a resort for communist party officials so it was more than a single cut above the usual facilities. We were told the staff used to stock the stream that runs nearby to ensure the officials would

catch lots of fish and go away happy! We met there a French pen-
sioner who used to be a colonel in the French army, and now
lives in New Caledonia but spends his time traveling around the
world. He has been everywhere at least once. There was also an
American, born in New Somerset, Pennsylvania, now teaching
English in Siberia, who was there to observe a monument that
was established in 789 A.D. and bears on its face one of the two
remaining examples of an obsolete form of inscription.

Monday, on the way home, Batbold suddenly pulled to the
side of the road. He had recognized the parked car of the district
president who was on vacation in the countryside. He returned
beaming—the district president had caught many fish and had
shared some with Batbold. A bit farther up the road the driver
stopped by a roadside ger. He took from the back of our vehicle a
container which we had assumed contained spare petrol, but he
returned with it full of mare's milk to take home to his and
Baatar's families. For a while he smiled and sang as he drove; we
pictured him imagining the warm reception he would get when
he returned to his home bearing both fresh fish and mare's milk
from the countryside. Heaven can hardly match this!

Occasionally we would see motorcyclists passing us in the
opposite direction and speculated that it must be a hard trip bal-
ancing your way across the potholes, ruts, and countryside pathways. Sometimes there were two riders on the cycle. Then we
saw cycles with *three* riders and were amazed. The topper,
though, was one cycle that had two riders and the one in the back
was holding a sheep between them as they roared down the road!

We were happy to get home, and happy to crawl into our bed
at home rather than spend another night in a hotel. That was
when we realized that the apartment has now become our
"home" and we are grateful for it. Nancy has done a superb job
of creating a warm, attractive, and comfortable place (as usual)
and we are thankful for it.

# Hard Labor and Keys

*John*

When we stopped overnight in Beijing on the way to Mongolia we were told by the hotel workers that China was constructing a new airport ten times larger than the current one. In America, we would just bring in the really *big* machines to carry out such a job. Not so in China. They do everything with manual labor and just take longer to do the job. They may take 30 years to construct their airport but it will get done and literally thousands of citizens will have had gainful employment during that time.

In many respects it is the same in Mongolia. The whole city is being crisscrossed this summer with ditches that are being dug to put in new telephone and (in our part of the city, so we are getting a double dose of ditches) hot water lines. This is a major effort for the city. They don't have enough pieces of large equipment to do the job so they are employing large cadres of laborers (men and women) to dig the ditches by hand. One such project is underway outside our windows — ditches going from one manhole to another. They start early in the morning (around 7:00 A.M.) and then work vigorously until 10:00 or 11:00 P.M. Their stamina is amazing. As Nancy said, they seem to be small but very, very strong, like the horses Chinggis Khan and company rode when they conquered so much of the world. They keep at it, hour after hour after hour.

First they dig the ditch using nothing but picks and shovels. The ground is filled with rocks large and small so it is very hard work. Somehow they manage to cut ditches that are straight and have straight sides to them — just wide enough for them to get their hips inside as they jump to the bottom to dig deeper. After they've dug to about 4½ feet they fill the bottom with sand, put in the plastic carrier pipes, and cover them over with more sand. The one piece of mechanical equipment they have is a petrol-powered tamper which they use to tamp down the sand. Then they put an orange plastic webbing down the length of the ditch and cover it to the top with excavated dirt that is thrown through portable screens placed over the top of the ditch. Then they use the tamper again to tamp down the surface. The stones that were removed from the screened dirt are tossed into trucks and carried away leaving a smooth, quite acceptable surface in the roadway.

Nancy has written about the children playing in the dirt. I just want to add a word picture to her story. One night we were sidewalk-superintending from our third floor window when I noticed there were two tiers of children similarly watching from atop their domain of garages and storage containers. It was like an arena with tiers of people watching the gladiators or performers in the middle. This scene is being re-enacted all over Ulaanbaatar. We've heard that the telephone lines will be fiber optic cables, thereby greatly improving the telephone service and, incidentally, making cable TV available all over town. We've also heard that our hot water service will be greatly improved as a consequence of this work but since we haven't had hot water for a month we're going to wait and see about that. We have noticed that there has been hot water in our pipes during the middle of the last two nights so maybe there is reason to hope.

Moving to the topic of keys. Keys must have special symbolic significance in Mongolia. Everything is locked up. To get to a classroom you may have to open a hall door, and then an inner door, and then the door to the classroom itself. Each door requires a separate key and all keys are kept sequestered in some location that is always far distant from where you are. So just to get into your classroom you must first find someone to get keys—in many buildings this is an extremely difficult task in and of itself. Then they have to go get the key(s). Usually at least one of the keys is not the proper one and another trip is required. After teaching, each door has to be locked as you leave requiring the reverse procedure to be gone through all over again. That is why we are making as a condition of using our teachers that they be given personal copies of all keys they need in order to gain access to the building, to their classroom, to the copying room, and to the room where the instructional supplies are kept if that room is different from the room where the copier is kept. This is a really big break in custom and tradition and I'm not sure it will actually occur. The directors I've talked with have agreed but I'm not at all certain they'll be able to bring themselves to turn over copies of the keys. We may just be asking too much when we ask them to give up their exclusive possession of the keys.

# mongolia: the circle in the clouds

# september 1997

## First Day of School in Mongolia

*Nancy*

When we woke up this morning and looked out the window it was unusually quiet. It was about 32°F by the thermometer on our balcony and we decided summer was definitely over. Around 8:00 A.M. we saw streams of families making their way along the streets and many of the children were carrying bouquets of flowers. The little girls were beautifully dressed with large bows in their hair—just like you see in Russia; the young boys were in suits.

It finally dawned on us that they must be on their way to school. We were also going to school this morning. We were being picked up by the director of "Future School," a kindergarten. This woman is a true "go getter" and had stopped by to see us several times to make sure she'd have an American English teacher because she had promised one to the parents of her students. It seems they didn't really believe her so she asked us to come to opening day and say a few words to reassure them.

The teacher we have assigned to this school is still in the MTC, and won't arrive until mid-October, so I guess this seemed like a fish story to the parents. Since they pay a lot of tuition money to these private schools we promised her we'd come to reassure them.

She came to pick us up dressed in a beautiful deel. These Mongolian women look elegant in their satin deels, trimmed in gold. (I, on the other hand, was dressed in a plaid wool skirt, white turtle neck, and black blazer — with leather gloves. John was attired in a blue pinstriped suit with Australian rabbit-felt hat, looking very dapper.) We were driven to the school by a chauffeur, and when we stepped from the car we were greeted with approving smiles. We were ushered through two lines of parents to a special room to await our entrance.

The moment finally arrived and we were taken through a classroom door to the sound of applause. All the beautiful children were seated at their desks with their parents standing behind them. It was one of those moments you never forget. The director spoke first and then asked John to say a few words, which she interpreted. (She had asked him beforehand to speak slowly so she could do a good job.) He assured the parents that they would have an American teacher and that she'd be here in October. In the meantime, since two of our other teachers (elders) didn't have to start their classes until October, they would start teaching their children the next day. We were once again greeted with applause. Then selected children walked forward and presented us with bouquets of flowers.

It was a beautiful beginning to a beautiful fall day and an exciting new school year for the Hopkinses in Mongolia.

# Our Life Simplified (Somewhat)

*Nancy*

We have a new arrival in our apartment and it came just in time, as school starts today. This means we'll be teaching, full time, in addition to our part-time morning classes at the Ministry of Justice and community classes in the evenings, both twice a week. Since teaching, preparation, and supervision will occupy most of our time there's not a lot left for household duties. Therefore, our new arrival will save us a lot of time. It sits under the kitchen sink, out of the way, but contributes greatly to lightening our personal daily needs. It's a water filter, shipped over from the States.

The missionary department provides these wonderful devices for the single missionaries but the couples have to purchase them. Now that we've been here almost three months and have burned out one electric kettle trying to keep up with our personal and visiting missionaries' needs for safe water, we decided to bite the bullet and buy a filter. It was shipped from the U.S. and arrived here about ten days later. The cost of the air freight was more than the filter but in the 13 months we have left over here it'll more than pay for itself in convenience.

One of the main health problems here is Giardia, which is contracted through the water. In addition, there are many other bacteria and little things living in the water which love to make their home in your intestinal tract so these mechanisms have three different filters through which the water flows. The filters are changed on a regular basis: #1 every 2 months, #2 every four months, and #3 once a year. Every once in a while we see a missionary struggling with Giardia — diarrhea, weight loss, lack of energy — and it's usually because they ate in the countryside or were not careful with their food preparation. Fortunately, there is

111

a "Giardia kit" that is kept in the mission for just such occasions. I believe it contains several pills which usually knock out the Giardia with one blow.

Other things we found this week: cranberry sauce, salad dressing, cheesecake mix, Frosted Flakes, American butter (the latter two at the Byangol Hotel), lemon squash (barley water — the Queen's favorite drink), canned chicken breasts, and canned ham. Last week John found two commercial-size boxes of instant Quaker Oats and we bought the only two they had. We promptly came home and had oatmeal for dinner and then again at breakfast. Oh, the little pleasures in life!

We found most of the above in a new store which is carrying Tesco products. This is a grocery chain in England whose brands we recognized right away so were excited with the new find. More foods are being imported every day. We jump right on them and our pantry is becoming quite full.

On a subject other than food: we haven't had hot water here for over a month. Even when we did, it was gone before 7:00 A.M. In most ways it's "no problem" as the Mongolians would say. I have learned that doing our laundry in cold water with Tide actually makes our clothes whiter than all those years of using warm water. We were boiling the water we use to do the dishes so that didn't matter. However, cold baths are no fun no matter where in the world you are. Even boiling a kettle or two of water didn't provide very much in which to bathe. Then a couple of elders told us how to warm our bath water and we've had luxurious baths ever since. We fill the tub with cold water at night before we go to bed. Then we throw in an immersible heater and drift off to Never Neverland. In the morning we have a tub full of scalding hot water to which we add enough cold to create the perfect temperature. We now scoff at those who are taking cold showers every morning.

# Our Life Complicated (a Lot)

*Nancy*

I recall reading a number of years ago, when I was heavy into gardening, that when you're planning a garden plot you should take into consideration the established paths of dogs and children and not put your effort there because, beautiful garden or not, they'll continue their same paths. Mongolians are the same with fences.

As I have noted before, there is much walking here (John has had one pair of shoes re-soled twice) and the Mongolians have preferred paths. There are also many buildings with fences around them. If one of these fences is on one of the preferred paths a section of bars is either eventually bent so the pedestrians can walk through or a section mysteriously disappears altogether. When we arrived there was just such a fence between the main market and our apartment building, but one section had been removed which enabled us to hop the wall and travel to and fro with our groceries. It was most convenient.

For some reason our landlord has decided to enlarge the area of our fence and now the two pathways we had (the original gate and the hole in the fence provided by some accommodating Mongolian) have been covered. The only outlet left to us is to go over to the schoolyard, make a left over two very small fences, and then plunge back through a hole made earlier by a frustrated shopper. I really do expect our old pathway to be opened once again. I noticed today that the space between two of the bars on the new fence in that area has already been widened a bit. Little ones can fit through but not we bigger folk—yet.

So we take each day as it comes and most bring something new. Some are challenges and some are old friends. Our new Mongolian friends touch us with their sincerity and shame us with their facility for new languages. Enkhmaa, our young facilitator and friend, received her mission call this week to the Russia Moscow Mission. She and her best friend have switched from speaking Mongolian or English to Russian so she can brush up on it. Instead of reading her English Book of Mormon she's now reading a Russian one. *Dosvidaniya.*

## Basking

*John*

The streets and sidewalks here are so rough it is very hard on shoes. I'd already had my loafers heeled-and-soled once and it was time to do it again. A couple of days ago, as Nancy and I were returning from buying some videocassettes (for dubbing English lessons) and 20 little notebooks (to keep track of events in the schools where we work), I noticed the sidewalk shoemaker wasn't busy and decided to stop and get my resoling done. It led to one of those quiet, gentle, basking-in-the-sun moments that I will try to convey to you.

To begin, you have to understand that the sidewalk is the shoemaker's place of business. Every day, rain or shine, including Sundays, the shoemaker brings his two duffel bags of tools and materials to the same place on the sidewalk that outlets from our residential area to one of the busier streets. People pass by on their way to work, to school, or to catch a bus. He unrolls the cloth in which he keeps his tools; unpacks his supply of heels, soles, thread, polishes, glues, etc.; and is ready for work. Sometimes his wife and son come to sit as well, to spend some time with him because he works long, long days.

When I stopped he got up from the cement block where he sits (all day, every day!) and reached into one of his duffel bags. He pulled out a pillow, put it on top of a second cement block that sits there all the time, patted it, and bade me sit down. Once I was down, he pulled out a pair of rubber sandals for me to slip on while he took care of my loafers. Basic, I thought, but the pillow and sandals filled all the needs one would have while they were getting their shoes resoled.

Next he pulled out a range of sole materials and carefully arranged them on the sidewalk. He proceeded to pick them up one at a time, say something about each, and hold out one of the fingers on his hand. As the fingers proceeded from left-to-right on his hand it was clear that we were moving along a quality scale but I didn't know whether we were proceeding up or down the scale! I was prepared to buy the best he had, because the wear-and-tear on shoes is so great, if only I could tell which was which.

I pondered my dilemma while he went through an elaborate charade with my old soles. He tore off the small piece that was coming loose and gestured toward it with contempt. Then he tore off another small piece to show me what poor quality it was and made a "Ptah" sound with his mouth. I got the point but still didn't know how to convey to him: "Enough, already. I'm ready to buy the best you have." He resolved my dilemma, thankfully, when he picked up the resoles at one end of the line and lovingly patted them. I nodded in concurrence and the deal was made.

He couldn't let sleeping dogs lie, though. As he pulled and tugged to get the old soles off he kept up a running display of just how cheap and miserable they were—tearing them into small pieces to show their poor quality, shaking his head and muttering in disgust. Along the way he kind of demanded that I participate in this ceremony of ridding myself of this inferior material. Finally I let him know that *he* was the shoemaker who had put on the replacement soles that he was condemning with such disgust—a fact he hadn't realized since Enkhmaa had handled the transaction for me! With that, he subsided in his demonstrations and let me alone while he proceeded to the resoling task.

It was a lovely fall day in Mongolia. The temperature had been around the freezing mark in the morning but the sun quickly warmed the air and was shining brightly in a cloudless, deep blue sky. Lovely. It provided a perfect opportunity for me to lean back against the wall behind me, bask in the sun, and either contemplate my muse or just watch the world go by. I was doing the former when a little girl jarred me out of my contemplation. I had half-a-dozen videocassettes and the 20 journals sitting on my lap and the little girl thought I was trying to sell them! It was charming I thought—one of those piquant moments which seem to abound in Mongolia. Then I returned to my musing only to be jarred back to reality by a teenage boy who wanted to get a better look at my wares! I immediately began to wonder about myself—I knew I was dressed casually but did I look like I needed to sell these few items in order to hold body and soul together?

Then I was amused to see that I was so discomfited by the thought that I got up from my pillowed cement block, put my cassettes and journal on the pillow, and moved to shield them from sight with my body. Evidently I couldn't stand the thought that I looked like a street vendor! While I stood there, my mind took me back to my days at an (unnamed) Big Ten university where I was an assistant dean in the School of Education. As a fund-raising project, our ward staffed one of the refreshment booths at the football and basketball games, and I served my time in the booths like everyone else. I recalled that some of the education faculty members were so shocked (and dismayed?) to see one of their deans working in a refreshment booth that when they realized who I was they left the line rather than embarrass me (or themselves?) by having me serve them! And here I was, embarrassed myself by the thought that I must look like a street vendor. When I realized what I had done, I just shook my head at myself and resumed my seat on the rock.

But the idyllic feeling was gone. From that point on the pillow wasn't comfortable enough, the glue on the shoes/soles was taking too long to dry, all the work awaiting me began to loom large, and I grew impatient as the shoemaker seemed intent on proving to me that he was, indeed, a fine craftsman. He honed, and he peered intently, and he took time to put tacks in every strategic place to keep my new soles from becoming unattached while I was merely anxious to be off. I couldn't tell whether I was still discomfited by my self-image of being a street vendor or it really had been too long but it was clear the moment was gone. Back to the real world. Back to work. Get on with it, Hopkins. So, when he finally finished I hurried on my way, not fully appreciating that the man had done a fine job for me. Only later did I take the time to look and then I realized that these soles are likely to last me a good long time. So I smiled and waved to the shoemaker the next time I passed!

## Fence Watch

*Nancy*

About a week ago I wrote a journal entry about the fence that had been constructed around our apartment compound blocking off our easy access to the market. I knew it wouldn't be long until either a few bars or a section of fence would be removed to open the way again. It took only about ten days and our pathway is once again clear. Several bars have been removed and we may once again hop the wall, squeeze through the fence, and be on our way. Oh, these wonderful Mongolians!

## Fence Watch II

*Nancy*

It's several days later and the landlord has had the bar in the fence welded back in place. I was prepared to make a fast run to the market for a loaf of bread so we could have something to eat. It had been a hard day of teaching and it was a half hour before we had to leave for community class; we hadn't had any lunch and might not have time for dinner. And there it was! Welded down tightly. A little street girl was sitting on the other side and suggested (through motions) that I go up to another spot through which only the smallest and skinniest could pass. I indicated to her that I would be too big but she urged me on. I gathered up my resolve and went to the spot only to have my estimates confirmed. I didn't push it because I could imagine how embarrassing it would be if I got stuck there. So I turned, took the long way around to the other hole in the fence, and climbed through. As I passed the street girl she looked at me and shrugged. Oh well, maybe it'll be open again tomorrow.

## A Woman's View

*Nancy*

Friday night we left with the Coxes, the assistants to the president, and two sisters for a zone conference in Erdenet, a city located northwest of Ulaanbaatar. The only practical way to get there is by a night train which leaves around 7 P.M. (1900 hrs) and arrives at your destination around 7 A.M. (700 hrs.). There are three ways to travel—sitting, standing, or sleeping. We American softies chose to sleep, so we purchased space in a coupé.

On the way up, John and I shared our four bed "suite" with the assistants to the president; they slept on the two top bunks, of course. On the way back, we shared with the two sisters who, once again slept on the top bunks. (We've built up our physical stamina but, please, not the top bunk!)

When we boarded our railway car leaving UB, John and I struggled with one of our huge suitcases full of books and teaching materials to be distributed to the missionaries who are teaching in Darkhan and Erdenet. The two elders were also struggling with heavy bags of supplies that they had to distribute but we finally found our assigned compartment. They "oohed" and "aahed" over the wonderful accommodations as John and I eyed one another. They tested the beds which had a foam mattress pad on them (a new addition since their last trip) and marveled at the fact that there were already sheets on their bunks. They assured us we were in luxurious surroundings so we joined in the merriment of having so much luck.

At this point it either hadn't occurred to the elders that the upper window was down and wouldn't go up or they were just keeping a positive attitude for our sakes. (I was smart enough to know that it was they who were going to have to deal with the cold more than we.)

The elders showed us where to stow the large suitcase so it was out of the way, and did likewise with theirs. Then we settled down while they ran out to a *tutz* ("*toots*," a tiny kiosk) to purchase their dinner. We marveled as to how they must have been away from civilization too long to think these accommodations wonderful, but we marked it up to the fact that males look at things differently than females. When they returned with their "dinner" we noticed it consisted of a bag of greasy rolls. Ours, tucked away in a briefcase, consisted of peanut butter and jelly sandwiches—much more nutritious. As John observed to one of the elders that his meal lacked some of the basic elements for a healthy body the elder named seven of the basic food groups that his purchase might cover.

The train gently swayed back and forth on its way north. I noticed this wonderful elder taking a bite of his "nutritious" meal and then wiping his greasy hand on the leg of his suit pants. After this went on for a while I nicely inquired as to where he had his suit(s) cleaned and he replied that he'd not had it cleaned since arriving. (He'll be going home in a few months.) We asked if he planned on doing so before he left and he said he probably should. We teased him that it would probably dissolve when they put it into the cleaning fluid. It took us five minutes to convince him we were kidding. (A note about cleaning here — there aren't many such facilities and some don't press the clothes afterwards. Since many of the buttons melt in the cleaning fluid they automatically cut them all off with a razor blade — which *you* have to sew back on! Having been warned, I make sure they know we have American buttons which need not be cut off. I've only taken a pair of slacks — as a trial run — and they turned out well. So we took John's suit and it'll be ready in ten days — now I know why the elder hasn't had his only suit cleaned!)

We all settled down into a quiet evening on the train. The sister missionaries joined us and we played some games. Then it was time to retire. We had all avoided using the bathrooms but the time had come. John went first and whispered in my ear that he was sorry I'd have to use them. Then the first elder returned and said, "That bathroom is disgusting!" an indication that he did notice things after all! His companion returned with the same epithet. By this time I was dreading my trip. Needless to say, I concurred with all that had been said.

John and I had changed into sweat suits, following the recommendation given to us earlier in the day by one of the elders. With that window open we were glad we had done so. The train crew came around with sheets and pillowcases (we brought our own pillows) which we bought for 350Ts each. We made our beds and crawled under the covers. The elders climbed up top and I suggested they stuff the extra pillows into the open window to at least cut down some of the cold blowing in. They were both cold all night but never said a thing to us—we heard it from others.

I slept especially well—didn't even hear all the commotion that takes place during a three-hour stop in Darkhan. I'm a child of the trains, having grown up when they were the chief mode of long-distance transportation. My dad used to take me on his business trips when he went by train and I always loved them. So this was a trip back to my childhood, and I nestled comfortably on my bunk. (I only wished I had put my socks on because the sheets and blankets were shorter than I am.)

We arrived the next morning in Erdenet, just in time to go to an apartment kept by the mission for senior couples. We washed up (with hot running water!) and changed. The Coxes hurried on to the zone conference and John and I set out with an interpreter to visit several school directors.

Following a very busy day we once again boarded the train at 7:00 P.M. for the trip home. The assistants stayed overnight to bring baptismal clothes back to the mission home so two sisters stayed in the compartment with us this time and the Coxes were able to enjoy a quiet time, which they seldom have. And this only after the president had interviewed all the sisters and elders returning to Darkhan on the same train.

This truly was a "luxurious" train. The compartment was very clean and well maintained and I wished the elders could see it. I don't know if it was just the car we were in, but it didn't matter. We had lucked out and were going to enjoy it. There were even artificial flowers on the little table under the window. And this window closed! Then, one of the Darkhan sisters from another car stuck her head in our compartment and said that she'd found out that at the end of car opposite from the "public" bathroom, was another one that was especially maintained by one of the female attendants. If you paid her 100Ts you could use it. I was thrilled! Before retiring I took 100Ts in hand and walked to that end of the car. There, in a nicely appointed compartment, sat one of the attendants and her son. I showed my money and the son jumped up, went to a door, and unlocked it. As he opened it I could smell perfume; almost expected music to float forth. It was immaculate! Flowers in a vase, a pink bar of soap and matching hand towel, even toilet paper! Well worth 100Ts. I would have paid 200!

Once again we slept well, although John tells me he sat out in the corridor for a while as he had become quite warm. I felt us stop in Darkhan this time and heard the milk sellers shouting their wares outside the window. I knew our Darkhan elders and sisters were departing the train for their apartments at this mid-night hour and silently prayed that the Lord would continue to bless them in their work. I lay back down and was soon asleep for the remainder of our 12-hour trip.

We arrived back at Ulaanbaatar around 7:00 A.M. and Bat-bold, the mission driver, was there waiting for us. He drove us and the sisters back to our apartment building where we found everything the same as when we'd left—no hot water for our baths. (We later found out that the railcar we had traveled home in was owned by Gok, a Russian-Mongolian copper conglomerate which had a large factory in Erdenet.)

## Fence Watch III

*Nancy*

Several days have passed since the landlord welded the pieces of fence that had been loosened so we could traverse to the market. A new section of the original fence has been broken loose to let us through again but it's not going to last long since they're building new sections of a larger fence every day. They'll go in front of the smaller, original one. In any case, I was able to go to the market twice today, unimpeded, with a smile on my face. It's the Russians vs. the Mongolians. (Russian School #3 owns our building as well as the school next door and all their employees are Russians.) Mongolians 3, Russians 2.

## Winter Is Here

*Nancy*

It is the tradition in this country to turn the heat on on September 15 — everyone's heat. It is government-controlled and I just picture someone sitting somewhere waiting to turn a valve that will make us all warm. Well this year, in order to save money, they decided to delay it until October 1. Guess what? It snowed on September 15. We woke up to snow on the five mountains that surround the city and flakes floating past our window.

The couple who lived in our apartment previously had been kind enough to leave their down comforter so we have snuggled underneath it each night, keeping warm and comfortable. Several nights ago I added a pair of silk long underwear. John is still hanging tough.

Today when I taught school, I was well-layered in order to be prepared for whatever temperature it might be in my classroom, but because my room is on the sunny side of the university it was quite comfortable and I was able to remove my sweater. However, when I taught community class in the evening I left all the layers on, including my coat.

This morning around 7:00 A.M., two Mongolian missionary sisters came to our door to borrow something and as the one turned I could see the back of her jacket was all puffed out. When I felt and asked about it she said it was her pillow which she stuffed there to keep her warm during their morning Book of Mormon reading.

But the real sign that winter has truly arrived was when Baatar, our driver, appeared in a felt derby-type hat and over-coat. He really looked kind of elegant.

We had one large suitcase we hadn't yet unpacked because it contained all our winter gear. It seems that each day I have opened it to get something out so I think this Saturday we'll finally unpack it, store the summer things in it, and put the winter wear in our closet.

The elders and sisters are now wearing their down jackets — most without the linings. John and I have put the linings in our raincoats and for now haven't resorted to our long down coats. Fortunately it's not that cold yet. But, it did seem to happen all at once. The saying here is "The day after Naadam (July 11) is autumn." Well on September 15, winter arrives but the heat doesn't until October 1! We wonder when the hot water will come.

## Fence Watch IV

*Nancy*

Russians 3; Mongolians 3; John and Nancy ½. (We were able to squeak through the fence before they put up the final barrier.)

## Teaching English in Mongolia

*Nancy*

Our primary responsibility here is to serve as directors of the English project sponsored by Deseret International Charities (the name by which we're known here). In addition to our administrative duties we also teach — a requirement for all of us in order to receive and maintain visas to stay in the country. We are each required to teach 16 hours a week and, even at that, more schools would like our services. As our numbers increase we are still unable to fill all the requests we receive.

John and I have taught both at the Ministry of Justice and community evening classes ever since our plane hit the runway in June. In September we also started teaching at Ulaanbaatar University. I have been deeply touched by this people and their intense desire to learn and, presently, their strong desire to learn English—age being no barrier.

In our Ministry class are the First and Second Secretary to the Minister of Justice, lawyers, accountants, the chief of detectives, and economists. A number of them already speak Russian, some Russian and Chinese, but they are now diligently pursuing English. We have made fast friends with these people, whom we greatly admire. In the evenings we offer free English classes for all who would like to learn. Rich and poor stream into the building, bringing with them family members, neighbors, and friends. Our beginner classes are huge—nearly 100 showing up the first night. This is a community service that all we missionaries perform. We offer five classes: Beginning, Beginning 2, Intermediate, Advanced, and TOEFL. Couples as well as single elders and sisters, take turns teaching these classes. Each term lasts two months.

There is a line in the song "Getting to Know You," from the musical *The King and I* which applies to us over and over:

> *It's a very ancient saying, but a true and honest thought.*
> *If you become a teacher, by your students you'll be taught.*

Our lives these last few months have proved that lyric as we work among the people of this ancient country.

As one who fears learning a second language I am constantly impressed with their resolve to struggle with sounds so different from what they're used to: th—, v, f, b, w. I have seen the big, burly, chief of detectives who, when John first started teaching him, was afraid to try to speak in English. Now he seeks out opportunities to speak to us, stumbling as he tries to recall the right words and proper sentence construction, inserting articles which aren't used in any other language. He told me the other day that he missed class because the president of Malaysia was here on a state visit and they went to the "countryside" to see horse racing. It was necessary for him to be there to oversee the security. He was able to tell me all of this in English. I have learned patience as I follow and admire their attempts to form words and sentences.

There is an extreme shortage of books here. Most of the students learn without texts and diligently copy every word we write on the board. It is also necessary for us to photocopy much of the material we use which we pass out to them and then retrieve at the end of class, during which time they copy it all in their "blue books" When we do give them material they can write on and keep, we have to go around and personally assure them that it's all right.

I love my students. I was very fearful of teaching in a university—thinking it more appropriate for John with his degrees than me with my one. However, he assured me it would be like interacting with our grandchildren and he was exactly right. I have fun with them and they all have such a wonderful sense of humor—American-like. I can tease them and they laugh at my feeble attempts to explain a word by using one of the few Mongolian words I know. When they have trouble with "th" I try to pronounce their "l" and they roar in laughter. So I tell them I understand their difficulty.

In this country schedules change at the last minute as do classrooms. Each day I go to class I'm not sure where I'll end up teaching. The kids have become used to Mrs. Hopkins roaming the halls looking for her class so now they send runners looking for me, and when they find me wandering from room to room they call out with a big smile and motion me in the right direction. I'm so lucky to be here!

One of the current favorites at Ulaanbaatar University (UBU to John and I) is singing *Old MacDonald*. It's a perfect way to teach pronunciation with its "Ee-I, Ee-I, O" and its "chick, chick here," etc. We have a lively tape with which they sing along. John and I are both using it and since we save it for the last 10–15 minutes of the class both classes leave singing and you can hear "Ee-I, Ee-I, O" ringing through the halls. The head of the English department heard John playing it (she's a wonderful woman) and told him it was one of her favorites. We've decided we're not the only teachers to use this method as the other day, when we were walking to the main street to get a cab, John was whistling *You Are My Sunshine* and a Mongolian fellow walking with his wife/girlfriend, suddenly turned and sang, "You are my sunshine." I asked, "Where'd you learn that?" He replied, with a big smile on his face, "In school." Elders Benson and Torgerson who are also teaching at UBU use music in their classes as well, but they take a keyboard with them and they perform live. Elder Torgerson was a vocal performance major at BYU.

I have one huge regret, which is that I can't learn and remember my students' names. There are so many of them and the names are so difficult for me to remember/pronounce that it is the one gloomy part of the job. John is great with the names but he's of Welsh ancestry and they have those terrible long names without any vowels and he can say them, too. I'm finally doing better with the people at church. Many of them shorten their names for us, so instead of Oyensura or Oyentsetseg they tell you to call them Oogie.

Mongolians don't hug each other. Thursday night in my advanced community class I was explaining a line in the poem "Casey at the Bat." It speaks about "Flynn a-huggin' third." Since I've been teaching English as an international language I have learned to become an illustrator, actor, and clown. Words just wouldn't convey "a-huggin" so I went over to one of the women from our branch, asked her to stand, and then gave her a big hug to which they all exclaimed (as in *The King and I*), "oh-h-h-h."

There have been a number of Mongolian women who have gone to the States on their missions and come back speaking beautiful English. The training they get as they see how the Church functions is invaluable to the Saints over here. But they have told me the one thing they miss when at home is getting hugs. So, every once in a while one will come up to us and say, "I just need an American hug!" We happily oblige.

We had a visit from Garry Flake who is with the Church's humanitarian service department in Salt Lake City and he named John country director for the Church's humanitarian services over here so he'll cut back on his teaching during the second semester. I know he'll miss the interaction with the students because he, like I, looks forward to being with them. The killer is the preparation. When we're not teaching we're preparing for the next day's classes. Every day is a fishing expedition as we search all the resources in the library that the Church shipped over for the original missionaries. We're in the process of updating the library with some newer EIL texts, hoping to find ones that are less culturally American. We don't want to idealize the U.S. so much that these wonderful people become dissatisfied with their own country.

John has been visiting schools in preparation for second semester assignments. It is best if he has an interpreter with him but on occasion there is none available as they're all at work or in school themselves. Twice this past week he visited a secondary school which would like our teachers and was without an interpreter. Both times a young student there, a member of the church, Oogie, appeared (coincidentally/miraculously) when John most needed an interpreter. She had her 16th birthday yesterday. "And a child shall lead them."

## Daylight Savings Time Ends

*Nancy*

Sunday morning at 2 A.M., daylight savings time ended in Mongolia. It was just like in the States — some people got to church an hour early and wondered where everyone was. We were fortunate enough to have read about it in the weekly English language newspaper or we would have been sitting there wondering with everyone else. Since the young missionaries don't have time to read newspapers they were not aware of the change. We tried to tell as many as we possibly could on Saturday evening, when there were branch confirmations of eight people in our apartment, but others showed up at investigators' homes to roust them out of bed only to be told they could have slept another hour.

It had already begun to be dark here by 7:00 P.M. (1900) so this just put the icing on the cake. The darkness is inching up on 6:00 P.M., then 5:00 P.M., and who knows how early it will eventually arrive.

The leaves have all turned yellow and many trees are bare. The lady who sweeps around our building seems to be fighting a losing battle as far as I'm concerned. She sweeps the leaves into nice piles, bags them, goes home for the day, and returns to do it all over again.

Another sign that the weather has changed are the gorgeous leather coats that have appeared. We've never seen such stunning looking coats. *Everyone* has one. There are short ones, long ones, and three-quarter ones. They're mostly black with a few colors here and there; not nearly all the brown that we see at home. They sure know how to work with leather here and the designs are very chic. There are more leather coats here than cloth! Men, women, teenagers—this is leather Mecca.

With the coats are the leather boots. Some go over the knee! These are a handsome people to begin with but put beautiful leather coats and boots on them and they could appear on any fashion runway in the world!

Add to this another national product—cashmere. They have the softest, non-shedding cashmere I've ever felt, which is made by the Gobi Company. So now that the thermometer hovers around freezing every morning, the Gobi stores that dot the city are experiencing an upswing in business and I've been right in there with them. There's usually one sales clerk and she races back and forth between customers as they shout their preferences of colors and styles. I was caught in one of these melees with John and Enkhmaa the other day. Enkhmaa wondered how we'd ever make our purchase with so much clamoring. It was then that I taught her a good old American idiom—"Money talks." I held out a 10,000 tugrug note and in no time we had the sweater in a bag, ready to go.

These are not luxuries over here—they're essential to keep you protected from the cold and wind. After all, this is the coldest capital in the world, and from what I hear you need every bit of protection you can get. So, you see, I have to buy my share. I tell John we're helping the Mongolian economy.

Lastly I want to mention poor Baatar's car! As driver, he gets all the couple missionaries to our various schools so we don't have to stand out in the cold. His car seems to know that winter weather is on its way. It's a 1982 Russian vehicle; big, black, with broken gas gauge, clock, radio, and speedometer. When we run out of gas he jumps out, gets a can out of the trunk, and pours some in (he never fills the tank). Then he runs to the front of the car, raises the hood, pumps some sort of lever up there, jumps back in the car, turns the ignition, and we're off again. But for the last week or so he's had difficulty getting it started. I don't know if it has a battery in it. John said he's seen it. When it won't start Baatar grabs a long crank he keeps at his side, sticks it under the front grill, and starts to crank! He used to use a gadget he had made that he propped against the gas pedal so the engine would kick in when he cranked. John finally convinced him that he knew how to hold the pedal down so now they have it down to a science. Baatar cranks and John pumps the gas. Sweet Baatar doesn't speak English. He lives in a ger with his wife and children. I don't know where he parks his car.

Now we share Baatar. We've used him all summer by ourselves because the other couples had voted not to retain him for the summer since they could walk in the nice weather, much to our good fortune. Plus, none of them were teaching during the summer—just John and I. As greenies, we had a lot of the city to learn and a lot of schools to visit and Baatar knew where they all were, having driven the couples for several years now. So, we'd hop in the car and say Ministry, School #23, Foundation, UB University, Labor Institute, Eermel Building, and off we'd go. As the weather is changing the other couples have decided to use Baatar once again so we all share him except on Fridays. We're the only ones who also teach on Fridays so we use Baatar all day. He'll take us shopping after we finish school—he knows where all the good stores are.

This morning he was late picking us up and he hates it when that happens. He apologized *(ooch-la-ri)* all over the place and I noticed his greasy hands, and there in the back seat was his wife, Enkhsaikhan, and her hands were greasy and dirty too. Obviously they'd had major problems with the car and it took the two of them to get us picked up and to the university. Fortunately the car has good strong handholds for the passengers because Baatar was determined we wouldn't be late for class as we sped through the city. We made it. He's very conscientious. John and I really like him. We feel safe with him. After all, *Baatar* means *brave*.

# october 1997

## The Circle in the Clouds: The Ger

*Nancy*

Recently, we were invited to have dinner with Dr. Lubsanjav, a noted professor who has dedicated his life to keeping Mongolian traditions alive. The evening we spent with him gave us a marvelous opportunity to experience many of those traditions.

We were given a location not far from our apartment where we were to be picked up. It was a cold and windy evening and we soon discovered that we should have had scarves around our necks and I wished I had something covering my head and ears. Not knowing who would be picking us up, we weren't sure who to look for. All we knew was it would be a white Toyota. As the wind whipped around our ears we examined each car that passed by and even walked up to a white Toyota that was parked near where we were to meet, only to be told they weren't there to pick up the Hopkins.

Eventually the professor (driven by his son) came by in a white Toyota pick-up truck. Following profuse apologies for being about 10 minutes late and for the humble truck in which he must pick us up, we started out for the apartment of our interpreter, Sumya. (Enkhmaa was getting ready to leave on her mission to Russia.) The professor speaks perfect English but John had Sumya with him when they first met so the professor extended an invitation to Sumya, too. It turns out that at the time Sumya was much more impressed than we were because we weren't acquainted with the renown of the professor — she was most impressed and a bit nervous.

We set out, closely packed into the small truck, on a journey that was to be one of our most interesting evenings since arriving in Mongolia. As the kilometers passed we realized we were traveling in a direction of the city we had not yet traversed. We were on a gradual but steady climb that took us to the northern outskirts of the city. We passed several ger districts and could see the bright lights of the city fading behind us.

The populated areas were becoming thinner and thinner as we approached the last ger district. The sun had almost set when we made a sharp left turn onto a gravel road that went through the center of that district. Then we began a really steep climb that wound its way around gers past children and dogs. After a block or two the driver began sounding his horn and in several instants we were before a fence and its large gate was being opened for our entrance. Before us stood a tall brick building, probably only two rooms wide.

We untangled ourselves from the truck and alighted with dogs all around us barking and wagging their tails. We were shown to steps which led us to the inside of the building and saw another series of steps. Climbing the first flight we were taken to the room on the right and it was a print shop with large printing presses and stacks of boxes filled with paper. Then we crossed over to the room on the left and were introduced to a son who had been educated in the United States. He bowed to us and as we offered him our hand in friendship he smiled and held his hands up so we could see that that would be a mistake as they were covered with ink.

Before we embarked up another flight of stairs we removed our shoes and were offered sandals. As we reached the next landing to the left we saw the women of the house gathered to make our dinner. One was kneeling on the floor rolling out little circles of dough on a wooden board and another was tending a baby. We nodded; they nodded. We were then taken across the hall and shown a very disheveled son's room which our host proudly pointed out was a typical American teenager's room. Another flight of stairs took us to two of his favorite rooms. On the right was our host's bedroom. Under an *open* window was a large bed which the professor informed us was his wife's. Across the room was a small cot which he claimed as his. At the head of the bed, where we would have a pillow lay a large white rock. I was curious but didn't ask about it. He showed us around the room and pointed out some priceless treasures, among them a personally signed book given to him by the Dalai Lama. There were other religious tokens and icons. I remarked about the open window with the cold wind blowing in and he smiled. To the left of the landing was his library. Filled from ceiling to floor were shelves of books in many languages, all of which he could read. After pointing out several of his favorite selections he showed us his English language section and proudly picked out a book from a series of New Testament Bible stories that were his grandchildren's favorites.

The best was last. We climbed one more flight of stairs which took us to the rooftop of his home and there before us perched a ger. The wind was really blowing around us and it was quite cold on top of that "mountain." He removed his slippers, we did the same. He stepped up three more stairs, opened a beautifully painted red and yellow door, and bade us enter. As I stepped into that warm, welcoming room, I entered another world.

A wood stove from which emanated a wonderful warmth was in the center of the ger. Around the edges of the circular room were chests and beds/couches all painted in red with Mongolian decorations painted on them. Pieces of art and religious icons were arranged on tables and chests. Family pictures were prominently displayed as well as that of the Dalai Lama.

Our coats were removed and Sumya and I sat on one side of the room on a couch and John and the professor sat on the other. (Upon entering the door of a ger, which always faces south, all visitors turn to the left. Then the head of the house usually directs the women to the right side and the men to the left. The place of honor is furthest from the door and in most cases, is where the altar — *khoimor* — is located.) We spoke of pleasant things. I have never felt so comfortable with a stranger as I did that night. I was as fascinated as Sumya with this man. In his library he showed us a picture of himself as a young man studying in China. He was so young and handsome and in his later years he still holds himself proud and erect.

He told us of Mongolian customs in the countryside. He told us that when babies are born they're washed in snow. This ensures a long, healthy life. He told us of the sacredness of the circle in the lives of the Mongolians. The ger is a circular habitat and the opening in the top is circular, therefore framing the sky in a circle. The original stoves in the gers were round and many of their painted designs are in the form of a circle.

As our meal was brought to us by his daughter he invited John to sit with him on the floor — John opted to sit on a low stool. Our host took his position across from John before a low table, crossed his legs, and remained there throughout the entire dinner. Several Mongolian dishes were served. He explained that his one departure from a native diet is his nightly can of beer — for medicinal purposes. Sumya and I remained sitting on the couch and small tables were set before us upon which our food was served.

Placed on a table next to me was a paper with hands formed in a series of varying shapes. At first I thought it was sign language for the deaf, but the more I looked at the ways the fingers and knuckles were outlined, the more it occurred to me that it was a way of teaching the ancient Mongolian script. This professor is waging a battle in the government legislature to get the teaching of script back into the schools. It is a political battle which he explained to us and it was interesting to me how the loss of a people's written language is instrumental in taking away their national pride and uniqueness. I asked him if the paper was, in fact, the way they teach children the script and he said it was. Then he promised to create a piece of calligraphy for us before we left for home that would have our names and all our grandchildren's names written in the ancient script.

I asked Sumya if she knew what the significance of the white rock was because I saw another one in a little religious niche that had been created next to the Dalai Lama's picture. She said she didn't know but by this time she was no longer tongue-tied in his presence so she asked. He said it was a stone from his birthplace in the center of the country and I understood. He told us the ger was a constant reminder of his roots in the Mongolian countryside; he had traveled much, read many books, learned five languages, studied in many disciplines, but in his heart is Mongolia.

How I hated this evening to end! But once you eat in Mongolia you don't linger. As we stepped out of that warm ger into the strong Mongolian wind I glanced over the valley that Ulaanbaatar sits in and thought, "I could be standing looking out over the Salt Lake Valley," it looked so much the same with its twinkling lights. In fact, I told Sumya to look and told her that's what it's like in Salt Lake City.

We descended the many flights of stairs, saying goodbye to the various family members in their various rooms as we passed. (Mongolian women do not eat with the guests.) I felt like I was descending out of another world and after replacing our shoes and walking down the last flight of stairs we once again entered the real world. We were ushered to the white Toyota truck. The dogs had taken up their barking and Sumya was petrified. John went over and petted and played with the dogs and she couldn't believe that he would approach the ferocious beasts. She held onto me and I scooted her into the backseat of the truck.

We were soon making our way out the gate, down the narrow, winding, stone "roadway" and once again onto the main highway. As we were wending our way down into the valley that UB sits in, I said to John, "Just think, if we were still at home we'd be sitting in front of the TV and missing all of this." God has placed us in the midst of these wonderful, innocent, brilliant people. How fortunate we are! Mongolian Proverb: A man who doesn't learn another language has no feet. We walk limbless before them.

## The Dust Bowl

*Nancy*

Last week we traveled to Baganuur, a city roughly 75 miles east of Ulaanbaatar. It was the first time we had gone east so we saw new sights. There were four of us — Baatar; Sumya, our interpreter; John and I. We had been asked by President Cox to finalize the arrangements for our teachers at the local school and check out the apartment they had found earlier. If all was found to be acceptable the mission would open this as a new area, sending a pair of elders next week.

We were impressed with how good the roads were and John remarked that we ought to convince the mission president to open more cities to the east. Baatar told us (through Sumya) that this road had just opened the day before and we began telling ourselves how lucky we were. We settled in for what we thought would be a 3½ hour comfortable ride but after one hour the road abruptly ended and we headed out across the countryside. It was Khara Khorin all over again! We grasped the handholds over the windows, fortunately provided in these old Russian cars, and braced ourselves for the bumps, swerves, and screeching stops.

Add to this the fact that most of Mongolia is desert-like in that it is dry and dusty. Early in the trip the heater wasn't working properly so Baatar offered me his coat to put around my legs. As the day progressed and the sun came up, things warmed up so we had the windows open. Dust was swirling around us and in the windows. It was coming up from under the car, through the bottom of the doors and, with each large bump John and I in the back seat were enveloped by a cloud of dust coming from behind the seat in the trunk area.

I marveled how Baatar knew which track in the dirt to take when two or three would trail off in varying directions. I mentioned it to John and he thought Baatar was heading for the sun and that proved to be accurate. We traveled for another hour like this when all of a sudden, Baatar put on his turn signal — there wasn't another car for 50 kilometers — and made a left turn onto a newly-built, blacktop road. I howled with laughter! In the middle of nowhere, he had hit right upon this strip of new highway which led to Baganuur and put his turn signal on, no less. Once again, I was duly impressed with the innate sense of direction these people have! I've been told that they are taught very young how to read the heavens, day and night.

We actually arrived at our destination in 2½ hours, dusty but
feeling fine. We carried out the business we were sent to do and
had lunch with the two ladies with whom we met—one the
administrator of the school and the other the head of the English
department.

Baganuur is a comparatively small town and rather remote
so having two Americans in town was an oddity, to say the least.
We received stares from the school children and giggles as they
parroted the English greetings we offered. One little boy rode his
bike alongside us for several blocks trying to drink in the
strange, round-eyed people with white skin. I was afraid he was
going to lose control of the bike and take a header.

Following lunch we started our return trip which was even
dustier than the trip out. Sumya, with her long black hair, sat in
the front and I watched her hair changing color as the dust built
up on it. John's white shirt had dust forming on the folds along
his arm and I could see a patina of dust building up on his dark
blue suit pants. We likened the trip to the old stagecoach days in
the western United States but agreed it would have been even
bumpier.

About an hour and a half outside of Ulaanbaatar we had the
inevitable flat tire. I got out to stretch my legs and peered into
the trunk while Baatar was getting out the spare tire. I couldn't
believe what it looked like back there. Everything was covered
with a half-inch of dust and sand which had come up from
underneath the car while we were traveling.

The tire was changed and I returned to the back seat of the
car while Baatar put the flat tire and tools into the trunk. Then he
closed the trunk lid. Can you figure out what happened next?
Right! We were enveloped in a cloud of choking dust. There was
dust in our eyes. Dust in our mouths. Dust in our noses. But, the
trunk wasn't closed tight enough so down it slammed again and
we were given a second dose for good measure. So before we

could start up again I grabbed our water bottle and gulped as much as I could and handed it to John for his pleasure. (You can't drink bottled water while bumping over the countryside without getting it all over you.)

We were once again on our way and I noted to Sumya that her hair was turning gray. She asked if we had hot water in the apartment building yet and I told her only between 3:00 and 6:00 A.M. I asked if she had hot water at their place and she answered that she did. I certainly envied her the hot bath/shower she'd enjoy when she got home.

John continued to get dustier and dustier. We started laughing about how we had become like the cartoon character Pig Pen, and that when we got out of the car a cloud of dust would follow us as we walked. Finally we hit paved road again and relaxed for those last kilometers into Ulaanbaatar. We were driven to our door and removed all our sand-covered belongings—John's briefcase was no longer black. We noted that the inside of Baatar's car had begun to look like the inside of his trunk and took a good guess at what he'd be doing all weekend. We decided to have the kids send us a can of Armor All for Christmas which we'd present to Baatar, who is meticulous about his car; it will blow his mind!

We dropped our clothes right inside the door and with fearful anticipation I went to the bathroom and turned on the spigot to be greeted with a stream of scalding hot water. A joyous scream of excitement issued from my throat! After I finished bathing and washing my hair, I found John on the floor with the vacuum cleaner and attachment removing the dust from his brief case and raincoat.

Having changed into our comfortable sweats we found something to eat (I don't remember what) and then called President Cox to make our report. It looks like Baganuur is a go and we're glad we went.

## Goodbye to the Ministry and UB University
*Nancy*

This week John and I finished two of our three teaching assignments and in two more weeks we'll finish the third.

We went to the university this afternoon for our regular classes. We were met by Elders Benson and Torgerson who told us the students were on strike so we probably wouldn't have any classes. We each went to check our classrooms to see if any students were going to attend and found in John's they were playing cards and not ready for English. Mine was empty. This was to be our last week of teaching there since John's new assignment as country director in addition to coordinating the English program will occupy most of our time. I really struggled when John said we would have to cut our teaching loads because I knew in my head that he was right but in my heart I had grown close to the students.

I saw two girls from my class in the hall and called them into the room and asked if I could take their pictures. I explained to them that I wouldn't be teaching them anymore. They asked if I was returning to America and I told them I would have a different assignment. I assured them they'd still have English teachers and they asked if it would be Elders Benson and Torgerson. I told them that it would be two other young Americans (a new group comes from the MTC this week).

I asked them to write their names on the board and then I'd take a picture with their names beside them. One of the girls wrote, "We are love Mrs. Hopkins." She then asked, "Is that right?" I erased the "are" and took their pictures. Then they asked if they could have a picture with me so I suggested we go find John and have him take the picture. We found him with his card-playing students and then they asked if he'd take the picture outside. We went out on the steps where they gathered together a number of students from the class that were nearby. I'll miss singing Old MacDonald with them.

It is sad to say goodbye to good friends and that is what the people at the Ministry of Justice have become to us. Last Tuesday morning, for our last class we took brunch in to them. Following brunch they asked us to meet them on the following Monday evening for "drinks." "Drinks" turned out to be a dinner at a nearby club that was very American looking; the dinner was traditional Mongolian *hosher* and *bodes* (American spelling).

One of the classes we had had with them discussed the "small talk" which Americans do at social gatherings. And so they attempted, as best they could, to make small talk in English. Following our dinner, during which the electricity went off, they expressed their appreciation for our being their teachers with the gift of a picture of a ger on the Gobi desert. On the back they had written their names in Mongolian and English. Their final gift was to pin on each of us a Chinggis Khan pin, next to our American and Mongolian flags. We'll miss our regular meetings with them and promised to be back next summer to resume our classes.

Now our assignment is to distribute the Church's humanitarian goods and propose future humanitarian projects to assist the Mongolian people. We have a few in mind.

## Missionaries to Mongolia

*Nancy*

We thought you might like hearing a bit about the missionaries here in Mongolia. Last week six more elders and three more sisters arrived so now we are 61 strong.

Two Mongolian members have been called to short-term missions to fill out our complement—one sister and one elder. With the arrival of the three sisters last week Sr. Erdenetsetseg was released. Elder Enkhbold will be released when the next group of elders arrive in December. Sister Erdenetsetseg was also her branch's Relief Society president and she did a marvelous job of doing it all.

There are a number of Mongolian sisters who are serving full-time missions here and many are in their own hometown, which makes it difficult not to visit with family members and friends. Many of the sisters who receive mission calls are sent either to Mongolia or Russia. Some have gone to the States where they receive marvelous training, not only in missionary work but also in how the Church should be organized and administered. The same applies to the young elders who are called from here. When they come home they are a real strength to the Mongolian branches.

Those who are called to Russia and Mongolia do not travel to the MTC but are sent straight to the mission field so they miss some of the benefits we receive by being able to be there and near a temple. Nevertheless, their testimonies burn within them and they are the sweetest spirits I've ever known. When they pray, you feel like you're listening in on a private conversation.

Our friend Enkhmaa will soon be leaving on her mission to Moscow. She is excitedly preparing herself and waiting for her letter of invitation from the Russian government. Not only do they receive a letter from the First Presidency but then they must wait to be invited by Russia. John and I are keeping our fingers crossed. Her day of departure is supposed to be November 4.

The primary work of the American elders and sisters here is to teach English. They must teach in a classroom 16 hours a week and that requires much preparation. There is an EIL library here in the apartment building where the couples and sisters are housed. The couple who lives in that apartment oversees the library and serves unselfishly as they have visitors day and night preparing for the next day's classes.

Since all American missionaries must teach, the Mongolians who are assigned them as companions must sit in the classroom without taking part. They also have to tag along while they're in the library preparing. I think how boring the days must be for them but their selfless act of sitting there makes it possible for many of their people to learn English. On the other hand, the American elder or sister must carry the entire teaching responsibility alone and doesn't have a companion with whom to share the teaching task.

With the exception of the senior couples, companions are never separated to teach in different classrooms. It is most disappointing for many schools who think they're going to get two free teachers instead of one companionship. It is difficult to explain that our teachers come in twos but teach as one.

We are presently teaching in 25 schools, mostly in Ulaanbaatar. There are others in Darkhan, Erdenet, and a new area opened just last week in Baganuur. Overseeing all this is a tremendous task as schedules need to be worked out and criteria met. Some days our apartment is "take a number" day as missionaries stream in with problems that have developed. I seem to work more with the curriculum and teaching ideas and John works out the problems with school directors/rectors/principals. He keeps a blue book on every school in which he records every visit and every problem and its resolution noted. He spends hours updating these books (now you know why I'm writing most of the journal entries). Frequently he jumps in the car and says to Baatar, "Mongolian Business Institute," or "Orkhon," or "Labor Institute," or "Ider," and on and on. Off they go to smooth out another problem.

Mongolia: The circle in the clouds

When we teach English all day, over a long period of time, we begin talking to one another as though we're not native English speakers—slowly, distinctly pronouncing everything, and not using contractions, e.g., "It is cold today," instead of, "It's cold today." After a lot of this we have to remind each other that we understand "Whaddayawant?" instead of "What do you want?"

For a while, the only English radio broadcast we got was VOA (Voice of America). We'd retire around 10:00 P.M., turn the shortwave radio on, and there they'd be teaching English—sometimes the same lesson we had just taught that day. It was maddening! I couldn't take it anymore! Enough with English! Then, a little over a month ago, the BBC began broadcasting on an FM station so we can now hear the news of the world before calling it a day and forgetting English teaching for a while.

These young elders and sisters put in grueling days. They teach English in the schools during the day and then discussions in the evenings. It is interesting to watch them grow. We see them blossom from chubby-cheeked childhood to womanhood and manhood. Their faces change as their spirits grow within them and burst forth for all to see.

We have heard from some people who are enjoying our web page. We have our children to thank for maintaining the page and for the original idea. John and I are computer illiterates so they set everything up for us before we left the States. Some readers have mentioned a desire to serve a mission upon reaching retirement age and we are pleased if our experiences have encouraged this desire. It is very hard work but the rewards more than compensate for the passing frustrations.

If you ever wanted to be an expert in something but felt you weren't, go to a foreign country and offer to teach conversational English. You become an instant expert and everyone clamors for your services.

# november 1997

## Okay, So Mongolia's Not Perfect

*Nancy*

Just so you don't think the Church sent us to Shangri-la for a vacation, here are some of the frustrations:

1.  *They only open one door. Even when there's a double door or whole wall of doors, a small door opens so everyone has to crowd through that one door and it's not first come, first through, it's "every man (or woman) for himself." You can always tell the Westerners who have just arrived because they keep standing there waiting for someone to let them through.*

2.  *When the first door opens you're faced with another door to actually enter the building. Because of the cold and winds there is a series of two doors and, I imagine for the same reason, the second door that is open is never opposite the one you just entered. You have to walk to your left or right to find the second door to enter the building.*

3.  *Every room in a building has a threshold you have to step over. I'd hate to count all the rooms I fell into when first arriving*

here. *I'm pretty good, now, and step over without thinking. The other day, however, while coming out of our bathroom, I about broke my neck. John asked one of his classes why these sills were necessary and the reply was, "All gers have them." Enough said!*

4.  *The steps on stairways are not even; some are deep and some are shallow (in the same staircase!) so don't be surprised if you hear one of us has fallen.*

5.  *There's no brown sugar.*

6.  *They don't have large shoes to fit feet like mine.*

7.  *Unless you tell them otherwise, when you take your clothes to the cleaners they cut all the buttons off and hand them to you.*

8.  *The heat isn't turned on until October 1, and then it comes on full blast and there's no way to adjust it. For those of you who know how cool we keep it in our Pennsylvania home, you won't be surprised to hear that it's November and we have the fan on.*

9.  *They don't carry the Eagles games.*

10. *The stores close for an hour lunch but that hour can be anytime between 9:00 A.M. and 3:00 P.M. Times posted on the door (in military time) don't really have anything to do with anything. However, if you wave money at them they'll open the door.*

11. *The Mormons don't have anything on the Mongolians with their "Mormon Standard Time." "Mongolian Standard Time" is always 20 minutes late.*

12. *It takes six full days to obtain a customs stamp to release a humanitarian shipment from Salt Lake.*

13. *The Russians won the war of the fence, for now.*

14. *Mongolians have an obsession with clean, shiny cars and shoes. Hope they never see my car! They carry a bucket and cloth with them. Saw a man sitting in his car in the rain, with window open, reaching out to clean the roof. Is that obsessive?*

15. *I say a Mongolian word and they don't understand me. I say it over and over and they finally catch on and repeat it and it's exactly the way I said it the first time. My students laugh at me so I have them say something beginning with "th" and they are suitably humbled.*

16. *We have to keep our shoes shined despite walking on sandy, dusty roads and sidewalks all day.*

17. *Our clothes are getting too big.*

18. *The sun shines every day.*

19. *We only get hot water between 3:00 A.M. and 6:00 A.M.*

20. *What's a "P Day?" Did a recent survey (at the request of the humanitarian department in Salt Lake) and couples are working an average of 60–70 hours each (not per couple) per week. Obviously we need a union.*

That may give you a taste of our lives here. Would you believe it when we say we love it? Just didn't want you to think it's perfect over here because then we might disappear from the face of the earth.

## The Hat

*Nancy*

Before we left home John was advised to wear a hat while in Mongolia. The UV rays are quite strong and since he had had a mole removed from his head which proved to be basal cell cancer we decided it's best not to take any chances. He decided to wait until we got to Salt Lake to purchase a hat but as luck would have it our son-in-law, Dan, had a marvelous hat he had purchased in Australia which he offered to the cause. It is a handsome, wide-brimmed hat which exactly matches John's coat. It's not a cowboy hat but it is similar.

John has become well identified with that hat. I have seen it carried through university halls by students as they chase down the room he's teaching in. It strolls along corridors in government buildings, meanders through the market, does a little sightseeing and a lot of "getting from here to there."

When someone has been sent to meet us who has never seen us before they're told to look for the hat. When we are to meet someone at Sukhbaatar Square it's the hat they look for. Enkhmaa asked him, when we first got here, why he always wears a cowboy hat. It has become his trademark. The hat became even more significant in the recent saga of a humanitarian shipment sent from Salt Lake to Ulaanbaatar to be distributed to the needy. As country directors it is our job to receive and disburse the items. But before that can be done the shipment must be cleared through customs. To do that one needs to prove that these are charitable contributions and should not be taxed.

John spent five full days "paper chasing" throughout Ulaanbaatar—freight yards, national governmental offices for official stamps, and city offices. On the fifth day, just when he thought he was finished, one more of many snags occurred. Another signature was needed. It would mean returning to another office, back across town. Then the magic occurred. A kind female official got on her "radio" and called the person in question. There was a conversation in Mongolian as to the problem. She looked up at John, said something into the radio, everyone in the room laughed, and she cleared the container. Sumya later told him that it was the hat! They trusted the American in the hat!

# Fence Watch: Russians—Game, Set, and Match

*Nancy*

It's been a while since we reported on the status of the fence around our apartment building which is maintained by Russian School #3.

You'll recall that as of our last reporting the Russians had completely closed off all *easy* access to the market next door by welding up the holes in the fence made by the Mongolians and installing an additional, taller fence next to the original fence. The only avenue to the market left (other than walking through the front gates, around the entire building, and then along the street to the front entrance of the market) was for us to go through the school yard, over two low fences, and then through a different hole in the schoolyard fence which meant bending low, stepping over a wall, and swinging yourself through using your arms. Coming back with several bags filled with food was always an athletic feat.

We were sure that before winter's end a more convenient hole would miraculously appear and life would be sweet again. About a month ago, a change did take place. Elder and Sister Hague from Washington State arrived. Elder Hague will be working with one of the banks here in Ulaanbaatar and Sr. Hague is teaching English and serving as librarian in our EIL library. Elder Hague walks with a cane due to having contracted polio as a child. The first day they were here we took them to the market, wondering if he'd be able to traverse the wall and pass through the hole at the same time but he did quite well, using his upper body strength to swing himself through.

That very night a change took place! In the morning, when we ran over to the market the hole had been enlarged and the top bar removed. A step had been created on both sides of the wall. Elder Hague! Elder Hague must have come out during the night and enlarged the hole and created those steps. On the way up to our apartment we stopped by theirs to ask them about it and they denied all responsibility in the matter. Two days later a homemade, primitive gate was attached to the two side pieces. We found the gate locked a couple times so we couldn't get through but now it remains open. Although it's not our preferred route, easier access has now been provided.

## The Deel

*Nancy*

The deel is the national dress of Mongolia, only varying in design and ornamentation depending on the wearer's ethnic group or clan origination. The differences are so subtle that they usually go unnoticed to the untrained eye. The style is the same for both men and women. It is commonly worn on the street, although more by the older members of the population than the younger ones. The younger generation wear theirs on special occasions and national holidays.

The fabric design varies from the bright and colorful for the women to the more conservative for the men. It's not unusual for a woman's satin "everyday" deel to be covered with glistening gold threads. I have been told that the more elaborately embroidered fabrics are worn by the married women while the single women wear the more subtle designs.

Men's deels are usually made of a dark, solid fabric — wool, felt, or "gabardine-like." The men belt theirs with a wide piece of either gold or orange fabric that is several yards long and wound around their girth with the ends tucked in. The women wear either the fabric "girdle" of bright green, orange, or gold or opt for a gold or standard leather, western style belt. Although you see deels year 'round, there are fewer worn in the summer, but come fall and winter they run a close second to the beautiful long, leather coats.

The deel is especially well suited to the coloring and build of the Mongolian people. They look lovely in them with their dark complexions and dark hair. They always look fashionable, no matter the age. Boots are the footwear of choice with this costume and a tighter fitting pant is worn underneath—something like tights. Some of the women's boots go to the knee for extra warmth. Many of the men wear the traditional boot with the turned up toe—their reverence for the feet and the ground—so the foot doesn't disturb the little bit of grass that there is here. The women's boots are much more fashionable.

Most of the missionaries who come to Mongolia purchase a deel before they leave—most of them custom-made by women in their branch. They purchase their own fabric, often in the black market, and then agree with one of the sisters on a price. By custom, the lining is a patterned cotton fabric and some new missionaries make the mistake of buying the incorrect fabric for the lining.

A coat is not worn over the deel as it *is* a coat. As the season changes the weight of the deel changes. Fall and early winter deels have an interlining similar to our quilt batting but made of felt. As winter deepens the lining becomes heavier. I have seen two variations of the heavier deel. One has the long haired sheep or goat skin sewn into the inner lining with the ends of the fur extending beyond the fabric edges. The other is a completely separate sleeveless garment made of the same animal skin which is worn under the deel. The second option facilitates the changing seasons or occasional temperature change.

The Mongolians are very proud of their national dress and are pleased when foreigners adopt them. Last year, when the General President of the Relief Society and some others visited here they were presented with beautiful deels and all the couples were also dressed in theirs.

We were honored several weeks ago to be presented with our own deels. Enkhmaa's mother, Tserendulam, a retired doctor, lives in the Gobi but came to UB to visit an ailing brother. She brought with her deels that she had made for John and I. While here, she came to dinner. Although it was the first time we had ever seen each other, the deels she had made for us fit perfectly. We were astounded! Not a measurement taken and they couldn't have fit better than if they had been. (I mentioned this fact to one of the sisters in our branch and she said the first time she saw me she knew what size deel I'd wear.) Needless to say we were overwhelmed with these beautiful gifts and Enkhmaa was all smiles.

My deel is a royal blue with a lighter blue floral pattern. It is trimmed in an orange, metallic embroidered fabric and very tiny buttons (which my arthritic fingers have trouble buttoning). Tserendulam instructed me that I must wear boots and stretch-pants underneath and I assured her I had just the right thing at home but that they aren't standard missionary dress.

John's is made of a dark blue, shadow striped fabric, trimmed in blue metallic to match mine. His buttons are the traditional men's buttons made of silver which have been designed so they are easily removed for laundering. Each deel is lined with the traditional floral cotton. Not only did they fit perfectly but the choice of fabric was exquisite and fit our personalities and tastes perfectly. Blue (or blue-y as Enkhmaa calls it) is my favorite color and the fabric chosen for John goes perfectly with his conservative "pin stripe" self. If we had chosen the fabric ourselves they were what we'd have probably chosen.

Dinner with us was Tserendulam's first western meal and Enkhmaa said she was a bit nervous. We had Yankee pot roast and potatoes and she seemed to enjoy it. We also had the traditional cabbage salad which, with potato salad, are the main types of salads served in Mongolia.

After dinner we donned our new outfits and took pictures. Enkhmaa insisted John wear his Australian hat for some of them. John has become identified by that hat all over Ulaanbaatar so it's strange to see him without it.

Although we had to communicate through Enkhmaa's interpreting for us, we developed an affection for each other and we've added Tserendulam to our lengthening list of Mongolian friends whose companionship we will miss when we return home: Baasanjab, Bilegdemberel, Gerelchuluun, Enkhsogt, Enkhbaatar, Zorig, Baatar, Batbold, Turbilig, Otgonbayar, Professor Lubsanjav, Erdenetsetseg, Undrach, Tungalag, Nemu, Oyanga, Buyankhishig, Ulzii, Llkhamkhuu, Osijarmaa, Enkhbold, and the list goes on.

Our cup runneth over.

## The Trans-Continental Bear

*Nancy*

As mentioned earlier, the new couple is the Hagues from Yakima, Washington. Elder Hague will be working on a banking project with the Mongolian bankers and Sr. Hague will be teaching English (what else?) and acting as our EIL librarian. The EIL library is a room in one of the couples' apartments which contains many shelves of resource books. The original books were shipped over by the Church and two retired librarians came over on a mini-mission and catalogued them. The library also contains a paper cutter, *the* stapler, pencils, paper, and the other bare necessities for teaching English. A small copy machine is located in the only closet in the apartment. Originally, this apartment served as the church offices.

When you're the librarian here it doesn't mean it's quiet and everyone whispers. Rather, it means people knocking on your door at all times wanting to prepare a lesson, make a photocopy, check out a book, get a picture or flash cards, find that special dot-to-dot book left in the copier, etc., etc.

The Hagues had a traveling companion with them who is on a very special adventure. He is a white, stuffed bear with a backpack over his shoulders. He started his travels at the Atlanta Olympics; in his pack is a log of all the places he has traveled and with whom. His name is Bear-lee There and he belongs to Mary N. Toop's Franklin Middle School class in Yakima and is part of a geography lesson.

Upon arrival in Ulaanbaatar, Mongolia, he was presented to Enkhmaa, who was leaving Thursday on her mission to Moscow, Russia. She will carry Bear-lee There with her, and after finding a suitable companion she will sign the log on the bear's back and send him on his way to his next destination—possibly with a missionary returning to the United States.

Bear-lee There is very lucky to have had so many people looking after him but will his children believe it when he tells them about it?

## Our Thanksgiving in Mongolia

*Nancy*

Last week several of the sister missionaries mentioned they'd like to do some sort of service project since they were feeling the need to do something for someone. They mentioned that one of the Mongolian sister missionaries knew of an orphanage not too far from the mission home so John and I quickly indicated our interest. We've been visiting hospitals, etc. to learn how Deseret International Charities could best help these organizations. As it turned out, *all* the young sister missionaries were anxious to make an afternoon of it. Both the sisters in Ulaanbaatar and the ones from Erdenet and Darkhan would be joining us since they would be coming down on the train to spend Thanksgiving with us. As we weren't having our official Thanksgiving celebration until Friday we decided it would be a great way to spend Thanksgiving Day. Thus, all ten of the sisters in Mongolia and John and I met at the mission home and set out for this "nearby" orphanage. As we walked, two by two, we chattered away with the sisters we hadn't seen for a while and the two that will be leaving for home in a couple of weeks. The "nearby" orphanage seemed to us to be pretty far away, but then we realized it was measured by Mongolian standards and anything short of four miles is "nearby."

Finally, Sister Buyankhishig turned in and we were relieved to get out of the 5°F weather. We went up several flights of stairs and, even though we didn't have an appointment, were ushered into the office of the director. Mrs. Tumenbayar invited us to sit down. We introduced ourselves. From down the hall we could hear music and singing. She explained that this was a home for street children who were brought to them by the police. Many of them lived in the underground tunnels that carry the heating pipes throughout the city. We have seen many such children around the market begging and I was startled once when walking to church to see a young boy disappear down a manhole. One of the senior sisters told me that last year there was a terrible rain storm and 300 little bodies washed out from these underground warrens.

The director told us there were 89 children housed there and answered our many questions. She explained that although they didn't have an excess of food or clothing the children were neither starving nor naked. She was most patient with us and our inquiries and then took us down the hall to where the music and children's singing was originating. We were told they were having a talent show. When the 12 of us entered the room en masse a small girl was singing a song. She gave us a huge smile and never missed a beat of her music.

Then the teachers, students, handyman, and night watchman all took turns singing or dancing. Huddled in one corner were four or five boys who looked to be seven or eight but were actually 13–14. Their small size belied their true age. Tearing ourselves away from the sweet faces and haunting eyes, we were taken on a tour of the bedrooms, library, arts and crafts/home economics room with its Japanese treadle sewing machine, kitchen, and doctor's office. All the medicines for the facility were on one small tray. The doctor explained that when the children were brought in they often had skin diseases and dental and eye problems. They are usually so malnourished that they fall two or even three categories below the expected height and weight for their age. The doctor showed us the vitamin supplements she mixes and gives to them in a drink. While visiting the "dormitory rooms" we were told that when a family of children is brought in they are kept together in the same room.

Each room was well kept with beds neatly made. Each blanket was folded in a special way and a clean white decorated cloth carefully placed over it. Some of the coverings were hand decorated with cross stitch embroidery. On the wall of each bedroom was a chart showing the names of the room's occupants and their household duties. The rooms are tidied three times a day.

The kitchen was quite bare. A large, old (1979) stove sat in the middle of the room. On a far counter was a huge pile of dough rising. The director told us the children are fed four times a day and the meal consists mainly of bread and a soup made with cabbage and potatoes. "They're neither starving nor naked" went through my mind.

At the end of the tour we passed by the room where the talent show was being held and, as we looked in, children were dancing together, children and teachers were dancing together, teachers and teachers were dancing together, and all were having a wonderful time. We couldn't resist. We grabbed the hands of some of the little ones standing around the sides and then others got brave and joined our circles. We were silly and they laughed at and with us. One little boy who I had earlier thought looked especially sad and emaciated came over and took my hand. With that, the little part of my heart that hadn't yet melted disappeared. Their kindred who are still on and under the streets don't have anything to smile and laugh about.

What a blessing that God put us here that "our eyes may see and ears may hear" his little ones who have a need and that a generous Church and people stand ready with outstretched arms to succor them. I'm thankful on this Thanksgiving Day for The Church of Jesus Christ of Latter-day Saints and the generosity of its members. (We made several return visits to this shelter and brought clothing, school supplies, toys, and medical supplies.)

## The Coldest Capital in the World

*Nancy*

The Mongolians have been chuckling at we westerners for several weeks now as we've been wearing our down-filled coats. They chidingly ask why we're so bundled up and we reply that it's cold. Then they laugh and say "It's not cold, yet."

*Cold* came today. When we walked to church this morning it was –20°F. We had added a few things to our morning's wardrobe in preparation for the mile walk: I put on my expedition weight long underwear bottoms and chose a cashmere turtleneck sweater instead of a cotton blouse. John put on thermal bottoms under his suit and searched out his fleece helmet to wear under his hood as he had determined when it got much colder he'd need something better than "the hat" for his ears.

We had noticed, over time, subtle changes taking place in the dress of those that pass by our apartment building. First there were the beautiful leather coats and winter deels. A few weeks later attractive boots were added to keep the legs warm. About the same time, the Russian (or Mongolian) style fur hats appeared and made the majestic look even more so. During the last several weeks, fur coats replaced the leather.

It's interesting watching the local people dress to go outside. One of the other changes that has taken place is that the scarves have gotten longer. They have a specific way of wrapping these scarves to get the most benefit. Instead of placing the scarf at the back of the neck first, they place it around the throat, then to the back, but the placement has to be just right. It's like a man preparing to tie a necktie. One end of the scarf must be shorter than the other and the remainder of the scarf is wrapped around the neck, under the chin, then over the mouth and nose, and in some cases, around the back of the head and across the forehead so that only your eyes are apparent. This plays all kinds of havoc with hairstyles and lipstick.

You can tell how long westerners have been here by the way they "don their apparel." The new missionaries throw the scarves on western style, cross them in front of their chests and then put on their coats. Once you're outside, it's quickly apparent why it should be done the other way. The cold bites your chin, mouth, nose, and cheeks. If you do it Mongolian style there is a little pocket created into which you can pull your face, turtle-like, to keep warm.

As mentioned above, there are some disadvantages to this method. You get lipstick all over your scarf, and with the full head wrap your hair is as flat as a pancake! Since the Mongolian girls have such beautiful thick, black hair they either leave it long and put it into one braid which looks none the worse for wear when they remove the scarf or keep it short and just shake it out or run their fingers through. It's the western hair styles that take a beating; those permed curls just get flat and are full of electricity. There's no way you can look "cool" when you remove your head dressing.

Dumb luck has been with me because I had changed my hair-style upon arrival. Having had permed hair since I was about 12, when I finally convinced my mother I was too old for braids, I've carried on with the task ever since. Fully expecting to continue it here, I brought six perms with me. However, we've been so busy I've just let my hair go *au naturel* and it's now straight and brushed back. It's simple to care for and not too bad looking. I'll probably never get another perm (sorry, Carol, at Impact Hair Salon). Two weeks ago I went with John to a unisex barber shop and the lady there gave me a wonderful haircut. Anyway, the purpose of this last paragraph is to say that my hair is already flat so keeping my head and ears warm doesn't complicate my life.

When we left for church this morning we put on all the cold-weather gear we had brought with us. Thanks to LL Bean we were really comfortable but encountered a problem that we're going to have to work out—our glasses. The lenses of our glasses freeze over! I had had mine freeze over yesterday so knew I had to beware today, but John was so bundled around his face that by the time we arrived at church his glasses were completely iced over and I had to lead him over curbs and up and down steps. When I looked at him he had frost all over the parts of the scarf around his mouth down to and including the collar of his coat. I was stunned! Then I looked down and noticed that the collar of my coat was also covered with frost. We saw several sister missionaries standing across the street from the chapel and when we joined them we saw that their hair and eyelashes were covered with frost. When we were in the foyer of the church we were taught the trick of keeping your glasses clear—you take them off and put them in your pocket before you go outside. What a problem that's going to cause!

By the time we started the walk home, the temperature had risen to –10°F. We experimented with several tricks to keep our glasses clear and noticed that when we walked past the spaces between buildings, where the wind was blowing just a bit, our lenses cleared. It also helps if you use the turtle method of dipping in and out of your scarf instead of wrapping your nose and mouth completely. It also seems best to breathe through your mouth instead of your nose because your nostrils "freeze."

But, you know what? We love it! When we were first talking with the humanitarian services department we told them we had only one request which was that they didn't send us somewhere hot and humid. They were true to their promise. Thanks Elder and Sister Campbell.

# December 1997

## Elder Rolfson's Going Home

*Nancy*

Four missionaries will be returning home this week—two elders and two sisters. A new group of seven elders will arrive Wednesday.

You may remember the account of our overnight train trip to Erdenet several months ago. During that entry I mentioned one of the assistants to the president riding in our compartment had indicated he hadn't had his suit cleaned the entire time he'd been in Mongolia but that he planned to do so before leaving for home. As a further reminder, we then teased him that when it was cleaned, it would probably go to shreds. Well, he did clean his suit and parts of the pants shredded.

He stopped by last week to show us he had washed his pants and pointed to several spots where the material had given out. Then he proudly showed us that it was okay because he had repaired it with silver duct tape on the inside.

Like all missionaries, when we received our call to Mongolia, we received a clothing list which also included other suggested articles to bring. Our list included silver duct tape. At the time we wondered if it was really necessary to put that heavy roll in our luggage but we have found it to be essential. We've only been here six months and our roll is almost gone. We've used it to seal all the windows in our apartment to keep out the cold (it does a good job of preventing drafts) instead of using it to keep our clothes repaired.

While we were enjoying the revelation of Elder Rolfson's "patches," I mentioned it to several other elders and they lifted up their pant legs and showed me where they had repaired the hems in their pants with duct tape. Don't they ever use the sewing kits we're also told to bring with us? I purposely required our two sons to sew on all their own Boy Scout merit badges and patches so they'd have sewing experience before going on their missions. Duct tape was not on their clothing list.

## An Observation

Zero degrees does feel warm when it has been –20°F.

## Extraordinary Packagers

### Nancy

As you probably know by now, the traditional life of the Mongolians has been that of nomads. Those living in the countryside still live that type of life as they move their gers from place to place so their flocks can graze on the very sparse "grass."

Mongolians have perfected the task of taking down and putting up their gers. I have been told that two men can do it in about a half hour although I doubt that that includes all the felt insulation and outside covering. In any case, the women learned to be very efficient packers and I watched a sister in our branch who is now a city dweller use these skills the other day.

About a month ago we received a shipment of clothes, books, medical supplies, and other items from Salt Lake City. These items were for distribution to needy Mongolians and all four tons of it are almost gone. Most of it left our church building in the original bales in which it was shipped but those items that were earmarked for the members were opened and sorted by the Relief Society sisters in the district and branches.

The branch presidents with the help of the Relief Society presidents have begun placing orders for the members so they've been coming to the storage room to fill those orders. We watched Friday as an order was being filled for a small branch some two hours outside the city. Plastic bags are not readily available here so "packaging" the clothes for distribution to the various families was a problem John and I had discussed but had not had time to resolve. We were astounded as we watched these women create bundles by using the clothing itself. A pile of clothing was rolled into a compact bundle that was tight and then efficiently stacked. John and I just stopped our pitiful attempts to help, stood back, and watched their efficiency with unabashed admiration. I knew we were watching something that was inherent to them and we were only in the way.

## The Prime Minister's Dinner

*Nancy*

Mrs. E. Shurentsetseg is the wife of the Prime Minister of Mongolia and several weeks ago the Coxes and John and I received invitations from she and her husband to attend a charity fundraising dinner to benefit the poor children of Mongolia. It was to be held at a guest house called Ikh Tenger (great sky).

Well, this was some guest house! We left the city and traveled toward one of the mountain ranges that surrounds the city of Ulaanbaatar. At the base of the mountain we drove through a set of gates and then up a long driveway to the guest house, which turned out to be a mansion. Huge ice sculptures were lit by floodlights and a red carpet had been placed on the steps leading to the house.

As we passed each station in the car the policemen standing guard saluted us. As we stepped out of the car we noticed security men with radios directing the guests and their cars to their proper places.

The house was beautifully decorated for the holidays with much rope tinsel. They must have bought up every piece they could find in Ulaanbaatar as they had it all over the walls, creating Mongolian designs and imitating climbing vines. After removing our coats and hanging them next to the grand staircase (which was guarded so you couldn't sneak upstairs and check out the rooms), we were ushered into a reception area where the Prime Minister and his wife received each of the 100 guests (to which the list had been limited).

It was a formal occasion and the Prime Minister looked statesmanlike in his tux and Mrs. Shurentsetseg was lovely in an ankle length black lace dress that was trimmed with beads. Sister Cox's dress was one of the lovely silk ones she gets on her infrequent trips to Hong Kong and I was in my missionary dark blue suit dress with navy jacket. John and President Cox were in their missionary suits so were very unexciting looking. However, we were warmly greeted by the Mongolian Scout officials who have a special relationship with Deseret International Charities. The Scouts were co-sponsors of the event.

We saw a person from the U.S. Embassy with whom we had worked in planning the Fourth of July celebration, and the head of the Peace Corps with whom John has had some discussions, but, on the whole we didn't know anyone else in attendance. There were many beautiful women costumed in their native dress and Sister Cox and I studied the intricacies of the design.

Then came the big surprise of the evening. We were ushered into the dining hall where, along two walls of the room, there were tables filled with food. In the middle were large round tables that had been set with dishes, glasses, silverware, and bottles for drinks. But there wasn't a chair in sight. This was not a "sit-down dinner." It was a stand up dinner, holding your plate, utensils, napkin, and glass and eating as best you could. We all became contortionists as we tried to figure out how to do this. Sister Cox drank her Sprite and put the empty glass under her arm where it stayed the whole evening. I put my filled glass on my dish and anchored it with my thumb. John didn't even try. After a while it became apparent that we couldn't use the knives because we couldn't cut anything one-handed so they were discarded.

The food was delicious and it turned out the cold foods were on one side of the room and the hot foods on the other. There was plenty to eat. We each found our favorite and especially good were the finger-sized desserts.

Our evening was capped off when we left the dining room and went into the ballroom where an orchestra was playing. This night just happened to be the Cox's 40th anniversary so President Cox asked Sister Cox to dance—a very good dancer he is! John asked if I'd like to join them so there we were, two American couples, dancing on an otherwise empty dance floor to a Mongolian orchestra playing "our kind of music." Two or three songs later we decided it was time to leave so we left Ikh Tenger,

four Latter-day Saint missionaries who only five years ago
would not have been welcome in the country but thanks to those
pioneer elders, couples, and others who preceded us we now
enjoy a good enough reputation that it is thinkable for us to be
invited to some of the very best places.

## Mongolian Ice "Fallies"

*Nancy*

Several weeks ago, on a Friday, it snowed most of the day.
As you may recall, Ulaanbaatar is desert-like in that it has a very
dry climate so even though it gets very cold here it doesn't snow
much.

When it snowed we asked if the snow would remain for a
long time since it's not like we're used to in Pennsylvania where
it snows and then several days later melts and disappears. We
assumed that, since it remains cold here, the snow would also remain. We were quite surprised when the answer was, "No." I've
decided that what they really meant was, "No, it turns to ice."

What was an inch or so of snow is now an inch or so of ice. It
covers the sidewalks and the streets and I believe it is here to
stay until April or May. One advantage of this is that the cars
don't get as dusty and we don't have to polish our shoes as often.
The young boys love it as they hold onto the backs of cars and
slide along on their feet. We were coming back to the apartment
from teaching the other day and several boys were waiting to
grab the bumper on our car. I shook my finger at them. They
shrugged their shoulders and waited for the next "ride." Ugly
American! The ice has smoothed out the potholes in the roads
and our walk to the mission home has changed from stumbling
over loose stones and rocks to sliding into ruts.

I'd be scared to death to drive on these streets but the cars don't seem to have slowed down one bit. Fortunately (or unfortunately), they don't stop for pedestrians or for other cars because at the pace they move they'd never get stopped. At night the headlights reflect off the ice-covered streets and the ice reflects the sun during the day. The sun shines every day in Mongolia! You look outside and the sun is bright and beautiful and you step outside and are surprised how cold it is. It gets us every time!

It is necessary to look down when you walk because some spots are icier than others. You look out for the smooth ice because that's where danger lies. You look for the places where there is still loose snow that hasn't been packed down by automobile or pedestrian traffic. We were told that everyone falls twice during the winter. I've completed my quota but John hasn't had his first yet. He's sure had some near misses, though. The shoes that he specifically purchased for this purpose, with thick soles and heavy treads, are lethal on this ice so he's back to his black tassel loafers which have the rubber soles and heels put on by the Mongolian shoe repair man this summer. (By the way, he's not out on the sidewalk sitting on his stone during this weather.)

One of the senior sisters came well prepared. She has an apparatus with metal spikes that attaches to her shoes and digs right in. Even though I've fallen my boots give me good traction. The last and cheapest purchase I made before leaving home was a pair of Sporto boots that were polishable—a requirement of the mission. They were on sale for $29 and not bad looking. I hadn't unpacked them, thinking I'd only be wearing them in the winter, but we walk so much over here that the dress shoes I had were killing my feet and wearing out fast. In desperation I looked through my suitcase to see if there was anything I could wear that would be comfortable. It was still summer, but when I found these boots I put them on and they felt like bedroom slippers. I've worn them ever since and will find them difficult to give up when we return home. I'm on my second pair of shoelaces! The rubber soles and heels make me feel like I'm walking on air.

I fell the first time when I removed my glasses to keep them from icing up. I missed stepping off the curb and sprawled flat onto Peace Avenue, the main street that goes through the center of the city. (I leave my glasses on now and carry a second pair in an inside pocket.) The second time was one night when John and I were walking home behind the market and someone had thrown out a bucket of water and it had frozen into a sheet of glass.

Several other observations: the deels that are worn now are lined with sheepskin; scarves have been added around the necks of the older people; fur coats and hats are becoming increasingly plentiful and beautiful; some of the missionaries have finally put on hats; one of the elders wears a Santa Claus hat (and some Mongolians say "ho-ho-ho" to him as they pass); small children waddle as they walk; many cars break down; the slaughtered animals that are brought to the market for meat are stacked, frozen, like cordwood in the back of trucks; I found celery at the market and by the time I walked home (a very short distance) the leaves had frozen; the fresh bread we buy at the market is frozen.

We've been told this is a mild winter. Those who were here last year say it was much worse and the Mongolian people agree. I must say we expected and prepared for worse.

## Christmas Week

*Nancy*

It is interesting being a part of Christmas over here. The season takes on a whole different aspect in a country where the majority is not Christian. Even the Church members are still new to this observance so they try to absorb what they can from the missionaries.

Saturday afternoon was the district Relief Society Christmas party. It was held in the main hall of our church which is called "The Central Building." It was formerly a department store and movie theater. Some of our Mongolian friends tell us they remember going to the movies there when they were young. With much work, it has been converted into a wonderful meeting-house by a senior missionary who was here with his wife. They left for home just last week. He hired several of the members to work on the project with him and they were well taught by this master builder.

Back to the party. We have a new district Relief Society president who undertook the task of a party and she gathered together a committee of sisters who accepted their assignments with enthusiasm. They worried about decorations, refreshments, invitations, and entertainment, and when we walked into the meeting room it was simply but beautifully decorated; they even had two decorated Christmas trees in the front of the room.

It was their goal to invite every sister in the city and the nearby small town of Gorodok. The Church is growing so fast here that the organization has trouble keeping up with names and addresses. In addition, there is no postal service similar to what we are accustomed to. There are post offices with boxes to which your mail can be sent, but most can't afford a box. There are no mailmen who make home deliveries and no phone books in which to locate an address or telephone number. Most members don't have addresses or phones. All the invitations had to be hand-delivered so various sisters took stacks of them and set out to locate all the sisters. Their efforts were handsomely rewarded as the chapel was filled — we estimated 200 sisters. Some came in deels, some in jeans, some in Sunday best, but all were prepared to have a good time.

There were Christmas stories and readings, including an original poem by the first baptized member from Gorodok. There was singing and entertainment. There were games. I've written before about the innocence and sweetness of these people and once again I marveled at how they enjoyed what we think of as children's games. They enter into these things wholeheartedly and when "Santa Claus" arrived they were delighted. "She" started some games going and there were sisters of all ages trying to draw a picture of Santa on a whiteboard while blindfolded. Everyone was a good sport as was displayed by one of the older sisters who was chosen first to use her artistic skills. We all shared her amusement when the blindfold was removed and she saw the eyes she had drawn on Santa's chin and his nose where his ears should be.

Cookies, fruit, cake, and candy were passed around for our refreshment accompanied by bottles of Mongolian soda, which I finally sampled. You can tell the "greenies" over here because we're afraid to eat or drink anything we haven't prepared ourselves. After a while we just do it and they smile as they see we're finally "in country." It was okay.

Then the dancing began. It reminded me of World War II when the men were gone and the women and girls had to dance with each other. With great gaiety, the floor was absolutely filled with dancers! Eventually an older sister, Gallia, took my hand and we began to dance around the floor. Most Mongolian women are small but Gallia is fairly large and very strong! She guided me all over that floor as we bumped into other couples. She had her arm around my waist and pushed and pulled me here and there and I laughed during the entire dance—which I thought would never end! It was a Mongolian dance and lasted long enough that Gallia was able to teach me. I looked towards my chair at the edge of the dance floor and was about to return there when Oogie, a teenager, asked me if I'd dance with her. It was another Mongolian dance so I gamely agreed and she taught me *two* more native dances. It was fun. I don't know that I'll remember the steps but I'll probably get another try at the district party on Thursday.

As I mentioned before, the feet are treated with reverence in this country. As we were dancing around stepping on one another's feet I decided there are exceptions to this rule because not one person stopped to shake hands or apologize.

Members of the community also come to us for our Santa Claus suit (the mission has the only one), Christmas music (secular), someone to play Santa, and so on. Some of this creates a real dilemma for us. When we are teaching, we must *never* teach religion, or refer to or allude to it in any way, shape, or form, as it means we'll be sent out of the country. Our visas depend on our adhering to this rule. I was presented with an interesting situation this week when the aforementioned Oogie told me her class was responsible for the school Christmas program this year and they wanted to sing some Christmas songs. She asked if I could accompany them on the keyboard. I told her, "Sure, what will you be singing?" "*Jingle Bells* (okay) and *Silent Night*" (uh-oh). I told her that since there would be a religious song included I wouldn't be able to play. It was hard for her to understand and she pointed out that everyone sings it, Christian or not, and that it's just traditional. I had to explain to her that some people would really like to point to that and say I was encouraging and participating in promulgating religion in the schools. Then she told me they'd be singing it in English and no one would understand it anyway. I gave her credit for a good try but nevertheless had to decline.

So we watch our members as they walk the thin line between the Christian Christmas and the traditions of Mongolia and we serve as consultants to the secular side of the community.

## Christmas Day

*Nancy*

It turns out that Christmas in Mongolia is no different than that in the States when it comes to frantic activities leading up to and including Christmas Eve and Christmas Day. Seeing that 34 single missionaries in the cities of Ulaanbaatar and Baganuur are treated to a Christmas "almost like home" occupied many hours of cooking, baking, shopping, stocking stuffing, and other miscellaneous activities by Sister Cox and the senior missionary sisters. Actually, it seemed as if we'd been cooking and baking since Thanksgiving with all the farewells, new missionary arrivals, and other mission activities.

Christmas Eve was spent in the mission home where a missionary fireside was held. I was already tired from cooking and teaching English that day and found myself watching the clock because I knew I had a cake back at the apartment waiting to be iced.

In order to create a family feeling for the young missionaries on Christmas Day, Sister Cox suggested drawing names of the young elders and sisters each couple would host for Christmas dinner. Consequently, there was still much preparation to do back at the apartment.

When the fireside was over, we four couples walked back to our apartments and the sisters continued their food preparations for the next day—Christmas. After setting the clock for 6:30 A.M., I thankfully crawled into bed a little after midnight while Christmas music was playing on the BBC.

The alarm rang quickly and Christmas Day began. I could also hear preparations beginning in the apartments above and below me. John pointed out that a beautiful blanket of snow had appeared overnight, making everything clean and white.

We had decided with the elders coming to our apartment that we also wanted to perform a service on this day. We had some humanitarian goods that needed to be distributed and arranged to spend a portion of this Christmas Day with the former street children at the police shelter.

After visiting with the children and enjoying some music and games with them we returned to our apartment and had Christmas dinner.

The day passed in a flurry during which Doya, one of John's former TOEFL students and our new interpreter, called to ask if he could edit her term paper which was due the next day. So in the midst of everything, Doya arrived and they sat down at the computer to prepare her paper.

The food was good and fortunately there was plenty. We added one more plate for the extra guest and everyone ate with gusto. We cleared the dishes and John began to wash them (I cook—he does the dishes) when we realized it would soon be time for the district Christmas party to begin so I urged him to finish editing the paper and I'd pick up where he left off with the dishes. The elders hung around for a bit and then gradually left, with the exception of one companionship who crashed on our couch and loveseat where they took short naps before the party.

The dishes were finished (with the exception of scalding) and the paper almost completed. Baatar came by to take us to the Central Building where we entered a festively decorated hall. An hour and fifteen minutes late, the party began. After a while John had to leave so the paper could be delivered to the student. I was one of the judges for the dance contest so I stayed to the end and finally made my way home, enjoying the crunch of the snow under my feet.

When I came up the steps to our apartment I heard missionaries singing carols and saw John standing at our open door with an apron on. They turned, saw me coming, and motioned me by and I entered the apartment to enjoy the rest of their song. They moved on to the next landing to sing to another couple and I began removing my boots, hat, scarf, coat, and gloves. I collapsed and stared for about a half hour. Bed felt good that night although I didn't sleep well. John says I was overtired.


## 'Twas the Night After Christmas in a Mongolian Garage

### *Nancy*

The next day was pretty much ours until 2:00 P.M. when we were to be at School 38 so I could accompany Oogie and some others singing at the school's holiday celebration. After waiting two hours for the electricity to be turned on (because the school hadn't paid its bill) John and I had to leave because we had a another appointment. As we were leaving we heard much screaming and shouting and were told that the power had just been restored but it was too late for us.

The temperature had dropped a good bit while we were in the school and we tried to catch a taxi back to our apartment. We had to walk a good way to reach a street where there was more traffic where, finally, we were picked up. We considered it a real bonus that the car had a heater.

We arrived home with a little time to spare for our appointed pick-up by Baatar. Two months ago we had planned a surprise for him in cahoots with Batbold, the mission driver. I had been looking forward to this time for weeks. At the appointed time we went downstairs to meet Baatar but he wasn't there. This was unusual because he's always on time so we figured he must have forgotten our appointment. Batbold came by and was also surprised because he and Baatar are very close friends and he knows how dependable Baatar is. Batbold invited us into the mission car to wait a bit. It was warm in there and we were glad for the respite because the temperature was about –20°F. Finally, we came back to the apartment and started dinner.

After a while John saw Baatar's car coming towards our building so we hurried to get into our coats and ran down to meet him. Amidst his *ooch-la-ri's* we asked him to take us to the mission home where Batbold was hiding our surprise. After we got there our interpreter explained to us there had been a car accident on the slippery streets which entirely blocked all traffic and that was the reason for Baatar's delay. Fortunately Batbold was still there.

We had with us a package of things for Baatar's car that we had asked the kids to send us from the States: Armor All, a can of flat-tire fixer, and something else that Terri had wrapped. We gave these to Baatar with Sister Enktuvshin interpreting for us. Baatar was all grins and I could hardly wait to get these speeches over with so we could get on to the really big surprise!

*Finally* we all went downstairs, motioning for Baatar to follow, and went around to the back of the building where the garages are located. Batbold opened the door to the mission garage and we all entered. There was much talk as Batbold showed us a few things in *his* garage and I was dying! After a time I just blurted out, "Let's get on with why we're here!" Batbold rolled out two brand new tires and inner tubes and we indicated to Baatar that these were for him. It took several moments for the meaning of what was going on to sink in. I could hardly contain myself! I felt so much joy and happiness. Batbold was laughing and explaining to Baatar that these really were his new tires and that we had all joined in a conspiracy to get them for him. Baatar began to cry and then this quiet, giant of a man threw his arms around me and then John—not once but several times—and with tears in his eyes told us that we were like his parents.

Finally, the day after Christmas, I experienced the Miracle of the Manger in a garage on a cold winter's night in Mongolia.

## Gift of Wheelchair Makes Boy Happy*

*Nancy*

The first time we went to the Khanuul Social Center — which takes care of the medical needs of the poor here as best it can — we were introduced by Dr. Oyun (Doya's mother) to a young boy and his mother (Nyamdorj and Enkhtsetseg). They had come to request assistance as the boy could not walk and had to be carried on his mother's back. Because he could not walk, the boy was also not able to attend school.

As we left that day, the young single mother was leaving with the boy on her back. I asked how old he was and she said 8 years old. I could tell he was beginning to get larger and it was going to be more and more difficult for her to carry him as she had been doing.

A shipment from the Sort Center in Salt Lake City was already on its way, but we didn't know what was in it at the time of our visit to the social center. As I saw that young mother going down the street carrying her son in that fashion, I wished there was something we could do.

The container from Salt Lake City arrived and was delivered to our church building. After being unloaded, we were looking through things and wondered what was in a beautifully built crate. We dismantled the crate and what a thrill it was when we

---

*This article originally appeared in the *Church News*, March 28, 1998.

found two brand new children's-sized wheelchairs.

I wanted so badly for the young boy we had seen to get one of them, but those decisions are not ours to make. We help decide which organization gets these things, but let them make the actual determination to whom they are given.

Later we were invited to the center to commemorate International Handicapped Day and were told representatives would be distributing some of the items the Church had donated.

During the welcoming speeches, I looked around the room to see if the young boy and his mother were there. I saw them in the back of the room. After thanks were given, the wheelchairs and other items, such as crutches, were brought into the room.

The first name Dr. Oyun called was that of the young boy. His mother carried him up front and placed him in the wheelchair. He gave a little speech, saying thank you for making it possible for him to go to school. Naturally, the mother had tears in her eyes.

Another young boy was called next, and his mother carried him over to the second wheelchair and placed him in it. Oh, how I wish that whoever donated those wheelchairs could see the happiness their generosity brings.

While the crutches were being distributed, I looked at the first boy and noticed him exploring the chair. All of a sudden he realized if he moved the wheels with his hands, he could propel himself and his chair. A big grin broke out on his face as the full impact of what had just happened hit him. He would no longer have to depend on his mother to carry him from place to place as he became freer than he had ever been.

# mongolia: The circle in the clouds

# January 1998

## Brown Cakes

*Nancy*

My first experience with "brown cakes" was when a young woman appeared at our door, with three young children in tow, asking if I would help them make a brown cake for their mother's birthday. I was fairly new in the country and wasn't familiar with brown cake. I soon learned that brown cake was another name for a chocolate cake. It seems the members of the Church here had been introduced to chocolate cake by the senior missionaries and it had become an instant favorite. However, there are no cake pans to be bought here and the only available pans are ones brought by previous missionaries or purchased in Hong Kong when someone makes a trip there. We guard them fiercely!

So we found a recipe in a Betty Crocker cookbook which had been left in our apartment by an earlier couple and baked the cake. They didn't want to wait for it to be iced so I sprinkled it with some coarse powdered sugar that was available and they went happily on their way. Several more times young members came to our door and it was always someone's birthday and they wanted to know if I'd help them bake a brown cake.

During the past three or four months Duncan Hines has come to town. We bake so many cakes for missionary farewells, new missionary welcomes, and so on, that it was with open arms we welcomed Mr. Hines and his variety of cake mixes. With our teaching and project schedules it just doesn't leave a lot of time for baking from scratch so we all keep a number of boxes on hand.

After being here for several months it occurred to John and I that it would be helpful for new couples to have a handbook to orient them to the meeting schedules and the many things we found out by accident or mistake. After the handbook was drafted we gave it to the Coxes for their approval and sugges-tions. When it was returned there was a paragraph added by Sister Cox about brown cakes. It seems that many of the cakes we are asked to bake are not for mothers or sisters or brothers or missionaries but for the one making the request; it is just to fill their hunger for an American delicacy. I was dumbfounded as I recognized the many times I had been taken in. As I talked with other senior sisters about this they said they also had fallen prey to the brown cake ploy.

This weekend I was conned again. It turns out that when we later got together and talked, we found that only one senior sister had come away unscathed — she "just said no" because she was too busy. I sidestepped a request to "please help me learn how to make brownies" by giving away a box of brownie mix with an egg nestled inside and the loan of a pan. Then another young adult girl appeared at my door two days later and asked if I'd teach her how to make a brown cake for her aunt — she left for "home" with a box of chocolate cake mix and the loan of another pan. Turns out she went to one of the other couples' apartment and got the eggs and asked if she could make the cake there.

Then she went to another apartment and received another box of cake mix and made a cake there, too. We found out later she and her friends had a party. When another young adult called me on the phone and asked if I'd tell her over the phone how to bake a cake for her brother's birthday I said it would be too difficult over the phone and if she'd come over I'd show her an easier way. She hopped a bus and was here in about 20 minutes. I wasn't going to loan out my two brand new round cake pans so I gave her my last chocolate cake mix from the pantry and showed her how to mix up the cake. We baked it here and she was watching over the last layer in the oven (my oven is too small to cook both layers at the same time) when John and I had to leave for an appointment at the mission home.

When we senior sisters started comparing notes today we found we had been cleverly and sweetly used to fill the needs for a number of parties. You see, it's New Year's and this is one of the biggest celebrations in Mongolia.

## Silver Streaks Among the Snow

*Nancy*

We've been told there has been more snow than normal this year. I previously wrote how the snow turns to ice and all the hazards this brings. Now there's a new phenomenon—silver streaks down the middle of every sidewalk. A glide-path has been created on every sidewalk for the purpose of skating and sliding. One would expect to see young boys gleefully gliding along but this is almost a national sport. Fathers, mothers, and teen-agers of both genders run and slide down the sidewalks. Yesterday as I walked up to the state department store I watched a policeman skating along.

Being the old fogies that we are, John and I avoid these silver streaks and walk on either side, but while walking home from church on Sunday our sixteen-year-old friend, Oogie, skated down each one, holding on to my arm as she did so. Then she discovered that it would be even more fun if she held on to John's arm and had him run fast and pull her. Since he's about the only man in town still wearing tasseled loafers, I figured they'd both go down but they raced along without incident amid her happy screams.

I made another observation while walking yesterday. I have developed what I call "The American in Mongolia Hunch." One of the things I had to do before coming on this mission was make several visits to a physical rehab doctor to learn exercises I could do because I couldn't continue taking the anti-inflammatory drugs I had been using for years. He noted that I was not standing as straight as I should and suggested I be more aware of standing and walking in a more upright position. Yesterday I recognized that not only was I not walking as upright as he would like, I was hunched over as I kept my eyes on the ground to avoid the silver streaks and other obstacles that might send me flying. My shoulders were hunched up and neck turtled down as I attempted to keep my chin and cheeks warm by burying them in the beautiful mint green Gobi cashmere scarf I had wrapped around my neck.

Also on my walk I noted on several occasions that it's not just we foreigners who embarrass themselves by falling on the ice; three teenage girls were walking in front of me, arm in arm as they all do, and the one in the middle fell and took the other two with her. Their laughter got me to laughing and it took all four of us to untangle book bags and backpacks and get the girl in the middle up on her feet again.

My son, Chris, asked me this morning via the Internet if I minded that it was going to be 70°F back home in Pennsylvania and I could honestly answer, "No, I love walking in the crisp,

cold air with the crunch of the snow under my feet." While looking at the snow-covered mountains around us, John observed the
other day that it very much reminded him of the mountain view
out the window of our timeshare apartment at Snowbird, Utah.
Now, however, we don't have the benefit of the view for just two
weeks at Christmas; our pleasure has been extended to four or
five months.

## Frosted Windowpanes

### *Nancy*

The Mongolians tell us we're entering the cold part of the
winter; the newspapers tell us that we've just experienced the
warmest December on record. Yesterday, walking to church, the
temperature was about –25°F, but for some reason it always
seems colder walking home from church than walking to church.

One day last week many people were out chipping the ice
from the sidewalks and streets. It seemed as if the whole city had
been mobilized into snow and ice removal teams. Some were
using old shovels, some hammers or axes, and some used broken
shovel handles. John saw young boys using wooden pegs and I
saw some using cutting boards and old pieces of tin. Nearby our
apartment is a particularly bad place where the sun never hits.
It's also the place where the young boys hitch rides by grabbing
onto the bumpers of cars. A number of fairly well-dressed
women gathered into a work party there chipping away with
whatever they had. As a result of this all-out effort there are
many ice-free walkways.

This past Thursday night we boarded a train for Erdenet to
take part in a zone conference. When we climbed into our
assigned car we were hit with a blast of warm air so we made the
assumption we'd have a warm trip. However, after removing

our coats and stowing the books and food we were carrying to the missionaries in the cities of Darkhan and Erdenet we felt the cold nipping around our ears and noses. Soon we were changing into our traveling clothes—L.L. Bean expedition weight long underwear—making our beds, and crawling under the blankets to keep warm. We talked some and reminded ourselves once again that we were speeding—more like lurching—through the Mongolian countryside. It is so easy to forget where we really are; we get so busy with just doing the day-to-day things. Soon we turned off the lights, but not before I had taken my down-filled coat off the hook and put it on top of the two wool blankets I was lying under—I finally felt warm, everywhere except my nose. During the night John put on his hat.

We arrived in Erdenet about thirteen hours later and piled into a "taxi" to be transported to the senior couple's warm apartment where we cleaned up, shaved, and so on before the conference began. Sister Kinnison had prepared a breakfast of pancakes and eggs which we very much enjoyed.

During the afternoon John and I visited two schools where we met with their directors. While we were walking the sun was shining brightly (as it always does) and tiny ice crystals filled the air. Then our interpreter pointed to a rainbow in the sky. It was the first snow rainbow—or snowbow—I'd ever seen. It was more of an elliptical than a bow shape and was a beautiful background to the crystals. The silvery crystals continued to drift down most of the afternoon.

Since Erdenet is smaller than Ulaanbaatar, one is better able to enjoy the surroundings because there are very few cars on the street and not many people. While we were walking, the wind began blowing and whipping around my skirt so I got quite cold. I suggested we get a "taxi" to take us the rest of the way. Wrong!!

Since there aren't many cars, there weren't any rides!

Following a dinner of soft tacos at the Kinnison's apartment, we climbed the hill to the "taxi" stop to get a ride to the train station for our trip home. This time I had put on my longies and was quite comfortable during the walk. The streams of light emanating from the streetlights danced off the ice crystals that had fallen all afternoon. Joined by sisters and elders who would ride halfway back with us, to Darkhan, we crowded into a van and bumped our way to the train station. There was one set of tickets for railway car A and the rest for car B. President Cox suggested John and I take car A and we lucked out. There were curtains on the windows and plenty of heat. President Cox and the others weren't so lucky. They had no heat and slept(?) with their hats, coats, scarves, and gloves on and still didn't get warm.

After 12 hours we reached the countryside surrounding Ulaanbaatar. I dressed and went into the corridor outside our compartment. The windows were frosted over but I cleared a spot through which I could look. It was still dark but people were walking about. The scene reminded me so much of the winter ice scene in the movie *Dr. Zhivago*, except these were gers instead of mansions. The melody of *Somewhere My Love* started playing in my head. I saw people squatting in the sub-zero temperatures; some were feeding their stock, some were carrying wood into their gers to keep the stoves going so they could cook breakfast. Smoke curled out of all the chimneys and through the round opening in the top of each ger; a warm light glowed reminding me of Professor Lubsanjav's explanation to us of the significance of the circle to Mongolians. Could they have wondered who we were and where we were going as the train passed by?

## Out of Small Things Proceedeth That Which is Great

*Nancy*

> *A stable*
> *An upper room*
> *A garden*
> *A borrowed tomb*
> *A grove of trees*
> *A room above a general store*
> *Gorodok*

*Gorodok* is a Russian word meaning *village*. Gorodok is a village that supplied coal to Russia and thus achieved a reasonable livelihood for its inhabitants. When the Russians left Mongolia and no longer bought coal the mine was closed and the village is on a long decline to oblivion.

Now its gates with their Soviet red stars are rusted and hang on broken hinges. Many windows in the apartment buildings are bricked up or broken out. The present-day inhabitants struggle to clothe and feed their families. It reminded me of the coal mining and steel-mill towns of Ohio, Pennsylvania, and West Virginia with which I became familiar while growing up.

John and I had an occasion to travel to Gorodok this past Sunday with Elders Wilstead and Coil to fill a speaking assignment given us by the district president.

The 45-minute ride arranged for us by the elders was most comfortable in an old BMW that traveled over a smooth, black-topped road. Our car came to a stop just inside the old gates in front of a five-story concrete apartment building. Elders Wilstead and Coil explained to us this would be the first time they met in this building as the previous room they rented was without heat and this one promised to be better.

We walked up five flights and I remarked to the rest that I'm glad we didn't have this assignment when we first arrived "in country" as it takes some amount of stamina to reach the top. At the top of the steps the elders motioned for us to enter a room on our left and held aside a heavy piece of fabric which covered the door opening—the only thing keeping out the cold. The temperature outside was –20°F. on this Sunday so we hoped the promise of a "warmer" room would come true.

Red plastic chairs were stacked in the corner of the room and one brother was beginning to place them in rows. I noticed Elder Wilstead pulling a small electric heater out of a rice bag he had brought with him. Elder Coil busied himself getting sacrament trays prepared with the help of two young Aaronic Priesthood holders who had traveled with us from Ulaanbaatar. I had carried a small electronic keyboard with us so there could be some accompaniment to their singing; I set it up on one side of the sacrament table.

After I finished getting my things arranged (my music was propped against the bottle containing the water for the sacrament!), I looked up and noticed two sisters dusting off the chairs with rags they had brought from home. It seems that someone had tried to warm the room where they met previously by starting a wood fire on the floor. The fire gradually blackened the entire ceiling and then soot began to rain down upon the congregation. Before it was over, all members and chairs were covered with a heavy coating of soot; hence the need to meet in a new room this week and the need to dust all of the chairs.

Slowly the room began to fill so I began playing prelude music. Elder Wilstead was quietly arranging for prayers and welcoming members as Elder Coil and the young men continued to prepare the sacrament. They decided to be optimistic with the number of cups they put into the tray. Elder Coil sat with his back to the only window, which had recently been glassed in; the glass was now covered with a half-inch of frost and ice. We all kept our coats on until it was time to officiate and then the elders and Aaronic Priesthood youth removed theirs while John and I left ours on.

As I looked at this small room I was reminded of a visit we had made to another room slightly smaller than this one. It is in Kirtland, Ohio, over the Whitney general store. In that room many sacred meetings took place and I was struck with the realization that it doesn't take a large cathedral or well-appointed church building in which to experience the Spirit. These few members (18 were in attendance) gather together each Sunday to partake of the sacrament and receive instruction regarding the teachings of Christ and the Spirit resides with them. They sing the hymns that are familiar to us but new to them, without musical accompaniment. Their prayers are spoken in almost a whisper as they speak the name of the Savior with great reverence. The greatest cathedrals in the world hold no more spirit than that little room in Gorodok.

As I stood to speak I removed my coat and all those gathered there smiled at me as they sat bundled up. When I began to speak they were nodding their heads in agreement even before Elder Wilstead could translate my words. Our assignment was to speak on obedience so I had chosen to re-tell the story of Nephi and his brothers returning to Jerusalem for the sacred records and their genealogy. The Book of Mormon has not yet been translated into Mongolian, so the stories are told and re-told as in ancient days before books. When I finished, I sat again next to Elder Coil and quietly asked if most of those in attendance understood English and he replied that they didn't—there was only one girl there who was fairly good. I knew, then, that even though they may have not understood the words I spoke they knew the spirit of them.

John spoke next and had chosen as his theme the obedience shown by Christ at the time of his crucifixion. Once again they were nodding their heads in agreement as this wonderful story and example was told to them. These members are recent converts from the atheism of communism or the state religion of Buddhism and the concept of such a sacrifice is still new to them.

When the meeting ended and the sacrament table was being cleaned I noticed that only two unused cups remained in the tray and smiled with pleasure that the optimism shown when preparing the tray was well rewarded. Each member and investigator had come up to us and shaken our hand with a *bayarlla* (thank you) and *bayartai* (goodbye) before they left.

We learned a little more about this room. It is owned by a sister who lives in a ger and had been vacant for some time. As I previously mentioned, its window had long ago been broken out but she offered to replace the window, clean up the room, and one of the brothers gave the walls a coat of "pinkwash." Then she offered the meeting place to the Church at no charge and all agreed it is warmer than the old one. I did not find it necessary to put my coat back on after speaking.

The humanitarian department of the Church recently sent a container of goods to Mongolia from the Sort Center in Salt Lake. It contained books, clothing, hygiene kits, school kits, vitamins, and medical and school supplies. A large portion of these goods went to the school district that serves the village of Gorodok. In addition, some clothing had been set aside for members so this offered more relief to the families of Gorodok. To those of you in the Wasatch Front who donate your used clothing to Deseret Industries, let your hearts be warmed by the warmth your donations bring to the people of Gorodok, Mongolia.

## Winterizing Baatar's Car

*Nancy*

The temperature has been –20°F to –30°F in the mornings these past weeks and more than once as Baatar's been driving John and me to school or meetings, steam has poured out from under the hood and he mumbles and mutters and we say "uh-oh." Sometimes he makes a quick diversion from our appointed route and stops at an apartment building, runs up to someone's apartment, and comes running back with water which he pours into the radiator. Other times he just throws it into neutral and guns the motor to cool it off. We've decided if this is the way he has to operate each winter he must have friends in apartment buildings appropriately spaced all around Ulaanbaatar.

We talked between ourselves, wondering if they don't have antifreeze available here because that would certainly make his life easier. We tried to find that out with our interpreter but had so much trouble making ourselves understood that we gave up and just reconciled ourselves to the sudden stops and diversions. So, between running out of gas and having to stop while Baatar runs around to the trunk, gets a can out to pour in more gas and diverting to various friends' for water, it makes for an exciting ride. Fortunately we don't have to worry about flat tires anymore because of Baatar's new tires. Baatar never completely fills the gas tank, but we've found he's not the only one that operates that way. Many of the people here labor under the false impression that you use more gas that way. Also, they often turn their engines off at traffic lights to save gas. Some of the elders have tried to convince their drivers that it's worse to have to keep re-starting the engine; few have succeeded.

Back to winterizing: John finally asked Batbold, the mission driver and Baatar's friend, what he does for the mission car. He said they used antifreeze so John asked why Baatar doesn't. Batbold said that Baatar's car is so old and antifreeze is so much more slippery that it would leak out through the holes in his radiator more than water does. So this is Baatar's method: Every night he drains the radiator and in the morning boils some water, adds it to the radiator, and off he goes. Some others build a fire every morning and gently slide it under the front of their car to melt the ice in the radiator and to warm up the oil pan before they start it up. *This is every morning!* Baatar is a *very* patient man.

## The Mongolian Hymnbooks

*Nancy*

This past week I undertook a project that gave me a greater appreciation for the efforts of the early missionaries and others who were involved in translating some of our hymns into Mongolian and compiling them into a small hymnbook.

The hymnbook we use has 27 hymns in it, including Christmas carols and several Primary songs. It was photocopied on the mission office copy machine and, from what I've been told, the machine has never been the same since.

The Church is growing very fast and there will soon be ten branches instead of the three we now have. There will be more than one building in use here in Ulaanbaatar in addition to the current dependent branches in Hovd, Darkhan, Erdenet, and Baganuur, so the few hymnbooks we have will not be enough when all these branches get organized.

One of my assignments here is the music. I direct the district choir, teach keyboard on Saturdays, teach members how to conduct music, and present a monthly music department in the district auxiliary leadership meeting. Thus, hymnbooks sort of fall

under my broad responsibilities in this area. John and I decided
we should try to get new books printed, rather than ruin another
copy machine, and we asked the assistants to the president for
the master copy of the hymns so we could contract with a printer
to print them.

One of the elders dropped the folder off and I suddenly
became aware of the tremendous task performed by the original
translators, typists, and compositors. First, each translated hymn
was photocopied from the original church hymnal. Then, the
translators had to fit the Mongolian words to the meter and
measures of the music. Next, the typist had to select the font and
pitch to match the words to the notes with the appropriate
breaks. Finally, the lyrics had to be cut into strips and pasted
over the English words. They even included all the small musical
notations of meter, mood, and scriptural references; all were
translated, typed, and cut into tiny pieces that were each taped or
glued in the appropriate places. Then, of course, the compilers
had to compose the pages to take into consideration those hymns
which required two pages. They were true to the hymnbook and
included a translated message from the First Presidency in the
front.

As I opened the folder and paged through, I understood why
the elder had told me some of it would need to be re-taped
because tiny pieces of paper were falling out or flapping loose. I
realized I held in my hand many hours of painstaking work and
how could I ever let it go out of our possession!

The first thing I did was set about repairing and reconstruct-
ing the pages with transparent tape we had brought with us.
Then I remembered there were several pages in their hymnbook
that were misnumbered so I corrected them, using the same
method adopted by the original compilers—type, cut, and paste.
(Fortunately Brother Carlson had installed the Mongolian font on
our computer while we were still at the SMTC.)

There was to be one more hymn added—newly translated—the beautiful hymn *I Believe in Christ*. The assistants to the mission president had pondered how to add this two-page hymn and make it fit without having to do the whole book over again but decided just to give it to me and let me worry about it. Actually it was not a huge problem and with a small amount of moving things around it fit perfectly!

I still couldn't bring myself to let this original copy out of our hands so I photocopied each page and reconstructed the book. Mr. Nemu (our printer) stopped by the other evening to look at it and agreed to print it. He left carrying the next edition of the Mongolian hymnbook, a labor of love. He promised to keep it close to his heart.

## The Couples Are Coming—The Sister Missionaries Are Moving

### *Nancy*

Building 7, Microdistrict 5 is identified with the Mormon missionaries in Ulaanbaatar. At one time both elders and couples lived here. Then when sisters began arriving they moved the elders out and the sisters in. Gradually they were able to get the couples and sisters into the same stairwell, which made it convenient for borrowing sugar, eggs, and so on. It remained that way for several years but big changes are about to happen.

Five couples will be coming between the middle of February and spring—four arriving in February. Therefore, they're moving the four companionships of sisters out into the city, closer to the schools where they teach, and nearer to the people. Today, Saturday, January 31, they receive little sealed envelopes which tell them who their new companions will be and where their apartments are located. They've begun packing all their dishes, utensils, brooms, washing machines, clothes—everything—and then Monday is moving day. Our stairwell is all a'flutter! Batbold will move them around town in the mission vehicle, removing the water filter in each of their current apartments and installing it in their new ones. It will be one busy day!

After the sisters have gone the vacant apartments will have to be prepared for the new couples. Several of them need major repairs of water damage so our landlord, Russian School #3, already has a list and hopefully will begin the work early in the week. I'm sure it'll be a tense time right up to the wire but we anxiously await the arrival of an M.D. and his wife, a scouter and his wife, a missionary couple, and a new CES couple who will go to Darkhan. A team (husband and wife) of medical lab technicians will arrive in the spring. That will make a total of ten couples plus the Coxes in Mongolia. A record!

## Shopping

It's such fun to go shopping here. Everyone in the store gets involved. Several months ago we decided we needed a couple of rugs. The floors in our apartment are wide, wooden planks. In our case they've been painted blue but the prevalent color is yellow or orange. When the cold weather arrived, our floors were pretty cold and since Mongolian oriental rugs are very reasonable we decided to get several. We inquired as to where would be the best place to purchase them and asked Baatar to drive us there. Baatar *always* stays in the car while we run our errands but this day he came in with us. As we looked at rugs he would turn a corner up and look at the back, rub his hand over it, then turn it to the front again and rub his hand back and forth. Then to the back again where he read the label and mumbled a few words.

We'd move to the next one and he'd repeat the process. One by one other customers came over and soon we were surrounded with everyone talking in Mongolian, with the exception of one who spoke English and began advising us in our native tongue. But we kept turning to Baatar and watching his reaction as it is his opinion we trust.

They were all beautiful and the only decision as far as we were concerned was the size we needed. Then the salesperson pulled out a rug identical to the one we had been looking at and Baatar started his process again and the other onlookers joined in. They looked exactly the same to us, but when we asked Baatar thumbs up or thumbs down he chose one over the other and all the other Mongolians shook their heads in agreement with his choice, poking it with their fingers. So we paid our tugrugs, they rolled up the rug, and Baatar carried it to the car.

When we got home, I felt the rug was too small for the room but perfect in color. So, several days later we had Baatar drive us back to the same store and bought the twin. They now reside side by side, in our computer room. Who knows what the difference is between them. Baatar thinks we're crazy at times!

This past week I decided I wanted to go to the fur factory to look at hats and coats. It's ironic that the approved missionary list does not include (and even frowns upon) leather or fur coats and fur hats. Supposedly, they would make us look ostentatious and stand out in the crowd so we all come with our down-filled coats of various shades and styles and stand out in the crowd because everyone else is wearing fur and leather! When we take our coats off we look like chickens with feathers all over us. The men and women who are dressed in their beautiful native leather and fur designs are gorgeous and handsome and the most stylish I've ever seen. They'd knock your eye out on Fifth Avenue in New York City!

I just wanted to window shop. After we asked Baatar for his recommendation of a good place to look at furs, he drove us to a factory and its outlet. If you hadn't grown up in Ulaanbaatar you'd never find this place. We made turn after turn, down streets, up alleys, and over curbs. He finally came to a halt, turned the engine off, and motioned to a sign above a door. We know nothing about fur so we motioned Baatar to come with us (he had on his Russian fur hat) and the three of us entered this tiny showroom where beautiful fur coats of all species and designs were crammed onto a rack.

No, I didn't try one on but it was wonderful to run my hands over them. I might raise the wrath of animal rights advocates (even though, in general, I agree with them), but fur is one of the warmest coverings available for this climate. In many cases a family's livelihood depends upon the fur and meat provided by these animals.

I moved from the coats to the hats. They had a display case full of men's and women's hats. There were many of the traditional Russian style hats in all varieties of fur. There were a few very stylish women's hats and then a simple brown one which, when I put it on my head, was both soft and warm. Yes, I succumbed. The thing is, we're not well enough acquainted with furs to know what kind it is. They told us it was *beesan* but that's the Mongolian word for the animal. Before making the purchase we once again turned to Baatar to make sure we were buying a good product. He shook it (which is the way they handle fur over here to fluff it up), turned it this way and that, and mumbled. John and I kept watching for a nod or something to indicate we should buy it. Then the other people in the store became involved and the three female shopkeepers started a discussion with each other, looking at the hat, then looking at me, and then back to the hat. All the time Baatar's making no indication either way to let us know what he thinks. Then an English speaking customer asked me what the problem was and I told her there was no problem and that we trusted Baatar with these decisions and were waiting for him. She started telling me what a wonderful fur it was and the name of the animal and I was wondering if it meant bison, which is not a particularly appetizing thought. This went on and on. Baatar never did look enthused but by this time it was getting embarrassing with all the questions as to why I was being so indecisive. So without Baatar's wholehearted approval we bought the hat. As I think about it, it could be because it's not the typical Mongolian or Russian style hat but more one western women wear. In any case, it's small, soft, and warm. Everyone but Baatar had smiles on their faces as we left. We still don't know what he thinks.

An ankle-length fur coat costs about $300. Oh yes, a 9x12 oriental rug is about $100.

# mongolia: The circle in the clouds

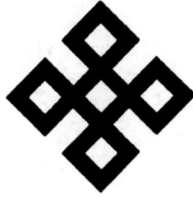

# february 1998

## Humorous English?

*Nancy*

Sr. Miller and I teach English to our branch Relief Society sisters. She teaches the intermediate/advanced and I teach the beginners. We each have ten sisters and we meet twice a week.

Tonight my class studied the present continuous tense: "Where is Betty? She's in the library. What's she doing? She's reading a book." After an hour of teaching and drilling I always try to incorporate part of the lesson in my farewell as they walk out the door. So tonight as they were leaving I asked, "Where are you going?" and one sister summoned up all she had learned and replied, "I'm going home." Another one replied, "I'm going to bed." And another middle-aged matron drew upon a couple of her new vocabulary words and said, "I'm going to a night-club." It broke me up! What a wonderful sense of humor!

## The Black Market, Revisited

*Nancy*

Okay, I know we said we'd never go back to the black market but sometimes in Mongolia you have to eat your words so we'll make ours into humble pie.

Four new couples will arrive Wednesday, along with six elders. We've been preparing the new couples' apartments for several weeks. We've not finished yet and it's Monday. To fully complete the job we need to put new flooring in the bathrooms and kitchens. We spent Friday afternoon with Baatar driving us around to every store we could think of that might have flooring but to no avail. We knew such a purchase could be made at the black market but after our experience last summer we were making that our place of last resort.

Well, "last resort" came and we arranged for Baatar to take us there on Saturday afternoon—his day off. Baatar picked up Doya, our interpreter, and they came and got us. As we began to climb the hill to the market things looked ominous. Having not gotten very far we could see a long line of cars at a complete stop. John let out a moan and patient Baatar turned off the engine to save gas and we waited for awhile. Then cars started going up the wrong side of the road on the left and up the berm on the right. A couple of cars turned around in the very tight space, probably to return on another day. John asked Doya to suggest to Baatar that we also turn around, but it was as if Baatar didn't hear her. Then Baatar started the car and we moved a few feet. I could see Baatar looking far ahead of us assessing the situation. Suddenly he jumped out of the car and started directing traffic. He was telling drivers to move and got several of them to get out with him and push a broken-down car out of the way. He also lectured the driver of a blue van on driving techniques. We moved forward a few hundred feet and I thought we were home free. Then the engine turned off again. John sat in the front seat shaking his head; Doya decided to take a nap and I was fascinated by Baatar.

I felt as though we were in a demolition derby but the objective of this one was to see how close you could come to the other car *without* hitting it. John was still shaking his head, suggesting once more we abort the trip; Doya was trying to doze and I was watching Baatar's eyes through the rearview mirror — I think Baatar had turned his hearing off as well as his engine. His intensity was amazing as he watched for where the problems were originating and a couple more times he jumped out, took charge of the situation, got the line moving, and muttered to Doya that the police weren't doing their job. Doya's father is an Ulaanbaatar policeman who, when younger, had the black market in his district. He is now one of the "top cops" in the city. This went on for some time until Baatar was able to clear the road and we reached the top without further incident, which amazed me. I've decided the Mongolians are as good at herding cars as they are their many flocks in the countryside. Nary a car was grazed or smashed into. As one terribly offending driver came dangerously close to us Baatar looked at him and just laughed. Maybe he was admiring his skill.

After turning the car around to face downhill we walked to the entrance. I think it might have been the exit because we were the only ones going the wrong way. Baatar told Doya to tell us to stay together. Then he linked my arm in his and he pulled me through that terrible crowd. It was scary and exhilarating. The crush of bodies was unbelievable and I understand now how people can get trampled when there is a panic. Baatar was looking forward and then backward, checking on us. John was behind us with Doya and I between him and Baatar.

We would never have been able to accomplish any of this without Baatar. I don't know how many acres the black market covers but if you don't know exactly where to find the item you're going to buy you could never find it among the crush of people and vendors. Most of the vendors are out in the open with their wares laid on the ground. Beautiful oriental rugs are piled in all their various sizes. Window curtains hang from stalls. Some of the sellers work out of shipping containers. If you can't find something you're looking for elsewhere you can always find it at the black market. They even sell nails and tacks individually. We would never be able to do any of this without our Mongolian friends.

Baatar took us right to where all the vinyl flooring was. Rolls and rolls of it were laid out by a variety of vendors. He told us to stay there and he went around checking quality and price to see which vendor was best. Of course I couldn't stay put. After a bit of waiting I wanted to look at the colors and patterns. I could see the ones Baatar was looking at were brown and fake wood—very unexciting. So I told John I was going to look around and Doya came with me. A number of the vendors had the same patterns and that reduced the number of difficult decisions. (It's hard to pick something out that someone else has to live with!) Baatar made his way back to John and the two of them came to where Doya and I were. I suggested one pattern and Baatar shook his head, no, not good enough quality. So I chose another one, close in color. I got the thumbs up.

While we were walking around the vinyl more than one Mongolian came up to John, pointed at his black tassel loafers, and shook their head. Several boot sellers tried to convince him to buy some good Mongolian boots. Then, while they were measuring off the meters of flooring we needed, the music that was being piped throughout the place changed to a very catchy song and I started swinging and dancing in place. I was really trying to keep my feet warm but doing it to the beat of the music. That seemed to hit the funny bone of many of the people around us and they were looking and laughing at me. Doya started laughing, too, and told me they thought I was funny. The fellow measuring the vinyl was getting a big kick out of the strange Americans — one wearing funny shoes and the other dancing.

We didn't have to worry this trip that our pockets might be picked or slashed because we had on our L.L.Bean down-filled coats with a secret pocket. We weren't aware of this pocket until a group of elders came over from the States and one had the same coat we have. He showed us this ingenious hiding place and even when someone sees us get our money out, they can't get at it. Thanks, L.L.Bean.

The flooring was measured and rolled back up. A small boy with a wagon came and they loaded our purchase on it. There was no way this little boy could perform the task so Baatar gave a fatherly smile (he has four sons) and pulled most of the load as they worked together to get it through all the people, up the hill, and into the trunk. We started down the hill, taking far less time to get down than the 40 minutes it took us to go up the two miles.

Baatar continues to be a very loyal friend. With the additional couples arriving on Wednesday there will be too many of us to share his car so another driver has been found to help. We specifically asked to stay with Baatar because he's seen us through a lot — from when we were Greenies to now, just past our halfway mark. As we were taking Doya home he asked her to make a very special request of us: for all the couples to come to his ger for Tsagaan Sar (The White Month) to have dinner with him. I reminded him there would be many of us and he nodded that he knew but his wife still wanted us to come. This is a great honor.

## Hardening Off Babies

*Nancy*

I've observed another similarity during the winter that reminds me of a gardening technique. When starting seeds indoors
there must be a period before transplanting them into the ground
called *hardening off*. It is a process of gradually exposing the
young plants to the unprotected weather of the outdoors. Each
day the plants are set out and then brought back inside, gradually increasing the time they are outside.

Mongolian parents do the same with their babies. They
swaddle the babies—wrap them tightly with their arms down at
their sides—and then put layers of blankets and quilts around
them, finally wrapping the bundle with a strap of some sort to
keep it all in place. It reminds me of the papoose carried on the
back of Native Americans. But these babies are carried in a
straight up and down position in the front, against the torso of
the mother or father—most times the father. The only part of the
baby you can see are the tiny dark eyes and small puffs of vapor
as their warm breath hits the cold. The baby is so stiffly wrapped
that it looks as though the parent is carrying around a board.

In the coldest weather, we see mothers or fathers just standing outside with these bundles. I can't even say "little bundles"
as all these layers create a fairly large package. They're not walking—just standing in the cold with their precious package. I've
never heard a cry coming from inside all those blankets. The only
conclusion I can come to is that they're exposing their children
very early in life to the severe weather of the Mongolian winters.
Recalling that babies born in the countryside are immediately
taken out and washed in the snow—ensuring a long, healthy life,
I have concluded that this is a continuation of this process as
they "harden off" their babies before planting their little feet on
the harsh ground of Mongolia.

# The Mongolian Flip

*Nancy*

Soon after we arrived we had a visit from the young elder who is the district leader in our branch. He and his companion asked if they could have their district meetings in our apartment. The entire time he sat with us he was spinning a pen around his fingers. It was very distracting and I couldn't believe this habit of his!

Every time this elder came to our apartment he did the same thing and I tried not to look at his hands. Eventually I was assigned to teach at Ulaanbaatar University and the first day of class I was dumbfounded to see most members of the class were sitting there spinning their pens and pencils around their fingers. It's a Mongolian thing! Not just an elder thing!

Soon after arriving the new missionaries start trying to accomplish this feat and many a pen drops on the floor during zone conference. Last week we had a farewell for Elders Dalley and King. As they sat up front during the goodbyes you could see it was time for Elder Dalley to go home. He had perfected the Mongolian Flip with a few variations. I've learned to no longer let it annoy me and instead observe the novices and the experts. Elder Dalley had become an expert.

So if you see a young man or woman spinning a writing implement around his or her fingers you'll probably find they served a mission in Mongolia. (After writing this journal entry I heard from Chris who served his mission in Taiwan that this is an Asian thing—not unique to Mongolia.)

## Tsagaan Sar—The White Month

*Nancy*

This Thursday begins the observance of Tsagaan Sar, the Lunar New Year holiday in Mongolia. Historically it is a time to visit family and honor the older members of the family. When the Russians governed Mongolia they outlawed the observance of the holiday and those families who chose to observe it had to do so in secret.

Now, once again, it is a time of feasting and gift-giving. It is a time for celebrating birthdays. Only recently have birthdays been recorded by day, month, and year. Previously all you knew was that you were born in the year of the tiger, or monkey, or dragon, or any of the twelve animals that designate the years. Then there's the red tiger, the blue tiger, and so on, all denoting a different time during a 60-year cycle. This new year will be the year of the tiger so all those born during that time will celebrate their birthdays. The first day of the three-day holiday is reserved for families and the remaining two days are when friends call.

While talking with the young women I learned that this is not their favorite holiday as it entails much cooking. Some have told me they spend weeks making anywhere between 2000 and 8000 *buuz ("bodes")*. Either way, it requires much preparation and is very expensive. In addition to spending a large amount on food, the host gives gifts to all those who come to visit—in some cases two gifts each. It's a great honor to have many guests stop by, but it's also a financial hardship for a people who have little income. One of the outstanding qualities of the Mongolian people, however, is their willingness to share what little they have.

This year has presented a special problem. The holiday is set by the lamas, and they decided the end of February would be the propitious time to celebrate instead of the end of January or early February as in other parts of Asia. However, it has been a warmer February than usual which has created problems for the storage of the *buuz*. Usually they are placed on the outside balconies where they freeze and keep until needed but that's not been an option this year. All of a sudden there's a shortage of freezers in the city as people are rushing out to buy them for their *buuz*.

When you receive many invitations it is necessary for you to pace yourself and not eat your fill at the first place as you may have three or four more places to visit during the day. Batbold and Baatar have invited all the couples to their homes and others of us have received invitations from church members and acquaintances that we either work with or have met during the time we've been here. Of course schools are not in session and the elders and sisters look forward to a break from teaching and a time of feasting.

*Buuz* are made of a mix of ground or chopped mutton and onion which is rounded into a ball and placed in the center of a small round of dough. The dough edges are then brought to the center and pinched closed at the top. I've watched the women and they make them very quickly with their fingers flying. They can create several types of designs around the top of the *buuz*. When serving westerners they usually take into consideration our preference and make some of ground beef. It reminds me of the mix we use when making stuffed peppers. After the rounds of dough are filled they are placed in a large steamer and cooked. I've heard of young missionaries having *buuz*-eating contests — much to their chagrin later that evening!

## The Translators

### *Nancy*

One part of the threefold mission of the Church is to perfect the Saints. One example of this effort is teaching one another the revealed principles of the gospel. In the United States and many other parts of the world there is access to a Bible, Book of Mormon, and other scriptures in the language of the country; lesson manuals have been translated and are available to teachers as they teach in the various auxiliaries and classes; young children in Primary are taught through music and stories, and visiting and home teachers take messages from the *Ensign* into the homes of the members.

The Saints in Mongolia have no such aids. Everything has to be translated, lesson by lesson, week by week. A cadre of dedicated Mongolian sisters sits at various couples' computers that have the Cyrillic alphabet and translate Relief Society, Primary, visiting teaching, and Young Women lessons. Several Primary songs are being translated so the children can understand what they're singing.

I greatly admire these sisters and the contribution they're making to the Church here. When you refer to them as pioneers they look at you in surprise and say they're just doing what needs to be done. Some are returned missionaries, but most are university students or recent graduates waiting for mission calls. Sometimes they work in pairs but many times it's a lone figure sitting in front of a computer screen typing out the next week's lesson. Last week two sisters worked at a computer on the fifth floor of our building for three hours. When the power ran out on that computer they came downstairs and worked on our computer for another four hours.

One of those translators, Erdenetsetseg, just received her mission call. She presently serves as the District Relief Society President and is one of God's choice spirits. Her big white envelope from the missionary department arrived last Friday. That evening the senior couples were gathered in one of the apartments for our Friday night gospel discussion and Erdenetsetseg was there, too, with her brother. President Cox was bringing the envelope with him to give to her. We were all excited to hear her news. Finally the envelope was placed in her hands and she opened it in front of all of us. When she told us she was going to the Salt Lake Temple Square Mission, we all cheered and clapped.

Erdenetsetseg will be leaving in April, just when another sister, Munkhtsetseg, will be returning from her mission on Temple Square. In addition to serving as a guide there, Munkhtsetseg has been the primary translator of the Book of Mormon. She will continue her translation work here; her computer has preceded her and waits in the mission office.

# Mongolia: The circle in the clouds

# march 1998

## Tsagaan Sar, The Feast

*Nancy*

How do you put into words the hospitality, love, and generosity of so many of the Mongolian people? This will probably be the most difficult entry I will write because words cannot convey the heart and spirit of such a people. I've had Mongolian friends tell me Mongolians are like their well-bred horses. They're small but deceivingly strong, have much stamina, are extremely smart, and are exceedingly loyal—they'll run for you until their heart bursts. My eyes fill with tears at the experiences we've had the last several days as we were invited into the homes of these dear people who prepared a feast for us and served it in a most gracious manner.

These are humble people who don't have a lot by the standards of our world. However, Baatar and his wife didn't hesitate one moment to invite all eight of the senior missionary couples to their homes. They scrambled to find enough chairs or stools, utensils, glasses, tablecloths, dishes, serving dishes, etc., but they did it. The entire family, children included, cooked and prepared food for days. How proud they were when they saw us all seated around tables that were so bursting with food that there was hardly room for one more thing. It was all carefully and precisely staged and when we went to Baatar's ger we could see he was as accomplished a host as he is driver. It is the same at Batbold's home, as husband, wife, and children scurried around serving us.

Baatar had arranged for his brother, Khavtgai (our branch president), to be there so he could interpret for us. Baatar, dressed in his deel, offered us greetings and welcomed us to his ger. Then, in the Mongolian tradition, he passed a ceremonial snuff bottle to each of us. He then told us it was traditional to begin the meal by partaking of anything that was white and most of us chose the little white candies that had been placed around the tables. While we ate salads and plates of cold meats and pickles he removed his deel to reveal western style clothing underneath and assisted his wife and children in serving.

How proud Baatar was and how proud I felt for him. As you've seen in the entries up to this point, John and I love Baatar and think of him as a son (or grandson, as John points out). Due to the language barrier we never knew a lot about his family, so this provided us with a wonderful opportunity to get to know more about him. Baatar's wife was married previously and she had four sons. Her husband died and Baatar married her and took on the responsibility of raising her children and then they had a girl of their own, Oyunga.

Baatar taught us the traditions of Tsagaan Sar as we ate. We ate buuz for the old year, buuz for the New Year, and buuz because it was the second day of the New Year. If we had known we were going to toast all the years with buuz we would have held back a little but almost all of us were good sports about the whole thing and ate as many as possible to guarantee the household good luck and a prosperous year. Those of us who have been in-country for a while knew a little of what to expect but the couples who had just arrived the week before were truly tested with all the different foods and drinks. They were wonderful sports in tasting this and that and being surprised at how good most of it was.

We've learned that you don't empty your plate or it is filled and refilled. Elders Wilstead and Coil stopped by last evening after having spent the day going from place to place visiting with members and investigators. They were both dressed in their deels and traditional Mongolian fur hats. Elder Coil is fairly new. He looked a bit green around the gills and asked if he could just have some cold water to drink. I offered him some homemade cookies, too, but he declined. He admitted before he left that he had probably eaten about 50 buuz and by the end of the day had learned that if he just held one in his hand after taking a bite he wasn't urged to eat more. Then Elder Wilstead came to the kitchen for a drink and picked up the same glass that Elder Coil had used. I suggested he use a clean one but he said they'd shared drinks with so many people during the day that a glass of water between companions wasn't going to make one bit of difference. He stood there wolfing down cookies, old veteran that he is, while we talked. Elder Coil continued gulping down water. As they were leaving Elder Coil picked up several peanut butter cookies and I knew he was going to be okay.

While seated around the table in Baatar's ger we could watch the buuz being cooked in a glistening stainless steel pot. It consisted of about four different sections piled one on top of the other so the steam could cook the small dumpling-like food placed on racks inside each section. This was a more modern cooker than I had seen before, and I was pleased that Enkhsaikhan had a newer, up-to-date cooker for accomplishing all this. It said something about the man. The meal they placed before us was amazing, all made without running water and a minimal number of conveniences and all cooked on a wood stove. I couldn't help but think of all the dishes they would have to wash before their extended family came an hour or two after we left. Then they'd had to do it all over again.

At the end of the meal two of Baatar's sons put on hats and presented each of us with a gift. It is an extraordinary gesture that is done in all the homes. Not only do they provide a great feast, far surpassing our Thanksgiving, but they also give each person a gift.

Later in the day we went to the home of one of the older sisters, Gallia. She is the mother of 11 children and proudly wears a medal presented to her by the government for her accomplishment. (She's the one who "guided" me around the dance floor during the Relief Society Christmas party.) One of her daughters had returned from Beijing for the holiday so she could help her mother prepare and serve the Tsagaan Sar meal. This time there were only eight of us but it was still enough to test their supply of serving utensils and other table settings they had. Fortunately for our sated appetites the bowls were tiny.

Before coming to Mongolia we had either read or it was suggested by someone that a good thing to have with you is a Polaroid camera. With this you can take pictures of your hosts and present them as gifts. We did this and have found it to be a wonderful way to show our appreciation for their hospitality. Gallia was the first one we've met who hadn't seen the magic of this camera and when I took her picture and presented it to her a few minutes later her reaction was priceless.

Like Elder Coil, John and I (and the other couples) were filled to the eyeballs with wonderful food. We were able to come home and loosen our belts (or sashes as some of us wore deels), but the Coxes had two more visits and had had one the night before. The next day they had several more and others scheduled for the next week. We're impressed with their ability and grace. We have one more this evening in the home of the doctor in the Khaan Uul district (Dr. Oyun) who distributed some crutches and wheel-chairs from the last shipment sent by the Sort Center now called the Humanitarian Center. (The name was changed while we were serving our mission.) We have another dinner appointment Monday evening with the director of the college in which John and I taught English and then another Tuesday afternoon. We appreciate the fact that our invitations are well spaced.

Tsagaan Sar is a family celebration. On Friday, as we looked out our window onto the street below, we saw many families walking together to the various apartment buildings to gather with other family members or friends. Some were dressed in deels while others were smartly dressed in more western clothing including their beautiful fur or leather coats and high leather boots. One family particularly caught my eye as they danced in perfect rhythm, skipping down the street. What a joyful occasion it was for them as mother, father, sons, and daughters joined together to celebrate spring and the Lunar New Year.

John and I speak frequently about how blessed we are to have been sent to these people. For so many years they've been repressed and hidden from the world and their sweet natures known to only a few. Our greatest fear is that as they reach out and the world reaches in to them they'll adopt some of its lesser qualities. When we first arrived, there were no children's toys of war and violence; they have begun to appear. Tsagaan Sar is a time of renewal. It's a time to celebrate birthdays and spring. It's a time for family to gather and in Mongolia everyone is "family" (or *ger-bul* in Mongolian).

Baatar and Batbold are not members of the Church as they are, now, honoring the wishes of their Bhuddist mothers. But after we were all seated in Batbold's home he said, "Okay President Cox, talk to Father." President Cox offered a touching prayer on the food and blessed the family and home of Batbold. I did not have the stamina of a Mongolian horse—I cried.

## Funny Things Happen in Mongolia

*The Black Market, Again?—Nancy*

Even we can hardly believe we went to the black market again. Now that winter is over, we decided John's taken enough ribbing from the Mongolians about his shoes and we decided to get some boots. We had our interpreter ask Baatar where to get ones like his and he said the only place to get them was—the black market. We both shuddered but Baatar said that it wasn't as crowded in the middle of the week so we went today.

There was no traffic jam, so we drove right up the hill and parked. There was no horde of people. We were able to walk through the gate unimpeded, but this time we had to pay so I'm sure Baatar took us *in* the *out* gate the last time. We followed him to the area where the boot vendors were and then the fun began. As boot vendor after vendor noticed this American looking at boots they gathered around him claiming their boots were better constructed and of better quality leather. Baatar went over every inch of each boot, inside and out. They eventually sat John on a little stool, in the midst of this ever-growing aggregation of aggressive entrepreneurs, and he began trying on boots. It reminded me of Goldilocks and the Three Bears—one was too big, one was too little, and the third one was (almost) just right! The problem wasn't the size of his feet but the size of his calves. Having been a swimmer, he developed these beautifully shaped calves that caused problems because of the height of the boot. It was a struggle getting them on and off and I laughed at Baatar working with him to do both. I had thought of taking a camera to get some pictures of the place but was afraid of it being stolen. I sure wish I had! It was comical seeing John seated on a little stool with all these people gathered around, kibitzing on which pair of boots to buy. It was like the day we bought the rugs and everyone in the store had to give their approval on our choice. It reminded John of the day he was sitting on a little stool on the sidewalk, basking in the sun, while the shoemaker put new soles on his loafers—only to be confronted with people who attempted to buy the videotapes and school booklets he had purchased for our use!

John finally compromised on a pair. They are a little big but Baatar said he should just wrap enough rags around his feet to make them fit but I suggested the big socks we had back at the apartment would do just as well. Then Baatar began haggling over the price. Once everyone agreed there were smiles of approval and many heads shaking in the affirmative. Baatar put the boots over his arm and we started for home after a pleasant morning of shopping at the black market. Imagine that.

## The Photographer

*Nancy*

Several months ago one of the elders came to our door and said that a Mongolian tenant in our building had a favor to ask of John, so John followed him past two stairwells and up the steps into another apartment. It turned out this tenant had friends visiting from the countryside and wanted his picture taken with them. John came back to our apartment, got the Polaroid, and returned to the other apartment.

As it turns out they didn't want just any picture taken; it had to have the television in the background. So they moved the furniture around to the point where everyone in the countryside could see that they had a TV. John came back chuckling.

A couple days ago there was a knock on our door. Two girls were standing there with the same Mongolian gentleman. He was making motions that looked like he wanted to see or show something. Since he's also the handyman we thought perhaps he wanted to show our apartment to some prospective renters.

We motioned them in but when the girls started taking their coats off we knew we had misunderstood. John said, "Uh-oh." Then the other handyman came in, making the same peering motions. Finally it dawned on us that they were trying to indicate that they wanted a picture taken. By this time the first handyman had walked into our living room and was turning our loveseat 180° so he and the girls could sit on the loveseat and the TV would show in the background! We took two Polaroid pictures and they excitedly went on their way.

Tonight, handyman #1 knocked at the door again and this time he had a one-year-old child with him all dressed up in a deel. We guessed he wanted another picture. It turns out (if we interpreted each other's hand motions correctly) that this was his number one son. John (foolish man) suggested we take it in the hallway but I'm a descendant of Eve and knew better—he'd want the TV in the picture. When I motioned in a quizzical way if he wanted it taken in the living room he quickly assented and took his place in front of the TV. By this time we had really gotten smarter and moved him to one side a bit so the TV would surely be in the picture. I snapped the picture, gave it to him undeveloped, he smacked a quick kiss on his son's cheek, and they were on their way.

## A New Desk

*Nancy*

Since we're now serving as both project director and country director John's been generating a large amount of paperwork. We had so many piles of documents everywhere we couldn't see the tops of any of the flat surfaces in the apartment. He kept saying we needed a filing cabinet and I agreed. (Sosor and I gave up trying to dust a long time ago.) In the last several days we mailed off the three-year report, the five-year report, and the monthly report to Hong Kong. There was finally time to look for a filing cabinet.

Having no luck the first several places we looked, John then asked Sister Enkhtuvshin for recommendations. She wrote several out in Mongolian so we could give them to Baatar. This morning he drove us to the one at the top of the list and we discovered that the best we could do was buy a desk which had four filing drawers as part of it. After being assured that they'd put it together for us the purchase was made.

Two of their employees went to the storeroom, brought out four boxed pieces, and stacked them by the door. After the deal was done they followed John to the car with the boxes and Baatar struggled to get two boxes into his trunk and the rest into the backseat with me. Then the two fellows *also* got into the back seat with me! John turned and looked and by this time we've been in Mongolia long enough to know that anything can happen at any time, so we shrugged our shoulders and laughed saying, "This is a journal entry." We set off for home. They carried everything up to the apartment, and in 45 minutes we had the lovely new desk. John commented that he was constantly amazed how the assumptions we make turn out wrong in Mongolia. Both of us assumed (without thinking about it) that the two men would jump into a company truck, follow us to the apartment, and then put the desk together. Wrong! Of course there is no company truck. This is Mongolia, not the USA, but usually we go about our business without thinking and are dumbstruck when we are snapped back to reality.

Erdenetsetseg was here using the computer to translate this week's Relief Society lesson, so they got her to ask us if the driver was coming back to return them to the store. We said we did expect him back. They waited outside for awhile and when Baatar was late returning came back up to the apartment, we gave them

1000Ts to take a taxi but as they reached the bottom of the steps Baatar arrived. Through our window we had noted his arrival and started down the stairs to meet him. Halfway down, we met the two store employees climbing back up to the third floor to return our 1000Ts. The honesty of these people is virtually unfailing. We took the Ts, piled into the car together, and Baatar returned them to the store.

## Tsagaan Sar Count

*Nancy*

Elder Cerveny ate 205 buuz (66 in one sitting) and Elder Ball ate 155 over three days. The latter tried to keep up with the former but after two days got sick.

## International Women's Day

*Nancy*

Sunday, March 8, was International Women's Day, and it is celebrated in a big way here in Mongolia. We had barely recovered from the festivities of Tsagaan Sar when people started inviting us to celebrate Women's Day with them.

The first event was sponsored by the Khan Uul hospital for its female employees, and it reminded me a lot of the Relief Society Christmas party except that the vodka, champagne, and wine really flowed. We were the guests of the hospital's head doctor and the district health commissioner for the Ulaanbaatar city government. Doya went with us but the music was so loud I had great difficulty understanding her. It was a short evening because we had another meeting at 7:00 P.M., so after soup and salad and several whirls around the dance floor—not John and I together but in response to requests made by several lovely ladies—we made our apologies and left.

That was Friday evening. The next afternoon we were invited to a small party organized by the Mongolian Child Rights Center where they were honoring couples who have been married for a considerable time. Since we've been married almost 46 years they felt we qualified, though, interestingly, it doesn't seem that long to us.

Since Saturday and Sunday are Baatar's days off we caught a taxi to the Wedding Palace. The Wedding Palace is where most of the marriages are performed in Ulaanbaatar. Actually, the Palace is the busiest on the days that the lamas declare the most propitious, so couples wait to be officially married on those days. They don't always wait, however, and often bring their babies and children with them to the ceremony.

We arrived at the celebration exactly at noon and were led into a reception area where five other couples were also gathering amidst television and still cameras. After a television interview on the steps of the palace we were ushered back into the reception area and seated at a table covered with cakes, cookies, candies, flowers, soft drinks, champagne, and wine. They provided an interpreter for us and what followed was a most interesting afternoon.

Among the company were one of Mongolia's most famous wrestlers and his teacher wife, a renowned artist and his medical doctor wife, the director of the Children's Arts and Crafts Center (which we had toured on Thanksgiving) and his very shy wife, Mongolia's esteemed poet and even more shy wife, and a noted scholar and his scholar wife. After toasts and remarks of welcome from the head of the Child Rights Center and the director of the Wedding Palace we were each asked to tell a bit about ourselves and our families, all of which was recorded on audiotape and much of it on videotape. Then each couple was presented with a plaque and two figurines. During the afternoon each couple was also taken into another room where they were also interviewed by a television team.

Things then became less formal and John and I sat back as laughter and song rang through the small room. It turns out these distinguished people had all gone to the university together and were telling stories about one another. The poet wrote his first poem while there and it was dedicated to the artist. One of the others wrote a love letter to his future wife and the others opened it and all read it before it was delivered to her. Stories were being told faster than our interpreter could keep up with so she just told us the better ones. It was so much fun watching them recall the days of their youth that we just sat and laughed with them and felt the warmth of their love for one another.

The director of the center initiated the singing by standing and singing a song about mothers. Then the wife of the wrestler, a teacher for 25 years, sang a song about the family. One lilting Mongolian folk song followed another as our various companions sang and after a few lines everyone would join in—well, almost everyone. The director of the Children's Arts and Crafts Center has a beautiful, robust bass voice which made the rafters reverberate and it was especially touching when he sang a love song to his wife. The director of the Wedding Palace stood with her glass raised and sang a song which everyone once again joined. By this time John and I had been lulled into a very warm zone of comfort. Can you guess what came next?

The poet, sitting to John's right, spoke up and said, "Now, let's have a song from John and Nancy." I was mortified! Here were these beautiful people who had sung enchanting Mongolian folk songs and what could John and I ever sing? I tried to beg off but John was most agreeable. So we stood and I whispered to him, "What do we know that we could sing?" We discussed a Primary Song or two but knew they wouldn't understand them and then John suddenly remembered a song that many Mongolians know. After choosing an appropriate pitch we launched into a harmonious duet of :

*You are my sunshine, my only sunshine.*
*You make me happy when skies are gray.*
*You'll never know, dear, how much I love you.*
*Please don't take my sunshine away.*

*The other night, dear, as I lay sleeping,*
*I dreamt I held you in my arms.*
*When I awoke, dear, I was mistaken*
*and I hung my head and I cried.*

*You are my sunshine, my only sunshine.*
*You make me happy when skies are gray.*
*You'll never know, dear, how much I love you.*
*Please don't take my sunshine away.*

That evening, the short interview they had done with us on the steps of the Wedding Palace appeared on the television news. The next day at church some of the members ran up to tell us they had seen it. For several days following vendors at the market and others told us about seeing it. Then, on Monday night, while teaching beginning English to some of the Relief Society sisters in our apartment, they started talking about it and I told them we had had our video camera with us and taped parts of the afternoon. They asked to see it so we hooked it up to our television set (for educational purposes, of course). They knew each of the other guests at the party and listened as each sang. When John and I sang I was amazed at their reaction. They pointed out that all the rest of the singing that afternoon had been done by the wife or the husband but never both together, and we were the only ones that had sung together and in harmony. They said that made them feel proud. I was astounded at their observation.

We spent part of the actual Women's Day with Baatar and his family. He picked up his brother, Khavtgai, and us after church.

When he got out of the car to open the door for us I saw that he had on a new deel. Then he reached into the car and pulled out a beautiful bouquet which he presented to me. It had two beautiful roses in it—the first real roses I had seen since arriving here. He drove us to his ger where his wife had prepared a wonderful lunch for us. We were especially honored because the family sat and ate with us. Usually only the host sits with the guests and the wife and children prepare and serve the food. But this day they all sat with us and we enjoyed getting to know one another even better, thanks to Khavtgai's interpreting.

The last "celebration" was when my Relief Society English class surprised me with a cake, another rose, a ceremonial silver cup, and a watercolor of Chinggis Khan.

Do you think it will be hard for us to leave? You bet it will!

## What It's All About

*Nancy*

Training local leaders from among the branch members is one of the primary tasks of the senior couples. Almost all of us have assignments working on humanitarian projects and teaching English which take up the major portion of our time but we also act as "shadow leaders" for the local members.

It would be easier for us old veterans of church service to take over and do the jobs ourselves but we were wisely counseled before coming that we must teach and encourage the members to handle their responsibilities themselves. It is flattering to be "needed" and looked to for the necessary leadership here but we have seen several local members "crash" after they became too attached to an American missionary, whether it be a single missionary or a couple. When the missionary left, they felt lost and without direction.

President Cox has also instilled within us the realization that the members need to call on their own priesthood leaders for church ordinances instead of knocking on the doors of the missionaries for these services. In dispensing the humanitarian goods that come from the Sort Center in Salt Lake we make sure that it is Mongolians giving to Mongolians and not we Americans as we work only behind the scenes.

Several things have taken place recently which have given John and I great pleasure in our work. When we first arrived last June our branch president was not functioning. John attempted with great patience to motivate him to serve the members of his branch but months passed without his making an appearance at church. His two counselors carried on as best they could until one left for BYU-Hawaii and the other for a mission to Russia. At that point the only thing left to do until the matter could be resolved by the district president was for John to conduct the Sunday meetings with the assistance of a missionary interpreter.

While John was dealing with these matters I was developing the abilities of several branch members to handle the music for their meetings. Three of us, all senior sisters, had taken on the job of teaching the keyboard and conducting in their successive periods of missionary service. Soon after we arrived I was given that responsibility by the Coxes and have been teaching keyboard lessons in our apartment every Saturday since. In addition, there are monthly auxiliary training meetings where I conduct a music department.

Most Mongolians are very humble and somewhat shy. It is not natural for them to stand in front of a group and lead. They are much more comfortable, as we've been told most Asians are, working together in a group and functioning excellently in that manner. Therefore, standing and conducting a meeting, leading the music, or playing a keyboard necessitates their overcoming this natural shyness and requires a bit of urging and reassurance.

About a month or two ago (time flies here!) a brother John had trained was called as the new branch president and he took his place on the stand with a counselor. Two of the girls that had been attending the music training sessions were also on the stand handling their portions of the meeting with great aplomb. The sacrament was blessed and passed by an all-Mongolian assembly of young men. John and I sat in the congregation, holding hands, with big smiles on our faces as we observed the all-Mongolian presence on the stand.

During one of our music training meetings I talked with the young sisters about the necessity of their stepping forward and standing in their places. I told them of the great love I have for them and the way they could make me the happiest was that when we go home they don't cry but honor the great friendship we've developed by serving diligently in their callings and training others; that this is their church, not the American missionaries' church. We cried a little together and got on with the department.

A week ago last Sunday was a momentous event in the history of the Church in Mongolia. Three branches in Ulaanbaatar were divided into six. During the week I was anxious to find out just who would be left in our branch. I found out that Unruh and Gerelsaikhan would no longer be in our branch and we'd have to start all over again developing music people, this time for six branches.

Yesterday I slipped into one of the new branch's (Chingeltey) sacrament meeting and saw Unruh sitting at the keyboard playing the sacrament hymn and Gerelsaikhan conducting the music. My heart and eyes were full as they each looked up and saw me standing in the back of the room. They smiled at me and I gave them a thumbs up. That's what it's all about.

## Miracles

*Nancy*

This morning we awoke to see a picture of our new grand-daughter, Eleanor Susan Asplund, on our web page. What miracles take place in our lives while we are serving a mission!

Several hours later we visited a shelter for street children and it is the most deprived we have seen since beginning to represent the humanitarian services department of the Church.

With the help of the people at the Sort Center in Salt Lake City and the members of the Church who are generous with their donations we'll soon see another miracle.

# Mongolia: The circle in the clouds

# April 1998

## Leaping Forward

We've been hearing from the Mongolians that spring brings wind as well as warmer weather. While we watch the temperature rise (maybe the 50s this week) we are also beginning to see the winds pick up. Nyamaa, one of our drivers—the couples now have two—told us that it's mostly windy in the afternoon. As we walked to the mission home this morning the wind began to pick up and John remarked that it was a little early. I checked my watch and noted that it was 11:25 A.M., so it was just getting an early start.

We understand that the wind we've felt is nothing compared to what it will become. Ulaanbaatar sits in a bowl of sand surrounded by five mountains. Much of Mongolia is sand, so imagine what it's going to be like when the heavy winds come. We've been told that visibility is cut down, with blowing sand that stings the exposed parts of your body. Several missionaries who wear contact lenses have had to remove them and revert to their old spectacles because of sand getting behind the lens and becoming quite uncomfortable. It's been very mild so far but I've tasted sand in my mouth several times after being out. Elder and

Sister Kinnison who live and serve in Erdenet said that it can't be anything like Texas but then we know everything in Texas is bigger than anywhere else, so why not Mongolia.

Occasionally when we look out our window we see people holding handkerchiefs over their nose and mouth. Fortunately we've not had to be out when it's blowing that hard but I know we're not going to be able to avoid it entirely because it lasts through May. Spring is not the favorite season here. The Young Men and Young Women don't plan any outdoor activities during this time. Sosor, our cleaning lady, told me many of the old people die between Tsagaan Sar and Naadam (February–July) and blames it on the unhealthy air. (But she also says that drinking and smoking don't cause cancer.)

Once again the children are out running and jumping along the tops of the metal storage containers that are all over the city. A new crop of young ones is joining in and it's fun watching out our windows as they try, with the encouragement of their older brothers and sisters, to summon up the courage to jump some of the wider spaces. You just want to run out and give them a boost. Depending on the age, some of the older siblings lift them up and over but when they're deemed old enough it seems to be a rite of passage that they jump themselves.

John and I watched yesterday afternoon as a young boy worked as hard as he could to psyche himself up while an "old timer" urged, waited, and finally adopted the ruse of waving goodbye. After he took a few steps he turned to peek to see if his ruse had injected any urgency into the situation. That is when he noticed us watching through our bedroom window and drew to the attention of the "jumper" that he now had a bigger audience. Instead of turning and running, as they usually do when they see us watching, they smiled and waved back when we waved to them. John urged the timid one on with "power ranger" gestures and with real grit and determination he made the jump. Then he turned and looked at us with a huge smile at his accomplishment. Of course we gave him a huge smile right back (with a good deal of hand clapping and a few cheers thrown in for good measure). As I write this there are ten 8–10-year-old boys out there, one having just made his first jump over an approximately three-foot space while the other nine patiently waited. It was quite comical watching him rock back and forth and spit into his hands (for whatever good that does a jumper!) before each, "Okay, I'm going to do it this time" gesture. He finally took the leap and made it! None of his friends called out "chicken" or flapped their arms like a chicken at him. They all sat patiently on the far side of the gap and waited for him, which is the Mongolian way. The boys have gone now and the girls are there.

We removed the silver tape from around several of our windows so we could open them and let some "fresh" air in—a sure sign of spring. However, there is now a patina of fine sand on many things—desks, furniture, phone, computer, printer, fax, and so on. So out came the cloth napkins and towels to drape over the more important pieces of equipment to protect them.

Last week we turned our clocks ahead and leapt forward into spring.

## Vanity, Thy Name Is Nancy

*Nancy*

While getting our physical and dental checkups previous to leaving I asked our dentist what I'd do if one of the facings on my upper permanent bridge came off—which happens now and then—and he said, "Take some super glue with you and glue it back on." That sounded simple enough to me. I skipped merrily on my way with two tubes of super glue in our luggage.

Saturday evening the couples went to the opera to see *The Barber of Seville* performed in Mongolian. While there I felt the facing on one of the teeth come loose. Not to worry! I knew right where the super glue was and after we got home I'd glue it back on.

When we arrived home the electricity was off but that's not an unusual occurrence. The opera had started at 5:00 P.M. so it was only 7:30 P.M. and there was still light enough by which to fix ourselves a cold dinner and by the time we finished that the lights would be on. *Not!!!* It turns out that while we were all gone, someone came in and stole the breakers from the electrical boxes in the hall which blew the lights in all three of the apartments on this landing.

The building maintenance men were informed and came up to fix things. *Three times* there were explosions outside our door while they attempted to fix things, and each time we were sure we'd find bodies laying on our landing. Remember, they're fixing this electrical box in the dark—occasionally lighting a match with which to see—until John and several of the other elders either loaned them flashlights or held them. They also asked John for a screwdriver. (After the first explosion, they were on their own.) We knew by the sound of things we weren't going to have electricity for a while.

I retrieved the tooth facing from where I had carefully laid it in the dark so it wouldn't get lost and we proceeded to light candles and flashlights, and I set out to do this "no big deal" task. I sat in front of a makeshift make-up table with wall mirror, aiming all the candle power at the mirror so it would reflect back on my mouth. The glue was applied (gel type) and the facing wouldn't go on! I had done a dry run (pun intended) before adding the glue and it went on perfectly. I struggled and struggled and my hands got shakier and shakier and people are knocking on our door asking about the explosions and why wasn't the phone working (when our power is off, the phones in the building don't work) and John's trying to shield his "beautiful" wife with a hole in the top of her mouth from all curiosity seekers. The maintenance men knocked and returned the flashlight and screwdriver and by this time I had super glue on my fingers, on my lips, and on adjacent teeth and was absolutely beside myself.

We both took on the struggle—at one point I was laying flat on the bed with John, flashlight in one hand and tooth facing in the other, trying to insert slot A on the facing into slot B of the metal bridge. "Tomorrow is church and I just can't go to church like this!!! I'll stay home until we can get in touch with Turbileg's fiancée—a dentist! Oh, I have to teach Monday! I can't let the kids see me like this. You're just going to have to teach for me!" This went on and on. We got every type of tool we could find in the apartment to clean out the channel in the facing that fits over the metal protrusion on the bridge. We figured small amounts of the glue had dried in the channel, and things just weren't fitting anymore. We had brought one razor for a cutting blade with us and we used that. We used a small Swiss army knife. We used a pair of fingernail clippers. We used a straight pin. Now I could slide it on part way but looked like a snaggle-toothed witch with that one tooth hanging below my top lip.

Remember, we have no power so the phones don't work and consequently I can't get in touch with Turbileg's fiancée. Turbileg is a Colorado University-educated lawyer who works at the Ministry of Justice who has become a good friend. He told us early on in our friendship that if we ever needed a good dentist his Korean-born fiancée was trained in Japan and is an excellent dentist used by many ex-patriates.

John realized earlier than me that this is a lost cause and starts urging that we just call it quits and go to bed. The candles have burned down quite a bit by this time and we're sure to need them again so I reluctantly give in. I lovingly put the bridge facing in a small bowl in the middle of the dining room table so it doesn't inadvertently get brushed into the trash or some other disastrous thing.

I slept the night with a hunk of metal in my mouth which my tongue kept running over while the facing remained safe in the dark. Sunday morning arrived and John had gotten up during the night to draw a bath for me that would still be hot when we got up. I slept as long as I could with thoughts of that hole between my teeth. It was now Sunday.

New thoughts were racing through my head such as, "Even if I don't go to church, I have to direct choir practice in the afternoon." I retrieved the facing from its safe place and tried once more — without the glue. It sort of went on, hanging about ¼-inch below the other tooth. I looked at myself in the mirror from the front and from each side and I thought maybe I could do it. Fortunately it was Fast Sunday so I didn't need to eat. I would do it! (Yes, lipstick does cover dried super glue.)

It's now the end of the day and I'm exhausted from trying to keep my mouth closed and trying to look as if everything was normal. As the day wore on I felt more and more like the snaggle-toothed witch in Snow White and that everyone was looking at my tooth. I felt as if it were getting longer and longer so I was glad when I could finally close myself into the apartment. Since the electricity was still off, John had walked up to the mission office in the afternoon and called Turbileg who said his fiancée would be back in town and call us around 7:00 P.M. The power was restored around 2:00P.M.

Around 7:00 P.M. I was talking on the phone with Sister Cox when it sounded like the whole world exploded. They were working in the box again and our electricity went off.

# Who Really Runs Stairwell One of Building Seven

*Nancy*

Sosor is one of the early members of the Church in Mongolia. She's also been the couples' cleaning lady for most of those years.

I don't know what her name means in Mongolian but wouldn't be surprised if it's *whirlwind*. You can tell the minute she hits the building every morning (except Sunday) as her voice rings up and down the stairwell. We don't exactly set our clocks by her but she's generally here around 8:00 A.M. each day.

It's not unusual to get a lecture from her on topics ranging from "Don't open the windows because the Mongolian dust will blow in" to something about our personal safety. Soon after we first arrived I had my first run-in with Sosor. The vacuum cleaner that was in this apartment was useless so we purchased a new one. Sosor has a favorite place for stashing "valuables" and that's around and under our bathtubs. That old vacuum stayed there for weeks as she said she'd find someone who could use it. Sister Cox advised us after a week to tell her to either take the things or we'd throw them out. So, after a while we got rid of the vacuum. Boy! did she chastise me and for days went around the building repeating, "It is terrible that you did that. Some Mongolian could have used that. The sister missionaries needed that." My body went rigid when I heard her in the building because I knew she'd start on me again.

That period finally passed and Sosor and I are now good friends. She and I have worked together a lot in getting the humanitarian couples' apartments ready. She can't stand seeing me down on my hands and knees scrubbing or climbing up on something to hang curtains (on wire or string). She fills me in on Mongolian traditions while we work, such as during the winter you wrap a long woolen scarf around your stomach to keep it warm even when taking out the trash—which she does. There are many "Mongolians do this. . ." and "Mongolians do that. . . ." President Cox told us that when he and Sr. Cox were here as couple missionaries he was serving as branch president and Sosor was the activities chairperson. An activity that was supposed to end at 2:00 was continuing when he suggested to her that they should have the closing prayer. She replied, "To Mongolians, 20 minutes late is on time."

She doesn't throw anything away and continues to keep her stash under our bathtubs. She saves every scrap of paper that goes into our trash and with about 50 missionaries teaching English there's a lot of scrap paper around. If it's got English on it she smoothes it out and takes it home to study. Otherwise it gets burned in her stove to supplement her heat or to cook her food.

Sosor goes to college in the late afternoon. Some semesters she goes right after lunch so has to do all the cleaning in the morning. I asked her how old she is the other day and she told me to guess. Of course I made all my guesses low and her hearty laugh was enjoyable as her four gold teeth sparkled in the light. She told me she is 56 and that's old for Mongolians (some retire at 55). A perpetual student she is! She's taking economics, computer, and business management. She was trained by the Russians to be a "water engineer" (a plumber). She has two daughters that live in Hungary where her former husband also lives.

Our landlord doesn't always get the many repairs done that are needed in the stairwell so Sosor goes down and either sweet-talks or yells at the "handymen" until they come just to get her off their backs. Then she stands over them and supervises, tsk-tsking at the mess they're making but at least they get the repairs made.

Since she and I have been working together so much lately, the call "Oh, Sister Hopkins" goes ringing through the stairwell frequently as she wants me to look at this and that. When I'm looking for her and call, "Sosor" she *always* responds with "Oh, please, here I am." She has made friends with one of the handymen here who, she says, is the carpenter. It also turns out that he's the man that knocks on our door to have his picture taken with our Polaroid—always in front of the TV set. His name is Bayarsaikhan. She hovers over him while he works, supervising and clucking at him. He marches at a quick pace when she's around.

Friday we had a mission conference during which Sister Cox gave a history of the mission. It was very interesting as we learned of the first baptisms and trials of those original couples and six elders. Then she came to Sosor. As she was telling about the hardships of food shortages following the Russians' leaving, she said it was Sosor who stood in long lines to get food for the couples. Saturday when Sosor came to put the finishing touches on the new couple's apartment I told her of the tribute that Sister Cox had paid her. I was crying and she was crying. She reached out and touched my arm and said, "Don't cry, Sister Hopkins. Mongolians do things like that."

## Out of the Mouths of Babes!

*Nancy*

One of the sacrifices couples make when serving a mission is being away from their children and grandchildren. But when measured against the eternal blessings the sacrifice is small.

Our son, Christopher, and his family are living in our home in Pennsylvania while we're here and I was sure to leave at least one picture of John and me in a prominent spot so the younger children would remember us. David was three when we left and he was the one I most feared would forget us.

This past Sunday there was a Church conference held in Madison Square Garden at which President Hinckley spoke. Members from all over the east coast made their way to New York City by bus, train, and car. Chris and family were among those who attended. Due to the overflow crowds, he and his family were seated in one of the luxury boxes close to the podium where President Hinckley spoke. As he took his place at the podium, David said, "Hey! There's Grandpa!"

## Another Day at the Office

*John*

I had a meeting on the eleventh floor of a building in downtown Ulaanbaatar yesterday. After the meeting my interpreter and I entered the elevator to descend to the ground floor. We got to the ninth floor and took on several more passengers, making perhaps 10 of us on the elevator. The operator pushed the button to descend but nothing happened. He pushed the button again; still nothing. The occupants (other than myself) were not surprised by this development. Without anyone saying a word they began to jump up and down in rhythm, to help the elevator along. I'm standing there, like a lump, saying to myself that I'd be much happier if this were taking place on the second floor rather than the ninth when the elevator clicked into gear, began its descent, and deposited us all safely on the ground floor. Everyone left without giving the incident a second thought. Just another day at the office.

## Anniversary Reflections

### John

We entered the MTC one year ago today. Since today is also my birthday, the two have inevitably become combined.

I was thinking this morning about the past year and concluded that while some days seem to crawl (because you are tired and can't wait to get to bed!) the weeks and months and year go very, very fast. But the year has been jam-packed with new events, good events, worthwhile ways to expend one's time, energy, and talents. I said to Nancy that if we are at the stage of our lives where the years are ticking down to the end (which we are and they are) then it is good to pack as much into each year as we have packed into this past one.

We have done a lot, accomplished a lot, and grown somewhat. We have kept our brains and bodies active, stayed out of the ol' rocking chairs back home, and learned that we don't need all the material things that pack our cellar and attic (there's going to be a big yard sale in the fall when we get home).

We have grown closer to Heavenly Father and some of his most charming but needy children. Hopefully, through the web page, we have injected into the minds of a few other couples the idea that maybe, just maybe, they would like to go on a humanitarian services mission one day so they, too, can help Him a little.

We have been inspired by the example of many others, starting with the couples in the SMTC a year ago who were embarking on their third, fourth, or fifth missions. Today we see the endless drive, patience, and concern of our mission president and his wife, the cheerful fortitude of the young missionaries as they do everything that other missionaries do *and* teach a full load of English, and the quiet, sincere, humble modeling of senior couples who are serving with us. Taken together they make you feel that you would be grateful for the opportunity to be a ministering angel to them as *they* reap the rewards of their splendid service — which is so much more than you are able to generate yourself.

Since the years *are* ticking down, and since the end grows inevitably nearer, it just seems to me that the wiser and better course is to fill them with productive engagement. One misses the contact with the children and grandchildren, of course. But these days the existence of e-mail helps to moderate even that ill-effect.

It hasn't been peaches and cream every moment, of course. The principle that there is opposition in all things is still in effect. But there is a benefit to that, as well. We've been taught (and I think correctly) that the primary beneficiary of a mission is the missionary himself or herself. Our less-than-perfect moments have forced us to engage, and overcome, elements of ourselves that needed to be perfected. Hopefully we have strengthened ourselves in these areas. If one continues to serve through successive missions, and in each mission succeeds in strengthening at least one area, then I can see how the missionary himself or herself can, indeed, be the primary beneficiary of the mission. In musing on this topic, our mission president expressed the view that missions were the avenue to sanctification for older couples. That is, missions offer the opportunity for regular study, prayer, and good works that, combined with the strengthening of areas of weakness that I mentioned above, can produce such a depth and quality of communion that sanctification does indeed follow.

I think the president is on the right track. To me that is just one more good reason, among many good reasons, why more couples should prepare to serve a mission.

Shifting to another topic, yesterday (April 29) Sister Erdenet-setseg entered the MTC. As we mentioned earlier, she was so excited she was talking extension before she even left here! *Tsetseg* is the Mongolian word for *flower*. She is a beautiful flower in Heavenly Father's garden. I appreciate so much the symbolism of her entering the MTC almost exactly one year after we did. It isn't that we had anything at all to do with her baptism, conversion, or gifts. It's just that I feel gratified at this indication that our work here (the work of *all* the full-time and senior missionaries) can produce such fruit and can so enrich and bless the lives of such choice people as Erdenetsetseg.

Let me close by saying (again) it is very, very rewarding to be a part of such an endeavor and you really ought to be thinking about and planning to become a part of it yourselves. This is something you can and should do. It is both enriching and very fulfilling.

## The Winds Hit!

*Nancy*

A week ago Sunday (we've been busy!) we awakened to a morning sky that was reddish brown. The winds were swirling and we couldn't see three buildings away. At first it didn't occur to us what it was, but when we saw the drifts of sand on the floor inside our closed windows and balcony door, we realized it was the promise of things to come made to us earlier by the Mongolians.

Papers and plastic bags were flying through the sky like birds. Just the day before it seemed that all of Ulaanbaatar was out cleaning and sprucing up the city for spring. The wind had picked up all that debris out of the trash containers and rearranged it throughout the city once again.

We were speaking that day at one of the branches on the edge of the city, and had arranged for a driver to take us, but later in the afternoon we had choir practice to which we had to walk. I followed the pattern of the Mongolian women who had donned head scarves to keep the sand out of their hair. John wrapped his neck scarf around the lower part of his face. Even though we both wear glasses, sand was finding its way into our eyes and our mouths. There was no getting away from it!

During choir practice (we have 60–80 members these days) people were sitting there cleaning the sand out of their ears while singing. While walking home we passed a woman who had seemed to solve the problem by wrapping a sheer head scarf over her head *and* face; she walked along as carefree as if it were a clear summer day — although later some of the women told me that that method doesn't work either as the sand blows right through the scarf.

On Monday, while I was teaching my college English class I noted some of the students still removing sand from their ears.

Someone has said, "You don't need to visit the Gobi desert. Just stay around a while and it'll come to you."

# May 1998

## How Can You Tell a New Missionary to Mongolia?

*Nancy*

Hand two missionaries each a package of Oreo cookies. The one whose eyes light up in delight and says, "Really?" is about to go home. The other one, who just keeps talking and doesn't even notice what you've handed him, he just arrived!

## A Trip *to* Darkhan

*John*

Now that we've been here ten months the prospect of catching taxis to and from Darkhan (rather than taking the train or using one of our trusted daily drivers) was not at all daunting. Besides, I was going to be accompanied by the two assistants to the president, both grizzled veterans scheduled to go home next month. No problem.

One of the assistants and his companion swung by the apartment at 6:30 A.M. to escort me to the taxi pick-up point. As we walked he talked knowingly of the process. The first thing was to get the right vehicle. We would select from available Mercedes or "Beamers" (BMWs to we uninitiated). Failing that, we would drop down to a Russian car or possibly a newer van (although their suspensions were a little soft and thus given to uncomfortable swaying). It goes without saying that under *no* circumstance would we use one of those awful Russian Jeeps.

Having surveyed the field for the cushiest transportation, we would next negotiate the price. Some drivers of these expensive luxury cars might have the temerity to ask for 5000 tugrugs per head (about $6) for the four-hour trip to Darkhan, but we would hang in there until we located the drivers who would accept just 4000Ts.

Finally, from among those drivers who were sufficiently perceptive to recognize that they were haggling with veteran negotiators, we would select that driver who promised to maintain the highest average speed, thereby assuring we would breeze into the Darkhan zone conference early, unruffled, and poised for action.

That was the game plan. As you have guessed by now the reality was somewhat different. By the time we had picked up the other assistant, switched companions, picked up the Darkhan/Eredenet mail at the mission office, and walked to the taxi junction we were running late. Still no problem. The previous assistants had already assured us that there were even *more* possibilities after 7:00 A.M. than there were before, so this would merely add to the choices that lay before us.

At the pick-up point we were surprised to find there were *no* Mercedes or Beamers. Hmmm. They must be running a bit late today. We strolled the grounds, observing with genuine sympathy the plight of Mongolians taking the buses and how they were being crammed with bodies and merchandise. Those awful Russian Jeeps were over there; so we stayed away from that place. There were vans. But where were the Mercs, the Beamers, and the Russian cars?

I give the assistants credit. They approached every car that drove through the lot and asked about their interest in fares to Darkhan. Given that missionaries are not even *allowed* to do door-to-door petitioning in Mongolia, I kidded them about learning to handle rejection at this late stage in their missions. The minutes went by. Still, no one going to Darkhan. By now we were talking about offering drivers a premium to take us, rather than plotting our strategies for negotiating down their initial fare offers.

By 8:30 A.M. we were desperate. (There was a brief flirtation with the idea of taking a *bus* but, as it turned out, we weren't *that* desperate!) Finally. *Finally!* The driver of a small van was willing to take us for 4000Ts (we didn't even have to haggle). Sold! On to the van and let's get going! Well, not so fast. He had to have enough passengers to make the trip worthwhile at that price so we waited while he rounded up a Russian emigré and two Mongolian ladies who also wanted to go to Darkhan this day. At 8:45 A.M., two hours late, the six of us crammed in the back and the driver and his wife or daughter in the front were off to Darkhan.

It was during the trip that I learned that my two veteran missionaries were not veteran travelers. One of the assistants revealed this was his first trip out of the city—he had spent his entire mission in Ulaanbaatar. This prompted the other to note that he had spent just one tour out of Ulaanbaatar—in Darkhan—but had traveled by train, so this was his first auto tour, as well. All their presumed wisdom about taxis had been *told* to them by the outgoing assistant. They hadn't experienced any of it themselves.

Well, to continue. It's the spring as you know. In Mongolia that means the thoughts of men turn to repairing the ravages of winter on the roads. There were probably a dozen places where the highway department poured piles of dirt across the highway, signaling the start of a detour. Detours here mean you just turn

off the road and drive helter-skelter across the countryside until
you see another pile of dirt across the highway to signal the
beginning or end of that particular section of reconstruction.

It's hard to describe the amount of dust that is generated by
these excursions into the countryside. I was facing the rear of the
van as we traveled. On these detours there was so much dust accumulating on the roof and sides of the van that it was sheeting
down the back window in exactly the way water sheets down the
windows of your car when you are driving through a car wash.

After four hours of this, just as we were approaching the outskirts of Darkhan, we were stopped by a policeman. He checked
the driver's license and registration. All okay. But then, noting
the presence of foreigners in the van, he pulled us off to the side
and had the driver talk with another official. Five minutes
passed. Ten minutes dragged by in the now-sweltering van. The
driver explained that the foreigners each had to pay a 1000Ts
"tax" because we weren't registered with the national health program! The assistants explained to me that this was just a rip-off,
but it was only 1000Ts, we were late, and we should just pay and
get on our way. I agreed but the Russian didn't.

Then the Mongolian ladies got into the act. Even though they
were not being asked to pay anything they were outraged at the
rip-off. They demanded to see documentation. The official went
back into his little trailer and came back with a packet of papers
which he said represented the law on the subject. The ladies
couldn't believe it. In the still-sweltering van they started to go
through the papers, paragraph by paragraph, page by page, debating the issue with the official.

After 20 minutes, with our arrival growing later and later, I
took advantage of their respect for age and began to motion to
the official and the ladies to get on with it. I pointed to my watch.
I made circular motions in the air with my finger. They must
have gotten the message because the official began to write a

receipt for the money. With that the policeman motioned the driver on. After 30 seconds on the road we in the back realized that the official had become so flustered that he had written the receipt but never collected the money! The Mongolian ladies were delighted to have put the petit-official into his place and cackled to each other for a good while about this coup.

The driver wasn't as delighted though. Or at least he so claimed as he deposited us at our destination in Darkhan. *He* then demanded 1000Ts from each of the foreigners lest the official recognize him on his return trip and ask for the money we had failed to pay. The missionaries rolled their eyes at this new rip-off but we were very late so we just paid him and took off. I don't think the Russian did though. His natural disposition came to the fore and saved him 1000Ts.

We hit the meeting running. The assistants went immediately into their presentation. Since they hadn't had time to make the copies of it they planned there was a good deal of tap-dancing as they presented. We then went immediately into the testimony meeting that closed the meeting so our arrival was really in the nick-of-time. Afterwards I was able to make the two school visits planned for the day and prepared to journey back to Ulaanbaatar — alone. The assistants had decided to hang around in Darkhan, play a little basketball, visit with the Darkan/Erdenet missionaries a bit, and then take the midnight train back to the city. If you want to read about my equally interesting return trip read the next journal entry. But if you're already travel weary just skip it.

# A Trip *from* Darkhan
## John

The mission president and his wife weren't sure of the wisdom of my catching a taxi back to Ulaanbaatar alone. Both suggested that it might be better if I were to stay and catch the overnight train back with them and the assistants. But I wasn't concerned. As my mental picture had it, the assistants would use their Mongolian language skills to negotiate a price for the return trip with one of those Mercedes/Beamer drivers, tell him where to drop me off in Ulaanbaatar, and in solitary comfort I would settle into the cushy back seat, loosen my tie, and sleep my way home. No problem.

As it turned out, loosening my tie was as close as I got to that picture.

There was just one driver in Darkhan going to Ulaanbaatar. He was driving one of those hard-suspension, over-the-road vehicles that abound in Mongolia. No matter. I was just going to sprawl out in the rear seat anyway. So I nodded goodbye to the elders and spread my briefcase, coat, and hat across the seat.

As I closed the door the assistant told me through the window that the fare was just 4000Ts. That jarred me a little. I have pondered before the ethics of paying taxi drivers what they ask when I *know* that amount is less than is needed to offset the price of petrol, vehicle maintenance, and so forth. I was debating in my mind just how much more I *should* pay the driver when we got to Ulaanbaatar, regardless of what he had asked, when a Mongolian matron of substantial presence pushed her way into the back seat.

Oh, I thought, there must be another passenger. That hadn't occurred to me (for some unfathomable reason). Okay, I thought, I can handle this.

Matron proceeded to slide across the seat. At first she sat in the center beside me. Then she began to press farther until she was pressing hard against my right side. It didn't do her much good to press because my left side was already sealed against the door, but, as we've said in other journal entries, the Mongolians are the world's champion pushers and she was doing much to defend that claim!

At this point her mother entered the vehicle. She looked to be incredibly old and wise; I shall call her the Ancient One. She slipped onto the seat to her daughter's right. Plump Granddaughter, about 20 years of age, soon followed. Now there were four of us in the back seat, too many to sit in the usual manner. Matron began to attend to that problem. She lifted up and moved to her left until she was half on my lap! I should have protested at that point, you suggest. Anyone who has ever been to a bargain basement sale will understand why I didn't. Matrons of her age are exactly the people you watch for as they are the most prone to use their age (and sharp elbows) to gain advantage. Therefore I sat, silently resisting but not saying anything, as black thoughts formed in my mind.

Ancient One rescued me by slipping forward on the seat. Matron gave me a stern look but settled back onto the seat instead of on me. Father (or Grandfather?) slithered into the luggage area behind the seat. I strove to evict the black thoughts by musing how humorous it was that while I had been struggling with the ethics of paying more than asked the driver was solving the problem in a practical way by busily rounding up more passengers. A good demonstration of the merits of doers versus thinkers in this world.

Hope springs eternal, though. I said to myself that we couldn't possibly be traveling all the way to UB in this cramped manner — no doubt these were just short-trippers, going elsewhere in Darkhan or to a community right outside the city. This hope gained strength as we turned into a subdivision in Darkhan. We were going to off-load the additional passengers and their baggage and then take me to UB! Alas. 'Twas not so. It was the *driver's* home we were visiting. He picked up two bottles of water, a thermos, and a slim, languorous wife dressed entirely in black.

The next stop was the petrol station at the outskirts of the city. There all hope vanished as the driver collected 4000Ts from each of us — all of us were there for the long haul. The driver offered each of us a Chicklet in return. A nice gesture I thought, not realizing at the time that he probably thought of it as motion-sickness medicine. Having tanked up, we pulled out of the station. At that point, Ancient One turned, we looked each other full in the face, both of us gave rueful but friendly laughs, and with grins on our faces in our sardine can we began the four-hour, jarring, swerving, (literally) hit-your-head-on-the-ceiling journey to Ulaanbaatar.

About 15 minutes into the journey, Languorous Lady, immediately in front of me, slipped into a cotton jacket, cranked the air conditioning up to High (on this coolish Mongolian day), slid a CD into its slot, turned it up to High, and *reclined* her seatback into our already-jammed laps. As she slipped into sweet repose I had a mental picture of Elizabeth Taylor in the picture Cleopatra. From that point forward she roused occasionally to (a) change the CD (*My Way, Don't Cry for Me Argentina, Bridge Over Troubled Waters* and various Mongolian hits), (b) light a cigarette for her husband (yes, he AND the other passengers smoked!), and (c) slip her hand shyly into her husband's hand (he drove most of the way one-handed).

It wasn't for another hour or so, as she made herself ever more comfortable and the driver handled the car with skill and seemed to know most bumps in the road, that I finally realized this probably wasn't just an isolated trip for our host and hostess. In this age of western-style market economy life this is probably their occupation. I suspect they make their living by serving as a substitute for the decrepit inter-city bus service that is available between Ulaanbaatar and Darkhan. Thus the car is their home-away-from-home. At least that's the way they treated it.

The driver seemed to think that since over-the-road cars are built to handle rough terrain there was no need to treat his carefully. We traveled at speeds of 140 kph (100 mph), slowing to a mere 65 kph (45 mph) when the road became *really* rough. We flew over the potholes, road washouts, and detours. I suppose the cramming in the back seat was a good thing in one sense in that we were so packed together that we did not have any room to bounce or roll individually—we only did so collectively! Poor Father/Grandfather in the back did not have that support, or even the support of a seat, so he and the luggage slipped and slid together all over the area behind our seat.

We completed the four-hour trip in three-and-one-quarter hours. I celebrated by handing out some Snickers bars I had in my briefcase but never had room enough to eat. Ancient One gave me another one of her friendly looks. Matron looked surprised but managed a grudging, fleeting smile.

Languorous Lady accepted it as her just due.

We dropped off the family first. The driver said he knew the location of the circus, where I was to be dropped, but he missed several roads leading to it. When I tried to circumspectly suggest that he should turn to his right at one of these roads to get in the general vicinity of the circus, Languorous Lady picked up the cue and offered the same suggestion to her husband. In true male fashion he paid no attention for awhile but in his own good time eventually turned in the necessary direction. She discreetly offered directions from that point which were sufficiently timid that he could accept them and we arrived at the circus.

As I limped away (Ancient One had been standing on my foot for the past two hours) I thought how funny it was that after 10 months in Mongolia and daily observations of how they cram themselves into buses, cars, and taxis, I had still managed to conjure up (not once but twice!) blissful pictures of myself traveling in cushioned comfort through the rough terrain of Mongolia and how readily we lull ourselves into unreality.

But I had accomplished at least part of my business and arrived back in Ulaanbaatar. The suit will have to go to the cleaners to eliminate the smoke odor, and I could hardly wait to get a bath to get the odor out of my hair. Nonetheless I was home safely, back with Nancy and no worse for the wear and tear of the day. No problem!

## Not All Angels Sing

*Nancy*

Elder Lowther just completed the translation of *O My Father* into Mongolian. I have written before of the difficulties of fitting the Mongolian language into our western songs and it is a very slow process. It is done by the single missionaries who are close to going home and have become proficient with the language. Further, they can only work on the process during their P (for preparation) days so that it doesn't take away from their time of teaching English or their many, many discussions. After it is translated, the missionaries take it to several Mongolians and ask them to review the translation and make any suggested changes. So each new hymn that is added to the small hymnbook is a victory and cause for celebration. The hymn *I Believe in Christ* that was added a few months ago has already become a favorite in meetings and Relief Society gatherings.

Our choir has grown so large (60–80 members) after we performed at the last district conference that I wanted some new music the non-English speakers could understand as they sang. I had taken several arrangements of hymns that had been translated and "cut and pasted" the Mongolian words to the music, but because of the difficulty of the vocal parts they fell flat. (I am still learning!)

The Mongolian people are great singers but always in unison. They are unacquainted with singing in parts so the task of sitting while each section learns their harmony is boring to them. The choir is now singing soprano, alto, and men. We have performed some beautiful numbers of which they (and we) are quite proud. For the next conference we wanted to sing one English and one Mongolian number.

At one of the rehearsals I asked them what they would like to sing. Elder Lowther told me he had just completed his translation of *O My Father* and only had to show it to a few members for their review. Within the week he delivered a hand-written copy upon which corrections had been made—it reminded me of Lincoln's Gettysburg Address written on the back of an envelope.

The next hurdle was to get the words set to the music in the proper meter. I do not speak Mongolian and everyone is busy over here—especially the translators—and I had promised the choir the music for this coming Sunday.

Friday arrived and the typed words still sat in our computer waiting to be printed and applied over the English words so it could then be photocopied. John was traveling to Darkhan for a meeting and I knew we wouldn't have appointments here in the city. I set the day aside to get the task done.

I sat down at our dining table and prayed that Heavenly Father would help me. I knew we were entitled to special gifts when they became necessary to do the Lord's work, because we had experienced it many times before, but, I didn't know if it would be so this time. (Did I lack faith?) I completed my prayer and started on the first line of the hymn

# mongolia: the circle in the clouds

*O my Father, thou who dwellest*
*In the high and glorious place.*

I was trying to decide where the Mongolian words would be "broken" to fit the notes when there was a knock on the door. A little disappointed that there was going to be an interruption, I reluctantly answered the knock. There stood Sosor. "Sister Hopkins, may I please come in?"

Nine hours later, our heads foggy and fatigue overcoming both of us, we had completed the placement of all four verses but were still struggling with the first line of the first verse. She was laughing and saying, "You don't know Mongolian and I don't know notes." I told her I couldn't think anymore—I had to have a break to clear my head. We had both worked hard and she had to go home. I needed to run to the market to get some bread and we had to call it quits.

During our day together we had had discussions of the meaning of the hymn and specific words. I told her that the original poem for the song had been written by a woman. At one point she explained that when you're talking about heaven in a song the notes have to go up and not down—we were able to get that to work. I couldn't believe how patient she was with me as I wrote the words by hand under the notes of a working photocopy. C's are S's, N's are backwards and sometimes with two dots over the top, H's are N's, D's are triangles with a tail, L's are ^, G's are a right angle—like a T with the left part of the cross left off. There are several different E's and B's and a J is a star-like character. She encouraged me and we laughed at some of my feeble attempts. The Spirit touched both of us.

She asked before she left if I was going to work on it the next day (Saturday). I told her I taught keyboard lessons in the morning and that one of my students is a girl who is studying opera. She speaks very little English but I'd run the lyrics past her. She asked what time she'd be here and I told her 11:00 A.M.

We said goodbye and I ran to the market. As I entered the second door I saw two missionaries and asked if they were busy. The one is fairly new and the other not yet a year, but quite good with the language. I asked them to come over, look at the piece, and see what they could do with the first line. They waited until I got our bread and came back to the apartment with me.

They had the first line done in a wink and sang through the rest. Fortunately they are both musicians and had a good feel for what they were doing. They only made two changes, including the translation of the title, and the hard part was done.

Saturday morning while Unruhjargal (my keyboard student) was here, Sosor returned. I explained that the two elders had taken care of the first line and she read it over and pronounced, "It is good!" Then she asked to hear Unruh sing it.

Unruh sang *O My Father* for the first time in Mongolian to Sosor and Gantulga, one of my other students, and it was beautiful. Sosor had tears in her eyes. Then she asked me to sing it in English. I had trouble finishing. Every time we sing that song, whether in Mongolia or the United States, I'll remember Sosor and the day we spent putting the words to the music even though I don't know Mongolian and she doesn't know notes. God answers our prayers....

## The Choir Sings *O My Father*

*Nancy*

Sunday afternoon Elder Lowther and his companion, Elder Swenson, stopped by to see how the preparation of the music was going. I showed them the "completed" work and suggested they go over it again. They made several changes and then had to leave because they were on their way to church. Elder Lowther asked that we bring the working copies to choir with us where he'd have an opportunity to hear the words sung and how they sounded.

During choir (77 in attendance), we introduced the new translation by having Unruh sing it to all assembled. It was beautiful and for the first time in a building of The Church of Jesus Christ of Latter-day Saints in Mongolia, *O My Father* was sung by a beautiful Mongolian girl. The Coxes had stayed because Sister Cox was going to accompany us on the keyboard. President Cox sat in the back of the chapel—which was filled with choir members. At our last district conference the choir sang and there were probably about 50 members in it. During his talk, President Cox suggested that since the Mongolians are such beautiful singers he'd like to see even more in the choir. They responded! John said that President Cox was touched by what he saw and heard.

While standing in front of the assembled singers I could see John and President Cox in the back moving their hands this way and that and surmised they were trying to figure out where the choir will sit for the next conference! Elder Lowther was making changes here and there while we sang. Following the practice he checked a few spots with Unruh and asked her advice as to where a singer would place the words in relation to the notes.

Towards the end of the rehearsal I spotted Sosor sitting amidst the choir members. She was trying to learn the notes!

## Call me Altantsetseg

*Nancy*

Getting our students to converse in English is one of the most difficult tasks we have while teaching. I can understand their hesitation as I'd feel the same if I were learning Mongolian. The sentence structure is much different in Mongolian from English so constructing a sentence on the fly is a daunting task.

There is a pattern to Mongolian names. Although it takes about three months before the pattern clicks, once you are familiar, it's much easier to understand and pronounce them — although I still have to see them written rather than just hear them.

A couple weeks ago I accidentally hit upon a way to get one of my classes chattering in English. I asked them what their names meant and following are the meanings to some:

| | |
|---|---|
| chimeg = jewel | delger = blooming flower |
| jargal = happy | tungalag = clear |
| tsetseg = flower | tuya = sunlight |
| Enkh = peace | bolor = crystal |
| sengel = happy | ot = star |
| mandakh = rising | mung = silver |
| naran = sun | bat = sure |

Thus we have such names as: Batsengel, Batchimeg, Bolor, Enkhmaa, Enkhtuya, Davaajargal, Shurentsetseg, Munkhjargal, Bolortungalag, Munguntuya, Naranchimeg, Otgontuya, Otgonjargal, Otmandakh, Oyundelger, and Otgontsetseg.

One of the boys is named Battulga and it took us both a while to figure out the English equivalent. I knew Baatar meant strong or bold but then he drew a picture of a fire being held by an ornamental grate and pointed to the grate. I later found out that it was "trivet."

They then decided I needed a Mongolian name and named me Altantsetseg. Altan means gold and tsetseg is flower. Therefore, I am Goldflower.

Since Mongolians' hair is almost always black or very dark brown, any other color hair is considered gold. Therefore, my gray hair translates to gold.

There are many Altantsetsegs serving here among the humanitarian service couples, missionary couples, CES (Church Education System) couples, and, of course, President and Sister Cox. There's a lot of gold among the mountains of Mongolia.


## A Trip to the Gobi

*John*

Rather unexpectedly we made a trip to the Gobi desert this week. It is standard practice to disperse the missionaries around Mongolia once school is out for the summer so we went with the district president and mission president and his wife to see if there was a need for English teachers in Saynshand. This is a town 500 kilometers south of Ulaanbaatar and 200 kilometers north of the Chinese border. It is a nine-hour train ride from Ulaanbaatar. We left at 12:40 P.M. on Wednesday and arrived in Saynshand at 10:45 P.M. We spent Thursday there and caught a train back at 1:00 A.M. Friday and arrived in Ulaanbaatar at 10:00 A.M. the same day.

So many things worth recording happened on the trip. You may have noticed that the nine-hour southbound trip took ten hours. We were stopped for awhile on the way down so Nancy stepped out of the compartment and looked forward to see why the delay. She noticed many people clustered around the engine. Then she noticed some men carrying what appeared to be a tarpaulin up the slope toward the town. She thought it looked like a body bag, because it was heavy and sagged in the middle. I said it was probably a sheep. After we started moving again, the district president (President Enkhtuvshin) talked with a member of the train crew and found that it *was* a body. A man who the locals said had been depressed had committed suicide by jumping in front of the engine as it was pulling into the station. Naturally this cast quite a pall over the trip right at the beginning.

As we were pulling into Saynshand we could see in the station lights that the trees were whipping and the air was filled with dust. When we stepped off we found ourselves in a full-blown gale and the dust was really particles of sand being whisked by the wind. We hadn't gone more than 20 steps toward the hotel, perhaps 200 yards away, when big, warm drops of rain began to pelt us. In a few more steps, the rain was cascading down very hard and mixing with the sand as it came. We were heading directly into it so it was hitting us full in the face. The wind was blowing so hard we had to lean into it to make any forward progress at all, and with the sandy rain right in our faces, we couldn't see where we were going. It all happened so fast, and was so primeval in its force and impact, that it was really rather stunning. We had to go forward but found it so hard to make progress against the wind, and could only look up occasionally because of the wind/sand/rain in our faces (and we were afraid it was scouring our glasses), that we weren't certain we *could* go forward. Step by step we struggled on and after a while we were able to reach the hotel. It was a totally unexpected, breathtaking experience. Nancy had become so disoriented that she was near panic until President Enkhtuvshin found her, took her hand and led her to where the rest of us had gathered.

When we got into the hotel we discovered we were all totally soaked and plastered with sand on the front but *dry* in the back! The wind had been so strong there were no air currents to curve the water around us or enable it to fall down upon us and soak us from the top down. The two presidents and Nancy were wearing the clothes they were to wear the next day and they were sodden, wrinkled, sand-covered messes. We had to wonder whether this was another indication that the trip wasn't going to go well.

The wind was blowing so hard I had to take off The Hat and clasp it to my bosom as we struggled toward the hotel. When we got there the first thing I did was survey the damage because Nancy and I both believed The Hat would fall apart if it became wet. Well, it was positively soaked. It had protected me but suffered what appeared to be mortal damage in the process. Mournfully I placed The Hat on top of a dresser with the brim hanging over the edge to protect and preserve its jaunty little dip in the front. I hoped for the best but feared the worst. After all, my entire *identity* in Mongolia was wrapped up in The Hat. In the morning, lo and behold, The Hat was as good as new! It had dried perfectly! Though Dan had told us The Hat was made from rabbit felt I now knew with certainty that it had to be water rat.

In the morning we found that everything had completely dried during the night. Wrinkles fell out, sand brushed off, and we found we could offer a presentable appearance after all. One problem, though. The composition of the sand is such that when we were walking through it in the rain it built up on the soles of our shoes. By the time we reached the hotel it was at least a half-inch thick. By morning it had dried and had the composition of concrete. We banged and rasped and picked at our shoes with little success. Then we discovered that a few drops of water turned it into sand again and we had soon sluiced it off. Not without creating quite a sandy, dirty mess, though.

The mission president started us off with a prayer for progress during the day. We hadn't been able to make any appointments (or hotel or train reservations!) in advance and were just going to be dropping in on people unannounced, so we clearly needed all the help we could get for this to be a positive experience. We made our first stop at the office of the vice-governor, to pay our respects and let him know why we were in town, but he had gone to Ulaanbaatar the day before. The governor wasn't in either. Not an auspicious start to the day and not a favorable omen for the rest of the day.

Next we went off to the regional medical school and hospital that are situated in Saynshand. We found the medical building and it was so ragged and rundown that I proposed it for the Ugly award. Not much to lighten our spirits there either.

As we walked, we were able to see a bit of the town. It is a barren place. Its main feature is sand. It has better roads than Ulaanbaatar, and less traffic, but the main thing you notice is the shifting, omnipresent sand. The fences and buildings rise directly from the sand, with no softening grass, bushes, or trees. In that sense it is stark. But it is also clear of papers, cans, and bottles. The wind sweeps away everything that isn't fastened down. One had the sense that the sand could become quite an oven when the summer sun beat down but fortunately we were not to experience the blinding heat that day.

Unannounced we walked a bit diffidently into the office of the director of the medical university and discovered the answer to our prayers. She was charming. She was gracious. She was the epitome of leadership and management. She had left Ulaanbaatar to spend one year in Saynshand and 30 years later was still there providing motivation, direction, and vision to the fortunate people there. She escorted us on a tour of a university that was clean, well-organized, and better equipped than the national showcase medical university in Ulaanbaatar. She demonstrated pride in her students and they responded to her pride like polished mirrors reflecting desert sunshine. *Her* students were going to stay in the Gobi to practice after graduation, not hover in Ulaanbaatar, like the graduates of that other medical university. *Her* students were going to devote their lives to helping the people, not accumulating material possessions. *Her* faculty was going to learn English so the university could send them abroad to earn advanced degrees and develop medical specialties to teach back home. Thus, she was delighted to hear that we could, and would, send an English teacher or two to work with her students and faculty. But not in August, she cautioned. In August the climate is so bad that even the natives leave for the hills and woods in the countryside. Not our teachers, the mission president said. They will stay here. She just smiled.

The director invited us to dinner that evening. Since the alternative was peanut butter sandwiches in the hotel rooms we were quick to accept. We snoozed the afternoon away until we were picked up by the university van at 7:00 P.M. and were transported to a building that is half university dormitory and half university hotel. Fortunately we went to the hotel side. The door to the room opened on a table that was crammed with delicious salads and beautifully presented platters prepared by members of the faculty that afternoon. On the way back to the hotel earlier in the day we had stopped at a few stores, to ensure the missionaries who would be sent there would be able to purchase wholesome food, and had picked up some soft drinks, cookies, and other munchies for ourselves. The director noticed everything we bought and had sent her minions to purchase the exact same things for the dinner that evening. There on the table were the same brands of soft drinks, the same cookies, and more of the chocolate-covered peanuts we had discovered and purchased. We were especially surprised to see the chocolate-covered peanuts; I thought we had already purchased the town's entire supply!

Before dinner was over student entertainers were brought in. Students had worked together to make their costumes and had won awards representing the medical university in various talent contests. The director of the school's computer laboratory bustled about setting up the sound system and keyboard. Then she accompanied the singers and dancers on the keyboard. All were very good but the dancer particularly caught my attention as she performed one of those eastern dances that features graceful movements of the arms, hands, and fingers. I was struck with

wonder that we were actually there, in the Gobi desert of Mongolia, watching this person perform with such elegance, style, and
grace. The wonder of it brought brief tears to my eyes.

A little dazzled by the lovely evening the director of the university had pulled together on our behalf, with *no* prior notice,
we returned once again to our hotel. We returned quickly to
earth when we learned that our agent had been unable to get us
train tickets. On every evening but Thursday there is a 7:30 P.M.
train to UB as well as the 1:00 A.M. train, but since this was
Thursday there had been no 7:30 P.M. train to carry a portion of
the many people who wanted to go to UB for the weekend. The
ticket agent was unable to issue any tickets until word came up
the line from previous stations as to how many tickets had been
purchased down line, and whether there were any open com-
partments remaining. The district president had been checking
regularly since our arrival but now we were getting to the point
where we either got the tickets or resigned ourselves to staying
until 7:30 P.M. Friday. Nine o'clock came and went. Ten o'clock
the same. Near 11:00 P.M. we got the word—we were to go to the
train station *now*! We hurried pell mell out of the hotel and on to
the train station.

There was a compartment but we could get just three of the
four bunks. The mission president tried to outrank me and insisted that I stay in the compartment with the two ladies; he
would spend the night sitting in the chair car with the district
president. I was able to win the ensuing "push fight" by pointing
out that I didn't have any appointments until 3:00 P.M. Friday
and could get a nap when we got home, but that his schedule
began as soon as we arrived back in Ulaanbaatar. While we were
discussing and debating the district president simply took matters into his own hands. He knew a person in Saynshand (a former student) who was a friend of the lady who sold the train
tickets, and *if* there weren't someone already in the compartment

when the train arrived she would arrange it so that no one else could or would get the presumably already-sold fourth bunk.

We proceeded to the compartment. There we evicted a couple of American oil workers who then proceeded to evict a couple of train workers who had taken their compartment next door. After much shifting of baggage we sat down to see whether anyone would arrive to claim the fourth bunk. No one could settle in for the night until the matter was finalized so we sat and waited. Time dragged by. The platform cleared but there was still plenty of time for someone to arrive before the train left. Finally, at 1:00 A.M., no one had arrived, the train began to move, and the four of us settled down to get what sleep we could.

As we were drifting off the door banged open and lights flooded the compartment. But it was not the missing fourth person, thank goodness. It was only the conductor collecting the difference in price between the chair ticket I had purchased and the compartment bunk I was occupying. Once again we all settled down to sleep away what remained of the night.

The trip back was *cold*. We huddled under our blankets but no one slept well because it was so cold. On the way down, we were driven out of our compartment into the passageway by the heat; on the way back we were cold, cold, cold. When the train crew knocked on the door to awaken us in the morning no one was willing to get out from under the blankets. We stripped and folded the sheets to hand them back, but we stayed huddled under our blankets. The district president had told us at 1:00 that he had found another place for himself so we expected and waited for him to rejoin us, but he didn't do so. We didn't see him until we arrived at the station in Ulaanbaatar. There we learned that he had been unable to find a bunk for himself and had spent the night sitting up in the chair car. There are no blankets in the chair car. He had spent the entire night without adequate protection against the cold. The cold had so permeated his body that he was unable to stop his chin from shivering as we were driven home. Two days later I still feel how awful that night must have been with no way to protect himself against the cold and the seconds, minutes, and hours just dragging by interminably. I am grateful now that I didn't have to return in the chair car but I feel terrible that he had to.

The upshot of all of this is that there *will* be English teachers sent to Saynshand, the gospel *will* be taught during their personal hours, and the spread of the Church in Mongolia *will* continue. We met a fascinating woman and enjoyed one more fascinating, memorable experience. How blessed we are to be here.

## Moving Day #1

*John*

In case our previous journal entries have not made it abundantly clear, let me begin by stating outright that we are very organized people. Thus when we decided to give up the apartment we now occupy so the incoming English directors-to-be could live close to the library, we immediately began laying out our plans for moving from here to there (a few blocks away).

There were many factors to take into account, as everyone who has ever moved realizes. The new apartment would have to be cleaned and furniture moved around before we moved in. Then our apartment would have to be cleaned for the incoming couple. We would move in short stages, over a period of several days, because 1) we only have a few boxes and they would have to be filled, emptied, brought back, and filled again, and 2) we wanted to minimize the imposition on anyone else that might be occasioned by our move.

We made arrangements with Baatar to shuttle us back and forth on Friday from 2:00 to 5:00 P.M. Scrap that portion of the plan. When we went to the new apartment Friday we found the pair of missionary sisters had not yet moved out. We helped one of the sisters move and then left because the other sister (who was on a split) still had to return and do all her packing. As we were leaving, the cleaning lady arrived to begin the initial cleaning. Surveying the scene with her we agreed that it was pointless for her to begin that day. Instead, she would begin Saturday morning and we would begin moving a few things in Saturday at 2:00 P.M. Fine. We made arrangements with Baatar to be with us Saturday from 2:00 to 5:00 P.M. instead of Friday 2:00 to 5:00 P.M. and we all went home.

Saturday at 2:00 P.M. I carried a few bags downstairs to load when Baatar arrived with his car. Just before 2:00 P.M., Nyamaa (the couples' second driver) pulled up in his van. He announced he was there to help. Then one of the senior elders came out; he was there to help, too. Baatar arrived, ready to go to work. Sizing up the situation, we could see they were all determined to help so we didn't argue very much. I assured the senior elder that we only had a few boxes ready and that one or two trips up the stairs would finish the job.

So we started. Then Batbold arrived. He drives the mission car. At that point we knew the jig was up. The careful moving scenario we had laid out existed only in our heads. They were here to *move* us and, by golly, they were going to move us whether we were ready or not.

The pitiful few boxes we had prepared were gone in the first two trips. By now both of us were engaged in a frantic effort to find things for them to take—*now!* Out went the fans, the television, the VCRs, the copy paper, and the desk chairs. Out went the bags of kitchen things we had just purchased. Out went the

268

filled and partially-filled suitcases. Out went the keyboard; if anyone shows up for a music lesson they're just out of luck.

When everything movable was packed in the car and van, Baatar picked up two of his kids to watch the car and van while the drivers carried things upstairs to the new apartment.

When we arrived at the new apartment the door key wouldn't work for some reason. Turns out the cleaning lady was still there and had thrown the slide bolt. When she opened the door we understood why the key wouldn't work, but also realized the apartment wasn't ready to receive us. Down the drain went the rest of our plans. No careful moving of furniture to their destined places before we filled the apartment with boxes, etc. No sequenced unpacking of boxes. No careful segregation of things that belonged to the mission so they could be returned and not co-mingled with our stuff and the landlord's stuff. No nothing!

We did our best to tell the carriers which room to put their things in before they hustled off to get the next armful. Mongolians do everything at top speed. They hustled up and down the stairs so fast we hardly had time to decide where boxes and other items should be placed. We started at 2:00 P.M. It took them 20 minutes to carry down everything moveable. Then it took five minutes to drive to the new apartment. After an additional 20 minutes they had carried everything up the three floors to the new apartment. By 3:45 P.M. we thanked them, said goodbye, and sent them all home. No furniture was moved. No boxes were unpacked. Nothing could be done because the cleaning lady was still busy. So we closed the door behind us and left. Tomorrow we'll go over and see what we can do to begin putting things in order.

At the SMTC they stress one thing repeatedly to the people going on missions: stay *flexible!* We had another lesson in flexibility today. We certainly hope it does us some good because we are constantly called upon to *be* flexible.

## Moving Day #2 Onward
*John*

Since Moving Day #2 was a Sunday we could only go to the new apartment between church and choir practice. We did some more sweeping, moved some furniture around (and swept some more), and washed and scrubbed furniture, closets, shelves, and floors. (Is this getting the ox out of the mire?) Nancy had the good idea to move a couple of shipping crates (still being used from the time the first missionaries came here in 1992) into a closet and thereby convert it into a pantry. We have tons of shelf space in the bedroom and office but very little in the kitchen. Working out places to put foodstuffs was what prompted Nancy to come up with the idea to convert a closet to a pantry.

## Moving Day #3
*John*

We were rousted out of bed early Monday morning by a housefly that kept pestering us. We'd dive under the covers for a while, hoping he'd go away, but he was still waiting for us when we surfaced. So, up and at 'em. Since we couldn't complete our move on Saturday, today was fer-darn-sure *moving day!* Sosor was coming at 8:00 A.M. to help us clean the new apartment. Rather than have Baatar sitting around for long periods during the summer, waiting for us to complete this meeting or that, we got him a pager on Friday. We told him that on Monday (today) he needn't show up until we paged him because we had the empty boxes to refill, but that when we paged him he should come a-runnin'.

Given our early start to the day we were just about packed by 9:15 A.M. We paged Baatar and finished filling the last of the boxes. By 9:30 A.M. we were ready. All we needed was Baatar's car to shuttle us back and forth to the new apartment. No Baatar. Then the phone rang. The mission office wanted to know if we had paged Baatar. We said we had and were waiting for his imminent arrival. They said he'd called and they would call him back (somehow, since he doesn't have a phone) and let him know we were waiting.

At 10:00 A.M. Nancy couldn't wait any more. She took off walking with a bucket and rags in hand. I beeped Baatar again. At 10:30 A.M. still no Baatar. Another beep, with the same result. Sosor called at 10:45 A.M. and said she'd be at the new apartment at 11:15 A.M. Another beep at 11:00 A.M. At 11:30 A.M. Nancy called to say Sosor said this was a national holiday (another Mother's Day — the third one so far this year!). Ten thousand children were gathered in the middle of town celebrating their mothers and bringing traffic to a standstill.

I called the mission office again and asked if they'd heard from Baatar. Someone had. He'd called to say he was "fixing his car" and would be along as soon as he could.

With that, I, too, walked over to the apartment, carrying a few things. During the afternoon we finished the cleaning, shuttled back and forth with a few more crucial things (such as our bedding), determined to spend the night in our new apartment even if we weren't fully moved in.

Perhaps Baatar will appear in the morning. Perhaps. You can see we're still being *flexible.*

*Stop the presses!* At 8:00 P.M. Nancy finally tired and we stopped for the day. She prepared a quick meal of dried chicken noodle soup and pretzels (no bread or crackers in the house). As we were saying our prayer the phone rang (as usual). Batbold wanted us to know that Bataar had completed the repairs on his car and was *on his way!* We slurped up our soup just in time to see Baatar rounding the corner. Down the stairs we went and roared off to Building #7. You may recall my telling you in Moving Day #1 that the Mongolians do everything at full speed. Baatar was so chagrined at being unable to keep his appointment this morning that he *ran* up the three flights to our apartment with me struggling along well behind. I opened the door and he fairly burst through to grab up as many boxes as he could possibly grab before hurtling down the steps to his car with me straggling along well behind with just one box in my arms, thank you. Back up the stairwell he hurtled with me struggling to stay on the same lap with him. On the third lap I quit competing and let him lap me while I caught my breath.

Finally we had filled the trunk (which he locked each time to prevent pilferage while we were both upstairs) and I shrewdly volunteered to stay down and watch the contents he was loading in the back seat. Just as I was beginning to catch my breath he came laboring down the steps with a super-size suitcase that must have weighed a ton judging by how hard he was laboring to carry it. I leaped to help, by opening the door to the back seat, and circled the car to pull it in while he manfully lifted, turned, and maneuvered it into place. (Well, I'd already had a hard day by the time he entered the scene, right??!!)

We roared back to the new apartment and began the sprint all over again. I gave up on the last two rounds and let him lap me again. By the time we finished even Baatar was sweating. We finished at 8:45 P.M. — the same 45 minutes it had taken us to load/unload the first car full. We told Baatar we'd see him in the morning. Yes, we're crazy enough to do it all over again in the morning! Good night, Gracie.

# June 1998

## Moving—a Woman's View

*Nancy*

I don't think moving is any woman's favorite thing to do. It means a lot of packing, cleaning the place you're leaving, and then cleaning the new abode. It's no different in Mongolia but there are a few added twists—one of which is a shortage of boxes.

We've watched the Mongolians move and, being a nomadic people (even in the cities), they just tie everything up in tidy bundles and move out. It's fascinating watching them make these wonderful little packages! We've mentioned before that we just stand back and let them go to work when it comes to getting their things from one place to another.

We're not as instinctive as they are, so we struggle with too many belongings, too few boxes, and a general ignorance of the whole process. Maybe Mayflower, Allied, or United have truly sold us their bill of goods that we need to leave the professionals do it, so in the past we've left the driving and packing to them. I bet the Mongolians could make a moving company a great success in the States.

A few words on these fine men — Baatar, Batbold, and Nya-maa. We've mentioned before that they all work as drivers for either the mission or the couples. They are choice men. None of them are members of the Church* but they care for us lovingly and willingly. We didn't ask the three of them to come help us — we just planned on doing it ourselves with Baatar's help. Instead they joyfully showed up. They're best friends and tease each other constantly, Batbold saying that Baatar is "bad man," and loves to hear me say "No he isn't! Baatar is good man." They both laugh. Batbold and Nyamaa speak English. Baatar understands the heart.

What they did for us is consistent with the Mongolian culture. They just plain work well together. It is the typical Asian culture where the group works together rather than one excelling. It makes a western teacher want to tear his or her hair out when giving a test, because what we call cheating they think of as "working together" or "helping" the weaker ones. It's not just looking on each other's papers, either, it's calling out the answers across the room (of course they do it in Mongolian but I still know what they're doing). But when a job needs to be done they don't even have to be told what to do or how to do it. They step up to the task, each taking a share and working like a smooth machine. If someone lags behind they don't chastise or criticize, they give him or her a boost.

Now we live in what has become known in the mission as "The Staleys' Apartment." The Staleys were a humanitarian couple who left last November. They were a Scouting couple and Elder Owen Staley was here to help organize the first scout jamboree ever held in Mongolia.

Now that I have almost everything put away I have discovered an entire large cardboard box of pasta: macaroni, shells, spaghetti, and noodles of all shapes. Guess what we had for dinner tonight (macaroni and cheese) and what we'll be eating a lot of for awhile.

---

* All three have since become members.

Our sons reminded us that when they were transferred to a new city or apartment they had to move everything in two suitcases. *What?!*

## No More School, No More Books, No More Teacher's Nasty Looks

*Nancy*

I taught my last class at IDER today—a combined class of third level students. I had told them that it was going to be a short class and we'd take pictures to celebrate the end of the school year. I was astounded when I entered the classroom to find them all waiting for me instead of me waiting for them. (Remember, Sosor says "on time" in Mongolia is twenty minutes late.) They were all smiles. I walked in with three boxes of candy under my arm and a bag with still and video cameras. Mongolians *love* pictures. It's almost a religion with them, and if you don't have many pictures displayed in your home they wonder out loud why you don't. We didn't know this before we came. When they inquired I pointed out I carried them in my wallet, but that was not satisfactory. A fast letter home resulted in pictures we were able to prominently display and provided many opportunities for discussion of our family with everyone who visited our apartment.

When I pulled the cameras out of the bag the girls started taking their pony tails down and brushing their hair—primping just as we would in the States. We opened the candy and several girls started passing it around (it is consistent in the colleges and universities that the majority of the students are girls—38 girls to 4 or 5 boys). I started filming with the video camera. Since this is the "videocam" model I was able to show them instantly what they looked like. After I was literally mobbed and almost knocked over I decided I needed to plan this better. So I asked them to sit back down and I'd do it row by row and then let them see themselves by rows. It worked much better that way and everyone enjoyed seeing themselves and their best friends.

Then one of the girls presented me with a picture of myself taken with one of the classes the previous week. I noted to them that when pictures are taken, Mongolians never smile and since I was going to take some pictures of them outside I wanted them to smile. I mimicked their sober faces and they laughed.

The candy was gone so we all went downstairs and out the front door to take the still photographs. I had asked Baatar to wait for me since I'd only be there a short time. He jumped out of the car and volunteered to take the pictures. He also did a little stage managing and began clicking away amidst my calling out the instructions to smile.

Just as we thought we were finished, the wife of the director (she seems to really run the school) came out. She wanted to have her picture taken with us so we started all over. Declaring ourselves finished, Baatar returned the camera to me and I turned to wave as I was walking to the car. They waved back and I snapped one last picture.

We were driving out the driveway to the main road and making our usual left turn when I saw Baatar look back towards the school. It seems they were calling to us. We continued driving and then I saw one of the young men from the class jumping low fences and bounding across the school yard calling after us. Baatar stopped, the young man said something to me in Mongolian—had they forgotten their English so soon? I told him I didn't understand and he proceeded to talk with Baatar. Baatar spoke to me in Mongolian and I gave him my usual shrug of the shoulders due to my not understanding Mongolian. He responded by pressing on the gas pedal and taking us to the next road where he proceeded to turn around. I go where Baatar takes me so we returned to the school. The students were still standing in front of the building where they had been joined by the director of the school. He wanted to say goodbye and be in some pictures too. So a couple of the boys helped me out of the car, another student acted as photographer, and we took more pictures.

With a promise to Zorigt (the director) that I'd return in September to have more pictures taken with the college's first graduating class (in December, after we return home) we all said our goodbyes again. Baatar whisked me down the road, beneath the Bogd Khan mountain, around the Russian tank monument (a tank that had made it from Moscow to Berlin in 1945), over the Peace Bridge, and home.

## Can We Borrow a Cup of Sugar?

### Nancy

Tomorrow John will be traveling to Darkhan with the Coxes to a zone conference. That zone includes the two elders that are serving in Sukhbaatar—Elders Buck and Voros. I'm staying home and putting the finishing touches on our former apartment for the new couple that arrives Wednesday.

John received a call this evening from Elder Voros asking if he could bring some brown sugar with him because they have found a great recipe for a cake that requires brown sugar.

Brown sugar is a scarcity in Ulaanbaatar as well as the outlying cities. Sukhbaatar is quite far north, close to the Russian border, so we weren't surprised they couldn't find any up there. The occasional small baggie that finds its way to our market is very dark and often hard. The trick of using it is to mix it half and half with regular granulated sugar and then let it stand for a while— also putting an apple in the container to soften it up. So, I remembered I had such a mixture and we measured out the two cups called for in the recipe and it'll be on its way very early tomorrow morning.

I have a bag of brown sugar sent to us by our webmistress (our daughter Terri) and it's saved for very special occasions. The other bag we had came in a Christmas box and I must confess that we went through it too fast—making all the things that we'd missed—so we're being more careful with this one.

All of this is to say it's the first time we've been asked by someone to borrow a couple cups of sugar via long distance telephone.

## Rain Comes to Ulaanbaatar

*Nancy*

Friday we were sitting in zone conference and the clouds opened up. It was the first rain we've had here for months and it was a cause for excitement. As I sat facing the windows looking out onto the apartment building next to the mission office, I saw balcony doors flung open as families came out to enjoy the downpour. Mothers brought their young children out and many ran back to bring houseplants to set on the balcony ledges to be washed and watered by the rain. A day or two later several members told us the same thing was happening in their neighborhoods as all over Ulaanbaatar the blessing of the rain was enjoyed and appreciated.

When it came time for the missionary testimony meeting, every single one of them thanked their Heavenly Father for the rain that has been so desperately needed. There have been grass fires on steppes throughout the country including some close to Erdenet. The Kinnisons (the couple who live there) said they could see the smoke coming towards the city and there were days when it became difficult to breathe.

We read in the local paper where things had gotten so bad they had started to fire rockets into the clouds to "seed" them in the hope that it would rain and help put out the fires. It did work and most of them were finally extinguished — all but one I believe — and they could shift all their manpower to that one area. The newspaper was explaining why the clouds had been so black and heavy looking over Ulaanbaatar but they had brought no rain here.

Under the rear windows of our new apartment is a concrete area where the young boys play soccer. Their joyful voices fill our bedroom and office each evening. Following the downpour the voices were coming from another area — behind the concrete garages — so we couldn't tell what they were doing. A trip to the mission office revealed that a huge puddle had developed, and paper boats, pieces of styrofoam, and any other piece of debris that young boys could sail were floating on their imaginary ocean. It provided days of pleasure before eventually disappearing into the sand of Mongolia.

The soccer games have resumed.

## Humanitarian Couples in Mongolia

*John*

President and Sister Cox recently compiled a short history of the humanitarian couples in Mongolia. Because it helps explain the role we play here we have asked their permission to include some of this in our book.

> In 1991, Elder Monte J. Brough arranged for volunteers from the Church to come to Mongolia in response to requests from the Mongolian government for humanitarian assistance. In making those arrangements, Elder Brough explained that our volunteers would provide the service agreed upon and in their free time would teach the doctrines of the Church to Mongolians who requested or desired

to learn of such things. This was agreed upon. The first and major area for humanitarian assistance was and still is the teaching of English.

In September 1992, the first senior missionary couple arrived in Mongolia. They had no apartment waiting for them and no one to "show them the ropes" in Ulaanbaatar. However, an official in the Ministry of Foreign Affairs kindly gave them his own apartment as temporary housing until "Building 7" became their Mongolian residence. They were followed soon after by five other senior couples. All of them consulted and/or taught English in the schools and universities. That first winter was cold and food was scarce. Sosor, an early member of the Church, cleaned their apartments and stood in lines to buy a head of cabbage, some potatoes, a loaf of bread or a few eggs for them. Some nights the first senior missionaries went to bed without having been fully satisfied by their evening's meal.

By August of 1993, there were eight Mongolian members of the Church. The first six single elders arrived. Their charge was to teach English and begin to give discussions to people who wanted to learn about the Church. By May of 1994 there were 80 members of the Church. Since that time senior missionaries have come and gone. They have made their contribution, left their mark upon the people they have served and Mongolia has left its mark upon them. The membership has continued to grow from those early days until now there is one district with nine branches. There are missionaries in eight communities from Hovd in the west to Baganuur to the east, and Sukhbaatar to the north to Saynshand in the south. While single missionaries do most of the work of finding, teaching discussions, etc., the senior missionaries have a no less significant role in building the Church.

The most important vision to maintain while serving in Mongolia is that of service. We are very literally following the "Ammon" model for building the Church in Mongolia. *We have come to live and serve for a time....*

There are presently 12 couples in country counting the Coxes. Six of these are humanitarian service couples. Besides teaching English and administering the English project there is a scouting project, a banking project, a medical lab project, and country directors who bring in humanitarian goods from the Sort Center in Salt Lake City.

All of us work together to carry out the agreement made between Elder Brough and the Mongolian government in 1991.

# July 1998

## Hovd

*Nancy*

Hovd is the westernmost branch of the Church in Mongolia. From Ulaanbaatar it can be reached in three days by car over unpaved roads (where there are roads) or a three-hour flight on Mongolia International Air Transport (MIAT).

Since it was made a branch by Presidents Cox and Enktuvshin just recently it has not had visitors from district headquarters in Ulaanbaatar. It was decided during the re-organization of the district several months ago that a member of the district council and his wife would visit Hovd once each quarter when they would speak in sacrament meeting. (All the other branches receive these speakers every month.)

It was our lot to be the first visitors, so on June 20 we flew to Hovd with one stop in Muren.

Hovd, like Ulaanbaatar, sits in a bowl surrounded by mountains. I was surprised to see seagulls there but we did fly over a number of large lakes as we got closer to the city. As we were on our approach over the mountains, I saw what I thought was snow covering the mountains and the ground. I saw tracks in the snow where vehicles traveled. Then we landed on an unpaved runway with stones bouncing off the bottom of the aircraft and I realized that the "snow" was really sand. We were in desert country, again, similar to Saynshand. As the airport personnel guided us into our parking spot I could see they were all in short sleeves and sunglasses and when we deplaned we were hit by desert heat.

When we entered the terminal we saw the two very friendly faces of Elders Lowther and Swenson who were accompanied by a large man with a great beard. They introduced us to President Ganbold, president of the Hovd branch.

We were led out the front door of the terminal to a fence where one of the typical blue Russian trucks had backed up with all the luggage. They asked for our baggage tickets and President Ganbold proceeded to claim our luggage. Then, luggage, two elders, two senior missionaries, Ganbold's daughter, and Ganbold squeezed into a Russian jeep for the trip into town. Elder Swenson (long legs and all) crawled over the seat into the back with the luggage. I, fortunately, had worn a full skirt as I have learned while being here that straight skirts and dresses do not accommodate climbing into jeeps, four-wheel drives, and similar vehicles.

Included with our personal luggage were all the supplies we brought with us from the mission office. This included all their money for the next several months; batteries for the keyboard; instructional books; newly translated handbooks; forms, forms, and more forms; the newly translated Old Testament (not by our translators); some New Testaments; and an assortment of other instructional materials. But most important of all were packages and mail from home.

Since there has not been an agreement with a school in Hovd in which our missionaries can teach English, they are only sent there during spring break and the summer months. (It is a requirement of the Mongolian government that all missionaries teach 16 hours per week to obtain and keep a visa.) Elder Lowther has been in Hovd four times and this was Elder Swenson's first time. One of our responsibilities while there was to talk with some of the school directors to see if arrangements could be made for our elders to teach in their schools. The other thing we had been asked to do by the mission president was to meet with the vice governor to discuss some humanitarian aid he had requested from Deseret International Charities.

We were dropped off at our hotel and shown to our room. The elders explained that the water (cold only) was turned on for a short time twice a day and there was electricity only a short time each day as it was turned on at different times in various parts of the city for about one hour. They showed us the large cauldron of water that had been brought to our "bathroom" and a couple of empty two-liter Pepsi bottles with which we filled the toilet tank when it needed flushed. They asked the hotel proprietor to bring us a thermos of boiling water so we could have lunch. We had brought six instant noodle dishes with us in case the hotel wasn't preparing food that weekend. All we needed was boiling water as these handy items are packed in a styrofoam bowl, contain three packets of seasoning, and provide a small plastic fork with which to eat them.

Elders Lowther and Swenson then left (after giving us several critical Mongolian words) to begin contacting the people with whom we needed to meet. We tested the light switches and saw that, indeed, there was no electricity. We acquainted ourselves with our surroundings by looking out the windows and saw that we were next to several ger enclosures, each with one ger and assorted storage sheds and outhouses. One shed appeared to house grandparents. Several hundred meters away was a large public school which seemed to always be busy.

The hotel provided sandals; so we took off our shoes, slipped on the sandals, and relaxed on the bed while we waited for the hot water to arrive. It eventually came and since we had eaten breakfast very early in the morning, before Baatar picked us up for the airport, we were very hungry. We poured the water into the soup bowl and waited a few minutes while the dried noodles "cooked" and then feasted on this ingenious dish. We had brought plenty of filtered/boiled water with us, a can of Pringles, a can of honey-roasted mixed nuts, and six Snickers bars (for instant energy, of course).

After we ate we settled down to wait for word from the elders as to what appointments they were able to make. They returned around 8:00 P.M. (I think we had napped) and told us what our appointments were for the next day. We suggested we go down and have dinner in the restaurant and take potluck. Potluck turned out to be a dish with spaghetti-like noodles mixed with small pieces of meat and a few vegetables. We had Sprite and Fanta Orange to drink—our staple here. Since there was no electricity and there were only a few windows it was hard to see what we were eating, which might have been a blessing as I pushed a few things to the side that I couldn't identify. The elders ate with gusto and were regaling us with stories of the various things they have eaten while on their missions.

For couples who serve missions, it's a treat to be associated with these fine young men and women. There are real giants in those young bodies that can move so much faster than ours and eat a much more diverse diet. We regard it as a real privilege to work with them and marvel at what they teach us. As we attend zone conferences each month with them, and see tears streaming down their faces as they bear their testimonies, I wonder how we could ever have missed this opportunity. They arrive here from the MTC with baby fat still on them. After a month or so they have slimmed down and firmed up from all the walking. In addition, their spirits have grown to match their strong bodies. Their faces glow with the spirit of the gospel and their handshakes strengthen—too much so for some of us in our arthritic condition.

While we were having dinner, Elder Lowther told us he was working on translating the hymn *The Spirit of God.* Remember, he's the one who translated *O My Father* which Sosor and I then put to the music. (An entry will follow on the new technique of setting words to music.) He said he was having trouble translating the words "and Jesus descends with his chariot of fire." He had searched the scriptures to find that phrase to see how it had been translated, only to discover that it does not appear in that way. How the members love each new hymn that is translated. Before Elder Lamb returned home he translated *Count Your Many Blessings,* and Unruh, our young woman who is studying opera, goes around humming it. (They take their final version to her so she can sing it and make last minute suggestions.)

We eventually said goodnight (the missionaries have to be in their apartments by 9:30 P.M.) and went our separate ways. The vice governor was in the countryside so we wouldn't be able to meet with him, but we did have one appointment on Sunday with a school director. John and I were just ready to call it a day and were getting into bed when the lights came on—10:00 P.M. Hovd time and 11:00 P.M. Ulaanbaatar time. We laughed as we got up and turned them off. We could also hear the water in the toilet beginning to run.

Sunday morning we washed and John shaved in cold water. The elders came by and walked (ran) us to where the branch met. These are two tall elders with long legs so it took some effort on our part to keep up with them. The weather had changed and it was rainy and cold. Fortunately we had brought our coats with us.

The branch meets in the branch president's home. It consists of a long room where the family lives/sleeps/eats and a very small kitchen. The president was away on business and his wife got stuck in Ulaanbaatar because the plane had filled up before she could get a seat. Their two teenaged children had everything set up by the time we got there. A coffee table served as the sacrament table. It had two pristine white cloths spread over it. Two small stools were placed behind the table. A few members had already arrived and greeted us warmly.

As the elders busied themselves with last minute arrangements additional members arrived. It was really raining now and they were soaked. As we shook their hands we could feel how cold they were. I have no idea how far they had to walk. One young couple was carrying a baby tightly swaddled in a blanket and they laid her on the bed and unwrapped her so she could get warm. The meeting proceeded but was interrupted several times. First, the phone in the room kept ringing and Ganbold's daughter kept picking up the receiver and putting it back down. The caller was persistent so the son finally got underneath the table and disconnected the wire. A bit later a neighbor came into the kitchen and made some sort of ruckus over a can he needed with yogurt in it. Finally all was calm again. Elders Lowther and Swenson were seated on the stools behind the sacrament table; Elder Swenson, being the taller of the two, had his knees close to his chin. The sacrament hymn was sung and the sacrament administered, passed by the only Aaronic Priesthood holder, the teenage son. Several of those in attendance, such as the couple with the baby, were investigators. The rain continued and it was necessary for the son and daughter to place pails to catch the water coming through the roof.

Following the meeting we took pictures of the branch and noticed it was still raining so we visited with one another and took more pictures. Ganbold's daughter brought out their photo albums and we enjoyed seeing wedding pictures of the parents and more of the children as they grew up. Sprinkled among the later pictures were missionaries who have been assigned to the branch during the summer.

The members started leaving and I noticed the rain had let up. We left also, and walked most of the way back to the hotel without rain. Once again, we ate in the hotel dining room and this time the meat and vegetables were mixed with rice. Following lunch, the school meetings took place, the elementary school director having made arrangements for us to talk with the vice-director of the local branch of State Pedagogical University. As a result of these visits, several teaching possibilities were uncovered and further negotiations will take place. We sent the missionaries on their way and assured them we'd be fine for the rest of the day. They reminded us of the Mongolian words for "hot water" and left.

The rest of the day was the same as the previous day except for one intrusion. We'd been in Mongolia for 13 months and had not experienced any religious harassment until Sunday. We had the door of our room open to provide extra ventilation when a large gentleman entered and in a loud voice said he was the police (he was dressed in a sweat suit) and demanded our passports, which we had had to leave at the desk. He kept repeating the words, "Polezia, Polezia." John could smell the alcohol on him so got up and shooed him out of the room. Quite brave of him, I thought, due to the difference in size and age. That was not to be the end of him, however.

By Monday morning we had gotten smarter. We saved one of the styrofoam soup bowls, washed it out, put hot water in it from the thermos brought up by the hotel proprietor, and used it for washing and shaving; we had brought soap, washcloth, and towel with us. We had been told by the elders that because the arrival of the plane from Ulaanbaatar upon which we would be returning was so erratic, the way most of the people handled the situation was to wait until they heard it flying in and then they'd leave their homes and travel to the airport. Since we knew that seats are not guaranteed even though you have a ticket (remember, the branch president's wife got stuck in Ulaanbaatar even though she had a ticket), we said we preferred to go out early so we could get a boarding pass.

We participated in one more appointment before our 12:30 departure, and then President Ganbold, his son, and the elders drove us to the airport, checked our luggage, and got our boarding passes. We told them all to go ahead and we'd be fine so they left. We wandered around, took some pictures of the runway with its surrounding mountains, watched the few people who were there, and reflected on our visit.

As time passed, *he* (the large gentleman) appeared again. We had walked out by the runway a second time. I was going to take a picture of the many bags of wool that were to be shipped out of Hovd but *he* shouted at me that I couldn't take any pictures. In my mind, I laughed. As a child of World War II, when we *really* couldn't take pictures because of national security, I wondered what secrets were hidden in bags of wool but I didn't want to provoke him. John and I were a bit separated at this point, he walking further out on the runway where they were extending it and putting down some blacktop. We could still see each other and when *he* shouted to John "Come here!" in Mongolian John, not recognizing him, started walking towards him. I called to him that *he* was trouble and not to go over there so John changed direction and came toward me. The gentleman continued shouting, but since a real policeman was sitting there and not preventing our doing anything we knew we weren't breaking any laws with the exception of those imposed by the self-appointed *Polezia*. I wondered what he would think if he knew that John had been cleared to edit the white paper produced by the Mongolian Office of Strategic Services just a few months previously.

We sauntered back into the waiting room and after awhile heard the gentleman going around telling people "Jesus Christ" and pointing to us. We had no name tags identifying us as such but Hovd is a small enough town that everyone knows every stranger and what their business is. People were turning their heads, looking at us, and we just smiled. Mothers with small children with whom we had played gave us big smiles back.

The waiting room was really filled by now because the plane had landed. President Ganbold had returned with his son as his wife was on the plane. As she entered the waiting room she came over to us with a very warm greeting. We'd never met but we were the only Caucasians in the airport and dressed in dark suits. She was profuse in her apologies for having missed our visit and we reassured her it was okay.

It was time for us to board the plane and *he* was once again out on the field. He was being helpful and ushering old people out to the stairs up to the plane. He saw us walking towards him to board, turned, and with the index fingers of his two hands made an "X" and put a hex on us. John just shook his head and rolled his eyes.

My impression of him: he's probably left over from the old communist days when he probably did have some authority in the town. The Communists did not permit religious freedom and they killed many lamas and destroyed many Buddhist temples. Since democracy has taken over he has been replaced, but is humored or honored for his past service by being given access to places and documents. I suspect this is the case because he knew which room we were in at the hotel.

After the plane took off it was discovered there was one more person on board than they had tickets so they spent much of the rest of the flight trying to find out who might have snuck on board. They never did discover the culprit even though they checked all our tickets once again as we deplaned in Ulaanbaatar.

We claimed our two bags and walked through the exit doors where Baatar stood amongst the huge crowd. I don't remember a more welcome sight since we arrived in Mongolia. We were home.

## Setting Words to Music in the Computer Age

*Nancy*

Some months ago I wrote about the difficulty in taking lyrics that the missionaries and others translate and fitting them to the proper musical notes. It was a tedious task using the cut-and-paste method. After completing *O My Father,* Elder Lowther suggested it would all be easier if a scanner were used. Then the hymns could be scanned into a computer and the lyrics added, making the needed adjustments quicker and easier.

Before being transferred to Hovd for the summer he tried it with great success and showed Elder Cantwell how to do it. While searching in the computer for the translation of *How Great Thou Art,* which had been lost, Elder Cantwell found two more hymns hiding there waiting to be set to music.

Elder Lamb translated *Count Your Many Blessings* before he left for home and it's now ready to be presented to the members.

Our blessings are many.

## The Fourth of July

*Nancy*

We've been teaching our interpreter American sayings and idioms. She carries a small notebook in which she writes the phrases and their meanings. The other day — one of many while John attempted to get the container of goods from the Humanitarian Services Center (formerly the Sort Center) in Salt Lake City released by customs—everyplace we went was closed, they said "No," or they were in the countryside. As we sat in the car I said, "This day has been a washout." A discussion ensued about what I meant.

The Fourth of July at the U.S. embassy this year was a literal "washout," not an idiom. A downpour chased everyone except the elders (and a few hearty couples including the Coxes) inside the embassy to wait it out. The salads were swimming in a couple inches of water and some desserts had become soggy. Although the salads were quite unappetizing looking to me, it gave the elders a clear shot at the food table while everyone else sought shelter.

The games that had been so carefully planned by Sister Cox and Sister Parkinson were cancelled and those of us who were faint of heart returned to the comfort of our apartments while the optimists stayed.

I thought the best quote of the day was when the ambassador's wife said, "With all these missionaries and one nun you'd think we'd have better weather."

## Naadam—The Three Manly Sports

*John*

The Fourth of July is followed by the weekend of Naadam. While we Americans celebrate our independence from England, Mongolia celebrates their liberation from Chinese domination— soon thereafter to become a Russian satellite country.

The Mongolian word *Naadam* refers to three athletic events: wrestling, archery, and horse-racing. Only the wrestling is limited to men. Archery includes men, women, and children. The horse racing events are for boys and girls ages 4–16.

The whole city has been spruced up as it is a major event with international visitors streaming into town. Buildings have been painted and flowers planted in containers all over the city. Many, many tourists were in town. After being here for more than a year we feel like "old timers" in Mongolia. When we sit at a traffic light in the car watching the people cross the street we can say "Tourists!" right along with Baatar and we laugh.

It wasn't nearly as hot this year as last year (98°F, a record) so it was a bit easier to enjoy the opening ceremonies in the Naadam Stadium. All we missionaries, singles and couples, attend and sit in the same section—part of a reported crowd of 15,000. The missionaries outside Ulaanbaatar attend their local celebrations, which many prefer.

Just to give you a flavor of the national celebration which is held in Ulaanbaatar I'll offer some quotes from the newspaper:

> The main event in Ulaanbaatar opened, as tradition dictates, with words from the President, N. Bagabandi, and a melody played on the morin khuur (horsehead fiddle).
>
> Horse-racing is arguably the most dramatic of the events. Ulaanbaatar's races were mass spectacles involving more than 3000 horses from 13 aimags (states). In one race alone, that for horses of more than six years old, 600 animals participated. And, for the horses at least, the competition is sometimes a matter of life and death. Six horses died during the punishing races, held in 32° heat [90°F].
>
> As usual, races were held for horses of six different ages, with the young jockeys ranging in age from four to 16. In the archery events, 116 archers ranging in age from four to 86 took to the field for this year's competition. More than 50 children, including 21 girls, also took part.

Before continuing excerpts from the newspaper, let me add that the archery contests here are different from those we are used to. There are no round bull's eye targets, but instead a number of cylindrical objects placed on the ground with those in the middle being stacked about three high and colored red. The archers shoot their arrows through the air and then they skitter along the ground. The object is to hit the red cylinders in the middle.

First-time competitor N. Batgerel, 30 and from Bayan-Olgii aimag, took first place in the men's event, hitting the cylindrical target with 35 of his 40 arrows. The women's event was won by 24-year-old D. Oyunkhand of Arkhangai aimag, who landed 30 of 36 arrows. In the children's round, the boys' competition was won by sixth-grade pupil Enkhculuun of Ulaanbaatar, on target with 19 of 20 arrows. Another sixth-grader, Batmagnai of Orkhon aimag, won the girls' competition, scoring a perfect 20 out of 20.

"Mongolian archery is a unique sport, different from the sport developed in Japan, China, and Korea," said S. Batkhuyag, head of the Mongolian National Archery Federation. Mongolian archery is a tradition passed down from generation to generation, he noted. The biggest hurdle in the sport's development in Mongolia is the painstaking manufacture of the bows and arrows. A bow takes six months to produce and must be left to dry for two years before it can be used. Currently there is only one bow and arrow factory in Mongolia, in Darkhan, and a bow and arrow costs at least Tg 150,000 (approximately $200)."

The two-day wrestling event was won by Bat-Erdene, matching the record held by "the great Bayanmonkh in the 1960's, 70's, and 80's." It was his 10th national wrestling title. Bat-Erdene, a former world amateur sumo wrestling champion who now adds the title of Super Grand Champion to his slew of other honours and rank of Giant, proved that he is the kind of wrestler who appears once a generation.

The traditional field of 512 wrestling hopefuls was winnowed down over the course of two long, hot days, until Bat-Erdene faced Elephant D. Sumyabazar in the final bout.

It took Bat-Erdene a relatively brief half an hour to throw Sumyabazar, a silver medallist in freestyle wrestling at the Asian Championships and East Asian Games gold medallist. Sumyabazar was appearing in his first Naadam final. He put in an impressive showing throughout the tournament, but in the final was suffering from an arm injury sustained during an earlier bout.
Naadam produced seven new Falcons, the title awarded to wrestlers who win five bouts in a national Naadam, but no new Elephants (awarded for seven victories) or Lions (bestowed on Naadam champions).

In addition to the sporting events there are a number of cultural events—concerts, operas, ballets, and the traditional Mongolian Folk Music and Dance Concert performed by the national company. The missionaries attend as many of these as we can—and you thought it was all work, work, work!

Thus concludes our second and last Naadam.

## What's in a Name? In Mongolia, a Whole Lot of Research

The following is an excerpt from the English language *Ulaanbaatar Post*. I know I quoted extensively in the recent entry about Naadam but this information is best written by the professionals. The article was written by Jill Lawless.

> When Mongolians get new civil passports over the next year they'll be receiving more than an ID card. They'll also be getting new names. Or, more specifically, reacquiring old ones. Mongolian family names, abolished by the communist authorities seven decades ago, will appear on the new cards, alongside an individual's given name and paternal name. Bringing back family names—which for centuries helped identify a Mongol's tribal and regional origins—involves a mammoth genealogical project sponsored by the government and carried out under the auspices of the Mongolian Academy of Sciences.
>
> After the 1921 revolution, the family names were eliminated as a relic of feudalism. Henceforth, it was decreed, Mongolians would carry only two names—their given name and their father's given name.
>
> "Historical documents show Mongols used family names from the eighth century," says Ts. Tsedev, an official at the State Centre for Civil Registration and Information and one of the compilers of a new book listing more than 1300 Mongolian family names. He cites *The Secret History of the Mongols,* the most important historical and literary source on ancient Mongolia, which contains references to many family names. "The practice likely began when some member of an ethnic group living in a certain region became famous, for example in war, and the rest took his name," notes Tsedev. Bringing back

family names was first discussed by the government at the start of the democratic reforms in 1990. It is a popular move, regarded as a symbol of Mongolia's revival of pride and interest in its history and culture. But it is also a huge logistical challenge. The erasure has been so successful that a leading Mongolian genealogist has estimated only 40 per cent of Mongolians are still aware of their family names.

A straw poll among Ulaanbaatar residents revealed an even lower statistic—only two of 10 people surveyed knew their family name. "We had no way of knowing it, and it just wasn't necessary," shrugs Nasanjargal, a taxi driver.

Tsedev says rural Mongolians and members of the smaller of the country's 30 or so ethnic groups are more likely to have preserved their family names. But many Khalkh Mongols—who make up 85 per cent of the country's population—have no idea. Tsedev and his colleagues have spent a decade filling in the gaps. By travelling throughout the countryside, talking to elders and studying carefully preserved family trees kept by some families, they have compiled a list of 1300 names.

At one time these family trees were customary. In ancient times, Mongol Khans and high officials had their own official registrars to keep such records. These were destroyed on the order of the government in 1925. Finding the names again has been like piecing together a historical jigsaw. The result is a book—currently being readied for publication by the Academy of Sciences—that lists names by aimag and soum. "So if people know where they were born, they can find out their tribe and their name," explains Tsedev. He himself traced his family name in 1991 by going back to his home aimag of Uvs and talking to local elders.

The government plans to back up the book with an extensive publicity campaign involving brochures, newspaper ads and a television programme on how to trace your family tree. Family names are important for a number of reasons, says Tsedev. Historically they served as a guarantee against inbreeding—relatives within nine generations of the same family were forbidden from marrying. "And compared to just a father's name, a family name gives much more information about a person. If a Mongol knows his name he will know his family tree, respect his elders and keep in touch." "And every family has special things to pass on to the next generation."

As for the increasing number of Ulaanbaatar-born Mongolians who don't know their family origins, they are free to choose a name from the list, or to invent one of their own. "A person has the right to choose any family name he likes," says Tsedev. "For example, a lot of people would be happy to have the same name as Gurragcha (the first Mongolian in space). He can start his own family tree if he likes."

Tsedev says this process will be tempered by Mongolians' inherent honesty and respect for their culture—no one would dream, for example, of usurping the family name of Chinggis Khaan.

"It's a great thing to find out who you are and where you came from," notes the researcher. "You find out what your role is in the world."

Still, Mongolians will have to wait a little longer before that identity is officially sanctioned. The new passports, due to be introduced on July 1, have been delayed—in part because the government lacks the money to pay the British firm that is printing the cards.\*

# Go IU!!

*Nancy*

This one is for all you Indiana University graduates, former faculty, and "friends of."

Elder John H. Groberg, area president, has been touring the Mongolia Mission. During his (and his family's) tour he met with the single missionaries and couples, looked at building sites, inspected missionary apartments, and spoke at a fireside for members. It is the custom in this mission that when there is a visiting authority the couples have the opportunity to become better acquainted with them by having them to their apartments for a meal.

---

\* The Communists required every family to destroy their genealogy and many did. But others, at the peril of their lives, hid them in the mountains, buried them, or used other means of preserving them. We have been in the home of one government official who preserved his by memorizing twelve generations and his children can now recite thirteen. "And these . . . Who were among the Lamanites, did infest the land, insomuch that the inhabitants thereof began to hide up their treasures in the earth. . . . (Moroni I:18)."

Last Sunday we had just such an opportunity and to our delight found that Elder Groberg attended Indiana University in Bloomington where he received his MBA. His wife and he lived in the converted barracks that were named Hoosier Courts— often fondly referred to as "the Mormon ghetto."

It was fun to talk about so many things we had in common. The Grobergs were there some years before us but we share many of those wonderful Hoosiers as friends. Bishop Johnson served as their bishop.

We reminisced about the music students and what they added to the ward and the fact that we were so thoroughly intimidated that we didn't dare sing in the choir. We had wonderful Ray Hardisty stories—our crusty, loveable custodian.

Sister Groberg talked about a bed they bought while there that gave her backaches the entire time. She also spoke lovingly of a child's rocker they bought somewhere nearby which has been passed down through the family from child to grandchild.

Though just a graduate student, Elder Groberg was given the assignment to find a piece of land upon which to build a church building in Bloomington. He did so, the same piece upon which a large ward building now stands. At that time a first phase was built which was the Sunday School/sacrament meeting room. Just before we arrived, the chapel had been built, and while John was bishop, a cultural hall and large classroom wing were added. It was during that building phase that many of us participated in UFO's (United Family Opportunities) with family projects to raise the necessary funds.

We often speak of what a small world it is in the Church, but who would ever have believed that you could sit in an apartment in Mongolia and talk about Hoosier Courts and Ray Hardisty with a visiting general authority!

# Mongolia: The circle in the clouds

# August 1998

## Too Many Bosses

*Nancy*

It's terrible when we westerners drag sweet, low-tech people into the stress of our everyday work hustle and bustle, but that's exactly what we've done to Baatar.

During the school year, the companionships of the couples split and go every which way throughout Ulaanbaatar to teach English in universities, institutes, ministries, archives, and secondary and elementary schools. Since they are so widely spread it requires reliable transportation and clockwork timing. Baatar and Nyamaa drop one of us off at one school and scurry to another to make a pickup. Each driver's schedule is meticulously planned so that a daily pattern develops, with very few deviations, if any. We all know where each is at a given time and things go fairly smoothly.

It all changes in the summer because the couples don't teach. It's a more laidback schedule which changes from day to day depending on shopping needs, sightseeing, and occasional trips to the countryside.

This summer our schedule was determined by a 40-foot container from the Humanitarian Center in Salt Lake. It was packed full of medical supplies and clothing. Since it requires many visits to various governmental agencies to get a myriad of approvals our schedule was never predictable from day to day. It seemed best that we not tie up the other couples with our schedule and they decided to reduce their transportation costs by all sharing Nyamaa leaving us the use of Baatar.

When a phone call came and a Minister or his assistant could see us, we would page Baatar and he would pick us up. Fortunately for all concerned, the system worked because it took 41 days to get the recent container released by customs. Throughout that period we could not predict from hour to hour where we'd need to be. I say "we" but actually it was pretty much John, Baatar, and Doya. They didn't really need my smiling face so I stayed behind in the apartment and fielded some of the phone calls that came in.

It took several days to get the bugs worked out of the pager system but now we're all comfortable with it. With the container here we spend most of our days sorting medical supplies, loading them, and delivering them to many different hospitals and social welfare centers. The clothing is going to shelters for street children, shelters for abused women, orphanages, a clinical sanitarium for children with ricketts and anemia, and so forth.

Getting in touch with Baatar has become easier for everyone. His best friend Batbold can now page him, his wife, Enkhsaikhan, can beep him, the mission office can find him, and now that our English replacements have arrived they also can beep him.

One day while we were driving along to make a delivery the pager beeped and we teased him that it was Enkhsaikhan trying to get him. He laughed and told Doya that he now has "too many bosses!" (It also beeps several times a day to offer the daily exchange rate.)

Fortunately for Baatar he'll give up the pager at the end of August and begin the more consistent schedule of driving couples to their schools.

## The Brain Drain

*Nancy*

This past week we felt as though we had lost our brains — well, at least all the information we had entered into our computer during the time we've been here. Monday morning we went to the mission office for a conference call with President Cox and Elder McSwain in the Hong Kong office. John stayed for another meeting at 9:00 A.M. and I came back to the apartment. Before leaving the mission office I picked up two copies of the *Church News* which had recently arrived.

Upon returning to the apartment I unlocked both doors and went into the living room/dining room, turned on BBC for the news, and started reading the *Church News*. About a half hour later I walked to our office window to see if Elder Dolana had arrived at the container. He was bringing the director of the only blood center in Mongolia to see the large blood refrigerator that came in this shipment.

As I walked into the office I saw an empty space on the desk where our computer (usually) sat. The connections were all laid out neatly where they had been disconnected. The only thing I could think of was that John had taken the computer with him to his meeting. I called the mission office and, unfortunately, he hadn't. That meant only one thing. Someone had stolen our computer.

This all happened as I sat in the living room reading the *Church News!* When I returned to the apartment I had closed the outside door and thrown the bolt. Obviously it hadn't gone all the way into the chamber to lock. Still, I couldn't believe that someone could get in without my hearing them as the door is very tight, rubs when you open or close it, and has to be banged hard to get it clear shut.

John came home from the mission office, Sosor arrived to clean, Elder Dolana and Nadmid (his interpreter) came with Mr. Ulaankhuu from the blood center, Baatar and Doya came for their day's work, and eventually eight policemen arrived. The morning was shot!

Doya's father is a police officer in another district but she called him and he alerted the police here. Statements were taken. Black fingerprint powder was sprinkled over things. Phone calls were made, and so forth.

While this was going on, John and I were thinking of all the information we had lost. All the English project and country director files were in there. Our web page journal entries. My missionary journal. All our e-mail addresses — on and on. We were sick to our stomachs. Our genealogy (fortunately a backup computer and disks are at home), LDS Infobases, a brand new "Introduction to Mongolia" CD left in the CD-ROM drive, letters written in WordPerfect, the ELLIS program for teaching English, the Mongolian font, and many things I'm sure we haven't yet realized.

After all the questions were asked and answered (with Doya's help) and we signed our names, everyone left except Baatar and Doya. I still couldn't believe that someone was able to open that door without my hearing because there isn't even a handle on the outside. So Baatar walked out, closed the door, and in a few seconds we saw that door slowly, quietly open. My mouth dropped and I told him he's in the wrong profession.

I don't remember much of the rest of the day. I think we may have resumed delivering clothing and hospital supplies but we were thinking about our loss.

Several miracles happened. John had just begun downloading onto floppy disks the English project and country director files. The English files had been completed but he couldn't remember how much he had downloaded of the country director stuff. It contained reports of all of our investigative visits to the many hospitals, schools, social welfare centers, shelters, orphanages, and agencies in UB and other remote towns. It also listed the items we had given to each. Hopefully, many of these had been saved.

The other miracle was that our daughter, Terri, had an extra laptop at home she could set up for us. You see, we're really computer illiterates and if it weren't for our children we'd be in bad shape. The problem was getting it here. President and Sister Cox came to the rescue! Sister Cox had had to go back to the States for several weeks to take care of some family business (since their service as mission president and wife had been extended a year) and President Cox suggested she could bring it to us. She would be leaving Salt Lake in several days. Phone calls were made and arrangements completed and we continued our work.

Sister Cox arrived back in UB Friday evening. We contained our excitement to rush right over and get the computer until we thought they had had time to let down a bit and visit. Then John went over and the first thing we did when we got it up and running was to see how much was on that country director disk.

What a thrill when we ran the cursor down the directory and saw the names and reports of 52 of those organizations. Only four or five had been lost.

An aside—a couple that was in the SMTC with us had to return home from Hong Kong a bit early so they could have some medical matters taken care of. We heard from them after they returned home and they said their computer crashed after they arrived home.

*Beware!* Don't put your brains into your computer without backing up first! In Pennsylvania Dutch country they say, "Too soon old—too late smart."

## Feed My Sheep

### *Nancy*

Mongolia, like the Holy Land at the time of Christ, is populated by thousands of herds of sheep. The people easily relate to the shepherd, the sheepherder, the ewes, the lambs. Those who grew up in the countryside, still the majority of the population, took turns tending the sheep. They grew to love the lambs and the solitary life of the herder.

It is a privilege to be a missionary for The Church of Jesus Christ of Latter-day Saints. There are thousands of us throughout the world answering the call of our Shepherd. Some are proselyting missionaries who go from door to door or street corner to street corner preaching the restored gospel. Others of us are called to serve as humanitarian service missionaries and go about the world doing the things that Christ taught, feeding the hungry, clothing the naked, and healing the sick.

Behind those of us who are in-country humanitarian service couples is a large group of dedicated church employees and volunteers who support our work, and behind them is the generous membership of the Church. John and I feel it a great blessing and

privilege to serve in this capacity. It is hard work. I think it is
said of the Peace Corps that it's the hardest job you'll ever love
and so it is with us. Fortunately we've experienced good health
and relatively good strength for our 66 years.

As country directors it has been our job to seek out the poorest of the poor and find ways in which we can help them help
themselves or offer temporary relief while they get on their feet.
We have found ourselves walking the corridors of hospitals
which are inadequately supplied; we've visited with children in
shelters where they have been taken by the police from pipe tunnels under the streets where they lived. Just this week we found
a sanitarium for children who are being rehabilitated from the
diseases of malnutrition. This is a country with many single
mothers who are trying to hold their families together. We've
talked with many of them. Unfortunately this country also struggles with the scourges of alcohol abuse, unemployment, domestic violence, and the diseases that result from the use of tobacco
and alcohol.

There are heroes and heroines who are working diligently to
stem the tide of the world as Mongolia has become more accessi-
ble to the imports—both good and bad—of the modern world.
We try to find them. The Mongolia Child Rights Center is one
such place. We delivered clothing to them that they will take to
children in prison.

Sitting under the bedroom window of our third-floor apartment is a 40-foot container sent from the humanitarian center in
Salt Lake City. It arrived in Mongolia via ship and then rail to be
placed on the edge of a large concrete pad where the local children
play soccer. It is filled with medical supplies and equipment, clothing, sewing machines, fabric, thread, shoes, and winter boots.

After it was delivered some of the elders and sisters took part
of their preparation day and helped us unpack some of it so we

could do an inventory. After the count was taken, they repacked it and everyone was impressed with how clean and orderly everything was. The inside of the container was immaculate and each module expertly wrapped in heavy plastic and stacked on pallets. It was amazing to think of all the miles it had traveled without a thing being spilled or crushed. Our sincere thanks and appreciation go to those workers in the humanitarian center who are so expert at their end.

I want to tell you some of the specifics of what is/was in the container. A blood refrigerator for the one blood collection center in all of Mongolia (which up to this time was using a small domestic refrigerator), three centrifuges (there were none in the blood center), a first-aid module, an anesthesia module, an obstetrics module, a hospital supply module, a central supply module, two children's supply modules, one pallet of sewing machines, 20 bales of fabric remnants, 40 bags of shoes and winter boots, 47 bales of used clothing, 50 bags of socks, and additional fabric and thread.

Each module contains approximately 1000 pounds of goods and each bale weighs 100 pounds (a reason for being grateful we're still blessed with physical strength.)

We've been greatly blessed by Elder and Sister Dolana ("Dolan") who came this spring as a Medical Laboratory Technician couple and Elder Theurer sent by the missionary department to be our mission doctor. Although we had ordered the medical supplies in the container last December, before those couples came, they have been invaluable in explaining to us what the various pieces of medical equipment are used for and together we decide which hospitals, clinics, or labs they should go to.

Yesterday Dr. Sandwijav, the chief surgeon of the one oncology hospital in all of Mongolia, came with an old Russian truck and four of his handsome, English-speaking, young doctors to

load the anesthesia module to be taken to their hospital. I don't
know who was happier, us or them!

Several weeks ago a new convert who is a young neurosur-
geon, Dr. Bayarmaa, told us of her hospital's need for bedpans.
The entire neurology department had just one bedpan! Because
of the people they serve—stroke victims and brain surgery patients—they were desperate. I told her we had bedpans and we'd
bring them over the next day. We were stunned by the excitement of that young doctor and her nurses when we gave them
those bedpans and several urinals. (The nurses didn't know what
the urinals were.) They even called in the head of the department
to share their joy. When we presented them with a box of barrier
cream it almost brought tears to their eyes.

Dr. Bayarmaa introduced us to a young woman who had just
completed her internship and was leaving that Friday for the
countryside where she will practice among "the poorest of the
poor." There is little or no equipment where she is going and the
doctor asked if it were all right if they shared some of their
things with her. We told her we'd be back the next day with an
assortment of supplies she could take with her, keeping in mind
it would have to fit in a car. We wish those of you who donate
all these items could see the joy on the faces of the recipients
since our words cannot adequately describe it.

It is easy to find the poor in Ulaanbaatar. Getting out to the
countryside and more isolated towns and cities is a different
matter. This past weekend we flew to the town of Muren. (Elder
Cook spoke about being in this town at the last General Conference.) The people there are rehabilitating a children's camp and
asked Deseret International Charities to help them with money
for seeds so they could teach the children how to plant and raise
vegetables. At President Cox's request we met with the people
and then flew up to see the camp. After spending a day at the

camp we were leaving the next afternoon to return to Ulaanbaatar. We asked if we could visit their hospital in the morning
so we could see the conditions there. They were very happy to
oblige and while I stayed in our hotel room (with a reaction to
the food from the day before) John, Sister Enktuvshin, our interpreter, and Mr. Butkhuyag,* Director of Social Policies for Muren,
went off to make the visit.

Without going into detail as to what we found, let me just say
we will soon be sending some medical and clothing supplies to
Muren.

> *For I was an hungered, and ye gave me meat: I was thirsty,*
> *and ye gave me drink: I was a stranger, and ye took me in:*
> *Naked, and ye clothed me: I was sick, and ye visited me: I was*
> *in prison, and ye came unto me. (Matthew 25:35–36)*

## A Love Letter from Mongolia

*Nancy*

This is a love letter to the people in the Salt Lake Valley, the
Wasatch Front, and other parts of Mormonland where hearts are
big and hands are busy.

By the end of this week we had made our way to the back of
the 40-foot container. There were two modules of children's institutional supplies neatly stacked and wrapped back there. Earlier
in the day we had visited a children's hospital out of town,
towards the airport. It's pretty much out of the way and probably forgotten by most.

As with all of the buildings here it has seen better days. I
noted on the outside that it had been built in 1975 but it looked

---

*He later joined the Church.

like it had been built much earlier as there's just no money here for maintaining structures. I thought its outward appearance didn't bode well for what we'd find inside but, much to my delight, it was being kept as clean as possible—without hot water we were to learn later.

We met with the director—a tall, handsome young woman named Munkhtuya. As with all of our "cold contact" visits we could tell she was wondering why these two Americans were paying a visit to her hospital and what we could possibly want. It was clear from some of her questions that she thought we wanted to take away some of the babies there. We handed her our "name card" (business card) which is Mongolian on one side and English on the other. Then Doya explained who we were, who we represented, and why we were there. We asked her many questions to ascertain the conditions there, the number of patients, how many beds they have, and the main diseases they treat. During this fact-finding discussion we found out they have no heat in the hospital during the winter—and this is Mongolia! Then we asked for a tour of some of the wards and there saw "the poorest of the poor."

She showed us an approximately five-month-old, very ill child who had been abandoned on the streets, found by a church organization in Ulaanbaatar, and brought by them to the hospital. A young female member of that church was staying with the baby and it was covered by a colorful Noah's Ark quilt supplied by the young woman's church. Just several days ago another baby, four months old, had been found abandoned and brought to them but had died the next day.

It didn't take us long to see we had in our container just the things that would be helpful to them. So we made an appointment to return at 2:00 P.M. and went back to the container. John and Baatar climbed over bales of clothing, bags of socks, and bags of shoes and boots, and began dismantling one of the children's pallets.

Up to this time we had been working with medical equipment. Since this is not our field of expertise we have relied heavily on the Dolanas and Elder Theurer for advice. As John, Baatar, Doya, and I formed a line to work the boxes up to the door of the container I just had to open some of them to see the contents. Now I was dealing with something for which I was an expert. Quilts! Wall hangings! Soft stuffed toys! Wooden toys! They were beautiful! All new materials! On top of the first box I opened was a green-and-white-checked crib quilt whose color jumped out at me. I lifted it out and showed Doya, exclaiming to her how beautiful it was. We looked further through the box and saw more quilts and hand crocheted afghans and blankets. Another box contained beautiful new crocheted slippers and booties, and more of the same sewn out of fabric. There were newborn kits that contained handmade flannel receiving blankets—some crocheted around the edge—an infant shirt, booties, safety pins, soap, and other useful items. There were wall hangings that would brighten otherwise drab cubicles where three and four beds were crowded together. There were more bags of wooden toys and hygiene kits with wash cloths, towels, toothbrushes, shampoo. Being from Pennsylvania we were aware of the wonderful things that good-hearted people in the western U.S. were doing but had never seen any of them.

I was reminded of an account I read about Belle Spafford (former Relief Society General President). She was attending an international conference of women's organizations. When she was introduced a woman in the room stood and introduced herself. She was from Poland and wanted to thank Sister Spafford for the generous gift of handmade quilts that were sent to her country at the end of World War II. She said that her people were suffering from the devastation and cold that had resulted from the war. There were no supplies and then a train car full of quilts arrived from the women of the Relief Society of The Church of Jesus Christ of Latter-day Saints in the United States. She said they were beautiful and colorful and made of new fabrics and not only did those quilts warm their bodies, but their bright colors lifted their spirits.

This is what the items in these boxes were going to do for these children and their caretakers. We absolutely filled Baatar's van with boxes. There was a little space for John to sit in in the back, and Baatar, Doya, and I sat in the front. We unloaded our precious cargo into Munkhtuya's office and took some of the things out of their boxes to show her. She ran her hands over them and told us we were the first foreign charity representatives they had ever had at their hospital and the first ever to give them anything.

Thank you sisters and brothers, young men and young women, Primary children, and all others of you who give of your precious time to bless the lives of those much less fortunate. We are humbled and in awe of your gift of the hands and hearts. We love you for your desire to serve those whom you'll never see. And thank you, Humanitarian Center workers, for assembling, carefully packing, and skillfully sending these gifts from the heart. God bless you, every one.

# mongolia: The circle in the clouds

# september 1998

## The Proof's in the Pudding or The Socks Tell the Story

*Nancy*

It is the custom to remove your shoes as you enter the mission home (because of the sand) and as we have sat in various zone conferences we've gradually learned you can tell when it's getting close for a missionary to go home by his or her socks.

At first you can see they're getting a bit thin around the heel and toes; eventually they've worn clear through to the skin. I used to think, as a mother, how distressed their mothers would be if they saw them walking around that way. A few would try to hide their feet behind a chair leg or maneuver one foot over the other so that it was not as obvious. I've seen one elder wear two pair—of different colors—probably to make his mother happy.

It turns out this is a badge of honor. It means you've been here long, have done a lot of walking, and have learned to do without. The funny thing is that when they do go home and leave many of their clothes here there are packages of unopened socks among the discarded shirts, suits, and ties. I remember when one of our sons returned from Taiwan, the soles on his shoes were flapping as he walked out of the Jetway. I guess that was his badge.

John and I have been wondering for a while now if our socks were going to make it. (In the winter I wear them over my hose for extra warmth.) There is a lady in Doylestown, Pennsylvania where we live who is called the Sox Lady. Following World War II her husband was stationed in Germany and when he returned home he brought with him a sock knitting machine (sounds like the amount of luggage we'll be bringing home with us). His wife started making and selling socks to supplement their income and when he died she was able to support the family in this way. She eventually retired and now the store is called The Sox Lady's Daughter as a second generation reaps the benefits of that old German knitting machine.

The socks are all cotton and of various lengths and colors. Many of the football teams in the area buy their socks there as they can be made in various school colors, or white with stripes. The long ones are perfect for tucking under a pair of football pants. We've bought our boys' socks there for many years, so when we were preparing for our mission we went over and bought many of her black and dark blue ones.

After many months the heels and toes are no thinner than the day we bought them but they're unraveling from the top down. Each wash day the yarn and elastic that is raveling out tangles them into one large ball requiring us to straighten them out. I hang them up and John walks around with scissors cutting the threads off. Fortunately they started out long.

We've been served well by our socks and we'll end the race

about even.

## How're You Gonna' Keep 'em Down on the Farm After They've Seen Paree?

*Nancy*

We had a meeting in Hong Kong last week. They had a training session for the country directors from Laos, Indonesia, Cambodia, Thailand, the Philippines, India, Vietnam, Hong Kong, and Mongolia. Notice that Mongolia is the only cold-temperature country.

This was our first time out of the country and we felt like a couple of farm kids going to the big city. The first thing we noticed was the big new airport in Hong Kong. Then as we waited for the bus that would take us to our hotel we saw a TCBY store, a bookstore with English titles, and several other establishments that made the heart flutter.

When they came to take us to our bus, memories came rushing into our minds that had been pushed back into the recesses as we carried out our responsibilities in Mongolia. It was nighttime when we arrived and the bus had large windows through which we could watch as the lights of the city came closer to us. As we got into the city, we became aware there were also windows on the roof through which we could view the extremely tall buildings of the Pearl of the Orient.

When the bus arrived at our hotel we entered its luxurious lobby, checked in, and were ushered up to the 25th floor and our very comfortable room. We opened the curtains and saw below us Chinese junks, yachts, a large cruise ship coming into the harbor, and a variety of other seaworthy vessels docked along the pier.

I think the first night after our meetings we ate at McDonalds. Boy, did it taste good! Another night we had steak and baked potatoes. One night we ate with our friends, the Richards, who were in the SMTC with us and were then in Indonesia. We figured since we were in China we'd eat Chinese so we ate in the Chinese restaurant in the hotel.

Across from the hotel, The Excelsior, was a large, four-story shopping center. It was just like the ones in the States, and after picking up a few books to read on our way home we went to a drug store where I bought some hairspray that would finish out the mission. We also found some vitamin E, razor blades, and Cadbury candy bars.

Oh, yes, we also attended our meetings and received excellent instruction. There are about 108 senior missionaries in Asia at the present time. Those that we met with in Hong Kong are working hard to bring humanitarian goods into their countries, teach English, and teach the people how to be more self-sufficient. They're a remarkable group of retired professionals who are bringing all of their experience to these third-world countries, paying their own way to do so. Every single person there told of their love for the people with whom they're working.

It was interesting—after we'd all seen and tasted some of the things from our "former life" we were anxious to return to our various countries and finish our work. I lay in bed the last night and thought to myself that I didn't regret leaving it all behind, again, and returning to where things were a little less convenient. We love the people of Mongolia and the job we're doing here. How our lives have been enriched by Gansukh, Erdenchimig, Enkhmaa, Baatar, Doya, Enkhtuvshin, Gerelsaikhan, Gantulga, Erdenetsetseg, Ganchimeg, Narantsetseg, Batbold, Mendbayar, Enkhsaikhan, Unruhjargal, Oyuntoya, and on and on.

# post mission

## The Mongolians Outdo Us to the End
*Nancy*

We're sitting here in our Bucks County, Pennsylvania home. It's colder right now than it was in Mongolia when we left, so instead of putting another log on the fire we've called the local gas provider and asked him to come and replace the obviously empty gas tank that feeds the flames of our fireplace.

We're still unpacking things we had stored in our basement and it's been a combination of finding things which we had forgotten and not being able to find things we knew we had. It's both exciting and frustrating, but all the while we're thinking of the good Mongolian friends we've left behind.

While still in Mongolia I started packing several weeks before we were scheduled to leave. I was determined we'd leave with fewer suitcases than with which we had come. In my mind I wanted to get it all into four (half of those we came with) but it eventually looked like I'd have to settle with five. Then it began to look like five wouldn't do until Baatar and Doya came to our rescue. The afternoon before we were to leave they came to help us with last minute packing. They knew we still had a medium-sized carpet, several leather jackets, and a myriad of gifts to get into that last suitcase.

We should have known better than to worry about getting it all to fit. They're a marvel at packing. Baatar soon had the carpet folded to just the right size to fit in the bottom of the suitcase and then they began rolling the leather jackets, placing two heavy leather pillows (gifts) between them and all the other large and small gifts that had been brought to us during our last week. Former Elder Schipp had warned us we'd receive many gifts before leaving but I thought everyone who was going to give us something had already done so. *Not!* They did succeed in getting it all in, however, and I wished I had had them do the whole job and we'd probably have gotten out of there with three pieces of luggage!

As is the custom in the Mongolia Mission you have dinner your last night in-country with President and Sister Cox. It was during this wonderful meal we learned that our plane left an hour earlier than stated on our tickets as Salt Lake had not yet caught up with the fact that we were already on Standard Time, having changed our clocks in September. That meant having to get in touch with Baatar (he had given up the pager) to tell him he should pick us up an hour earlier than planned.

I didn't sleep well that night although we were both very tired. Being the worrier that I am, I wondered about those few last things we needed as we'd be staying overnight in Beijing, China. After we had retired a knock came on the door and it was Nyamaa, one of the couples' drivers, and he had a gift for us and one to carry home for another couple who had had to leave suddenly due to illness. They were two fairly good-sized wood carvings of Chinggis Khan on a horse in full battle dress. We decided we were going to have to carry them on board the plane in a rice bag along with an additional bag which had John's fox hat, two Russian fur hats for sons-in-law, and my Mongolian wedding hat *and* another bag with several pieces of artwork we had purchased.

Morning eventually came and we showered, had a small breakfast, and packed our last minute items. We sat down and waited for Baatar. Then friends began to come by to say goodbye; more small gifts came. Baatar, his wife Enkhsaikhan, daughter Oyunga, and Doya came—not just to carry down our luggage and drive us to the airport but with "breakfast." Enkhsaikhan had gotten up early in the morning to start a fire in their ger stove, make *buuz* (bodes), and *hyarum* (milk tea) for us. We were overwhelmed! They explained to us that Oyunga was supposed to be in school but she wouldn't go as she had to say goodbye to her American grandmother and grandfather. So they drove her to school and explained to her teacher she'd be absent that morning.

Enkhsaikhan and Doya and several of the other guests went into the kitchen and got plates, cups, and silverware and proceeded to serve a meal to everyone present and all others who arrived. Enkhsaikhan served us each three *buuz* and John "graciously" kept giving his to newcomers. Another larger gift arrived and Baatar and Doya tucked it away in a suitcase.

We had purposely asked people not to come to the airport because once you're there there are lines to stand in, fees to be paid, luggage to be weighed—all behind barriers that others can't enter. Two of my young keyboard students came, however, and luckily they did. Oh yes, I forgot to mention that we also were hand carrying a custom-made box with a *morin khuur* (horse fiddle) in it that had been given to us. So—even with the Coxes, Batbold, Baatar and family, we needed more hands to get us through the X-ray machines, and other checkpoints. After paying our excess luggage fees we went to another counter to pay our airport tax—all the while our entourage is on a parallel course on the other side of the red rope. The stamp man who shows up everywhere in Ulaanbaatar tried one last time to sell us some stamps. Then the Coxes, who have done this hundreds of times, asked us to turn towards them and they took pictures of us with the girls, then Baatar and family, and Batbold, and then Batbold took a picture of us with the Coxes. It was now time for us to leave through the gate to the international departures.

The next scene is hard to write about because saying good-bye to these dear people was very difficult. Baatar cried, Enkh-saikhan cried, Oyunga clung to us. It's difficult to leave someone who you probably won't ever see again in this life. These people were all a very important part of our lives for 16 months. Baatar watched over us the whole time as if he were our son. He and Batbold always looked out after the "old people" as they would frequently refer to all the couples.

We eventually got through the door, placed our carry-ons on the x-ray conveyer belt, and were in the process of collecting them again when I heard someone shout "Hoi!" I looked up and little Oyunga had dashed through the door, past the guards who were shouting at her, around the security gate, and, with arms outstretched and tears streaming down her red cheeks, ran to us for one last American hug.

# updates

During 1999–2001 we had the opportunity to serve a second mission in the Asia Area Office in Hong Kong as Area Welfare Agents. Mongolia was among the countries assigned to us as our particular area of responsibility so we had the rare opportunity (among missionaries) to return to our field of initial endeavor to see how things were developing. Then, from January 2001 to October 2001, we were reassigned to Mongolia on a full-time basis to establish employment programs for the returned missionaries and members there. Following are some of the changes we noticed from our first mission in 1997–98 to our subsequent return.

- The growth of the Church continued. Whereas there was an average of 35 persons being baptized each month in 1997–98, there were an average of 100–125 persons being baptized per month by the time we completed our second mission in the fall of 2001. And this was being accomplished by *fewer* full-time missionaries!

- As a direct consequence of this growth, the number of branches expanded from 3 branches at the start of our first mission, all of them in Ulaanbaatar, to two districts, 12 branches in Ulaanbaatar alone, and additional branches of the Church in outlying cities such as Darkhan (2 branches and their own church building), Erdenet, Hovd, Choibalsan, and Gorodok.

- The black market has gone modern. The government moved the market out of the hills north of the city to a piece of flatland conveniently located within the city. They even provided a roof over the various stalls and booths now being used by the various vendors in the market.

- Rampant commercialism has caused many first floor apartments to be remodeled into commercial establishments. Virtually every street in the downtown area of Ulaanbaatar is now a strip mall.

- The number of cars on the street has increased so dramatically there are major traffic jams every day. The days when drivers just smiled indulgently at one another, without shouting, seem to be slipping away fast.

- As in the rest of Asia, mobile phones are so ubiquitous, and used so frequently, that one gets the impression the people have grown an appendage to their ears!

- Food is so plentiful in the city that the government was able to pass laws prohibiting the import of foodstuffs aged beyond their expiration date. When we first arrived, we could occasionally get canned goods from the U.S., but almost always the expiration date had long passed. Now you can order your food and baked goods by fax or email and have it delivered directly to your door.

- Printed copies of the Book of Mormon, translated into Mongolian, were distributed to member families the week we were leaving (for the final time) in October 2001.

- The Russian landlord won the battle of the fence.

- The boy (Nyamdorj) featured in the March 1998 *Church News* wheelchair story (journal entry December 1997), and his mother Enkhtsetseg, played a continuing role in our lives. We returned to Mongolia shortly after Christams Day in 2000 for one of our periodic visits as an Area Welfare Agent. The first morning we went downstairs in our hotel, Nyamdorj and Enkhtsetseg were waiting for us in the lobby. Nyamdorj had had one leg amputated and his condition continued to worsen. We arranged for him to be seen by the mission doctor, who found that Nyamdorj's cancer was spreading throughout his body and no medication or surgery could stop it. When we were transferred back to Mongolia in late January on a full-time basis, the first morning we went to church, there sat Nyamdorj and Enkhtsetseg. This was their third Sunday in attendance. Nyamdorj told us, "We like this church." Six weeks later, we were able to attend their baptism. Nyamdorj's condition has since improved greatly.

- The metal containers under the couples' apartment windows where the children played have been replaced by brick garages and are no longer a noisy playground.

- The shoemaker no longer sits on his cement block at the entrance to our subdivision.

- Baatar, Batbold, and Nyamaa, the three drivers, have all joined the Church with their families. Baatar has already served as a branch president and all three will be strong leaders in the Mongolian Church. Three of their sons have served missions in the United States as of this writing.

- Baatar, Batbold, and Khavtgai (Baatar's older brother) have all improved their lot in life, and that of their families, by building western-style homes in which to live. Based on what they learned from the couples, Khavtgai has constructed a greenhouse to provide more nutritious food for his family and Baatar built a root cellar in his new home to preserve fresh and canned foods through the long winter.

- Buthuyag, the Director of Social Policies in the city of Muren moved to Ulaanbaatar and he and several members of his family were baptized. We were able to be present at his baptism and see the end of the story that began three years earlier.

- By 2001 many of the young Mongolian men and women we knew during our first mission returned from their American missions speaking excellent English, and we were thrilled to be able to converse with one another about our experiences and love for one another.

- Chapels have been built in Sukhbaatar and Gorodok (now referred to as Nalaikh).

- We continue to keep in touch with many of our Mongolian friends, via email for the most part, and are thrilled with their progress and contributions to the Church and to Mongolia.

# Mongolia: The circle in the clouds

# Index

If you enjoyed this book, you will enjoy these other books from Walking the Line Publications!

## Becoming a Great Missionary

A training manual for missionaries, members, and priesthood leaders. This wonderful book is available for the price of $20 (plus $4 shipping)

## The Atonement of Jesus Christ

## The Second Coming of Jesus Christ

Each of these books is available for $10 (plus $4 shipping).

## Obtaining Your Calling and Election

This book is available for $12 (plus $4 shipping).

WALKING THE LINE